Kierkegaard:
Construction of
the Aesthetic

Theory and History of Literature
Edited by Wlad Godzich and Jochen Schulte-Sasse

For other books in the series, see p. 167.

Kierkegaard

Construction of
the Aesthetic

Theodor W. Adorno

Translated, edited, and with a foreword by
Robert Hullot-Kentor

Theory and History of Literature, Volume 61

University of Minnesota Press
Minneapolis
London

Published by the University of Minnesota Press
111 Third Avenue South, Suite 290, Minneapolis, MN 55401-2520.
Published simultaneously in Canada
by Fitzhenry & Whiteside Limited, Markham.
Printed in the United States of America on acid-free paper.

Second printing, 1994.

Library of Congress Cataloging-in-Publication Data

Adorno, Theodor W., 1903–1969.
  [Kierkegaard. English]
  Kierkegaard : construction of the aesthetic / Theodor W. Adorno;
translated, edited, and with a foreword by Robert Hullot-Kentor.
      p.   cm.–(Theory and history of literature: v. 61)
  Translation of Kierkegaard.
  Includes bibliographical references and index.
  ISBN 0-8166-1186-6   ISBN 0-8166-1187-4 (pbk.)
  1. Kierkegaard, Søren, 1813–1855–Contributions in aesthetics.
2. Aesthetics, Modern–19th century.   I. Hullot-Kentor, Robert.
II. Title.   III. Series.
B3199.A33K5413   1989
111'.85'0924–dc19   88-14389

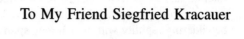

To My Friend Siegfried Kracauer

The boat appeared to be hanging, as if by magic, midway down, upon the interior surface of a funnel vast in circumference, prodigious in depth, and whose perfectly smooth sides might have been mistaken for ebony, but for the bewildering rapidity with which they spun around, and for the gleaming and ghastly radiance they shot forth, as the rays of the full moon, from that circular rift amid the clouds . . . streamed in a flood of golden glory along the black walls, and far away down into the inmost recesses of the abyss.

Edgar Allan Poe (1841)

Contents

Translator's Acknowledgments

I would like to thank the University Professors Program at Boston University which supported this translation during a post-doctoral year; Hobart and William Smith Colleges for funding my research in Frankfurt; and the people who offered their assistance: Kevin Sullivan helped resolve numberless difficulties, Lawrence Ryan was constantly generous in the discussion of textual issues. Ernst Behler, Rolf Tiedemann, Gary Smith, Steve Babson, and Benjamin Daise all contributed in different ways.

Foreword
Critique of the Organic
Robert Hullot-Kentor

This is an unlikely spot for a yiddish story, but nevertheless: The chancellor rushes into the throne room and informs the king that the harvest has been infected; whoever eats from its falls insane. He urges the king to seize what untainted stores remain and rule a mad people sanely. The king refuses; he will not be separated from his people. "Instead," he tells his chancellor, "we will make signs on our foreheads so that when we are mad we will know what has happened." The idea of a mark that would awaken them from history turned disaster bears some interest, but it is not beyond suspicion. The mark on the forehead is of sacrificial lineage and recurrence to it in difficult times is not a thought to crack open history, but its most dependable reflex. The effort to gain control has always had the form of sacrifice, not because domination has been mismanaged, but because sacrifice is the dialectical truth of domination. This is the point of Adorno's *Dialectic of Enlightenment* (1947). Domination inevitably implies sacrifice: the ego "owes its existence to the sacrifice of the present moment to the future";[1] abstraction, the modus operandi of scientific control, is nothing other than the sacrifice of the particular to the universal. Adorno's aim in tracing out this dialectic was to show that the historical effort to escape the compulsions of nature fails to achieve human autonomy because the nature that self-preservation is to preserve is destroyed by the logic of self-preservation. History is therefore a process of its own transformation into nature or—in Adorno's alternate formulation—into myth, the condition of necessity from which it meant to escape. This analysis of the dialectic of enlightenment implies an aesthetics, and here the interest of the mark on the forehead returns somewhat transformed: Adorno's aesthetics attempts to locate an image that would awaken history from its self-consuming progress as the compulsion to sacrifice. Such an image, however, would not be simple mimicry of the logic of sacrifice, but neither is it dialectically conceivable that the image would circumvent sacrifice. Rather, as Adorno wrote in one of his final formulations, it would be sacrifice that would become memory of nature as the expression of sacrifice: "All that art is capable of is to grieve for the sacrifice it makes and which it itself, in its powerlessness, is."[2] *Kierkegaard: Construction of the Aesthetic* was the first major philosophical study Adorno published; it appeared in bookstores on February 27, 1933, the day that Hitler declared a national emergency and suspended the freedom of the press, making the transition from chancellor to dictator.[3] References to *Kierkegaard* inevitably note this as ironic. There is nothing ironic about it: *Kierkegaard* is the study of the unconscious reversal of history into nature, Adorno's first analysis of the dialectic of enlightenment. According to Adorno, sacrifice "occupies the innermost cell of his [Kierkegaard's] thought."[4] The process of his philosophy is a sacrificial struggle against nature: "through sacrifice he asserts his rule,"[5] which nevertheless succumbs to nature because "sacrifice is itself mythical."[6] Although the ostensible claim of the philosophy of existence was to overcome the abstractness of idealism, abstraction remains its unwitting course in its sacrificial progress through the "stages on life's way": the aesthetic, the ethical, and the religious spheres. "Existence" itself turns out to be a pure abstraction of which nothing can be predicated, and the leap of faith is not an act of transcendence, but the despairing culmination of self-sacrifice. The truth-content of "existence," on the other hand, is in the sphere that "existence" rejects by its own progress, the aesthetic sphere of semblance: the sphere of melancholy, fragmentation, transience. In aesthetic semblance, existence passes away as the wish for a reality without sacrifice; it is the sphere of the memory of nature. *Kierkegaard: Construction of the Aesthetic* intends to recuperate the sphere of the aesthetic from the dialectic of existence: "not to forget in dreams the present world, but to change it by the strength of an image."[7]

Early Adorno

Although *Kierkegaard: Construction of the Aesthetic* was Adorno's first published philosophical work, he was not a novice. He had already written more than a hundred articles—mainly on music—as well as two extensive philosophical studies: a doctoral dissertation, *The Transcendent Thing and Noema in Husserl's Phenomenology* (1924), and a *Habilitationsschrift, The Concept of the Unconscious in Transcendental Psychology* (1927), an analysis of the concept of the unconscious in Freud and Kant. This latter work should have qualified Adorno for a professorship at the Johann Wolfgang Goethe University in Frankfurt, but its neo-Kantian sponsor, Hans Cornelius, rejected it—obviously hedging—as an "unworthy topic." Three years later, Adorno, age twenty-seven, submitted the Kierkegaard study, this time successfully under the direction of Paul Tillich. The order of these projects of course does not document when Adorno became interested in them; as far as the Kierkegaard study is concerned, it was not exclusively written in the three years following the completion of the Kant/Freud study. Its gapless density depended on a visceral familiarity with every word of Kierkegaard's extensive oeuvre. From a letter of Siegfried Kracauer to Leo Lowenthal, dated 1923, it is evident that the twenty-year-old Adorno was already completely familiar with Kierkegaard's writings and perhaps spoke an adolescent Kierkegaardese: "If Teddie one day makes a real declaration of his love . . . it will undoubtably take such a difficult form that the young lady will have to have read the whole of Kierkegaard . . . to understand Teddie at all."[8] Kierkegaard, then, was one of Adorno's earliest interests, which is not surprising. In the early 1920s, German philosophy was in the midst of a Kierkegaard renaissance, as it was called, and almost every major development in philosophy depended on how Kierkegaard was appropriated: the emergence of existential philosophy in Jasper's first publications, the "dialectical theology" of Barth and Tillich, and later in the decade, Heidegger's *Being and Time*, all drew on Kierkegaard's concept of existence as antidote to idealism. In this historical context the contentiousness of Adorno's decipherment of Kierkegaard's philosophy as the apex of idealism becomes evident. Although political turmoil and the war dissolved this context, Adorno's interest in Kierkegaard continued through the war and after. In 1940 he gave a talk, later published in English as "Kierkegaard's Doctrine of Love,"[9] to a seminar convened by Paul Tillich in New York City, where both had emigrated several years earlier. Whereas the *Construction of the Aesthetic* dealt exclusively with Kierkegaard as a philosopher, the 1940 lecture extended the analysis to his religious writings. In 1963, six years before his death, he wrote "Kierkegaard, One More Time," a study of Kierkegaard's last publications, their political implications and his polemic against the established church.[10] Apart from works directly on Kierkegaard, and there are several smaller pieces not mentioned here, Adorno's writings bristle with reference to him, often explicitly, frequently as sous-entendu. And in another sense all of Adorno's works draw arcs out from Kierkegaard because it was in this first major work that Adorno developed the fundamental ideas and forms of everything he ever wrote after it. Passages from *Kierkegaard* could be transposed seamlessly to his final works, as well as the reverse. In his review of the book, published only several days after it appeared, but after he had already fled the country, Benjamin was prescient: "In this book much is contained in little space. Very possible that the author's later books will spring from this one. In any case the book belongs to that class of rare and peculiar first-works in which a winged thought appears in the puppation of critique.''[11] The image, however, Adorno would dispute: the organic was not the measure of his work.

Enlightenment and Myth

Whether they admired the book or not, the other early reviewers of *Kierkegaard*, like most since, found it impossible to resume. F. J. Brecht wrote: ''To discuss this book is difficult; to sum it up without distorting it, impossible''[12] and then took the reviewer's prerogative to shoot and run and panned it in half a page. Helmut Kuhn found it brilliant but flawed: ''Its deficiency . . . is that its energetic and adroit thought does not solidify into binding and definitive concepts; rather it rolls by in expressive and polished formulations that are frequently overwhelmingly successful but also hovering and fragile.''[13] Another complained that the reading was fatiguing: ''the peculiarly swirling and swimming'' text made understanding difficult.[14] Karl Loewith called the book insightful in spite of its ''dictatorial, ranting and mannered style;''[15] if he had added ''arty'' and ''artificial'' he would have covered the field of invectives leveled at Adorno ever since. Loewith snipped out lists of themes from the book and packed them miscellaneously into paragraphs, quoting extensively. This was characteristic of the reviews. None of the reviewers considered why the book's style was so difficult or off-putting, or if what they all found interesting in it might have been inseparable from a style they took to be a blurring distraction. They all could, and did, deftly recite the problem of idealism, in Hegel, in Kierkegaard, in Adorno, but as a parody of the critique of idealism. Idealism floundered because of its inability to fulfill its claim of overcoming the division of form and content, of bringing its object to speech. All of Adorno's reviewers took their pose of masterful distance from the book as assurance that they could not possibly be implicated in such a difficult problem. It occurred to none of them to bring to bear on the form of the review a central insight of the book: that abstraction is the mark of the mythical. Bound to clear-headedness yet unable to organize a work they shattered into a chaos of partial themes under the pressure of summarizing it, their vision swarms with an archaic anxiety.

Chapter and Paragraph

It is hard to find other words than paragraph and chapter to describe the basic organization of *Kierkegaard*. Apparently, seven chapters are composed of a sequence of paragraphs. But these concepts are misleading as any attempt to read straight from one paragraph to the next, even one sentence to the next, makes evident. The parts are not related to each other by way of the compulsion of argumentation, logic's instinctual life; while they are completely logical, they do not develop by way of a subordinating logic of chapter and paragraph.[16] Adorno's ideal of form was that "every sentence should be equally near the center-point."[17] The parts refer to one another and complete one another by a principle of contrast. Topics develop without any schematized preparation and are taken up again at later points without any reference back to earlier discussions or any attempt to sum up the thoughts that have been developed. There is no "as we have seen," no "as we will see later," no introduction, summary, or conclusion.[18] There are no transitions other than those made by the material itself.[19] Not any more than new music would settle for paraphrasing expression would the *Construction of the Aesthetic* settle for paraphrasing Kierkegaard. The only solution to idealism is to fulfill it: to achieve the self-expression of the material. Each section of the book studies details and fragments of Kierkegaard's oeuvre as a microcosm of the whole. The image of an outdated travel guide, for example, studied at the beginning of Chapter 2, shows the decay of a meaning that should be canonical. Adorno continues to follow through the figure of the separation of a canonical meaning from the text in other images. This antinomy emerges as the figure of an objectless inwardness, one from which both meaning and the world of things are absolutely separate: "there is only an isolated subjectivity, surrounded by a dark otherness."[20] The construction pursues a compositional nominalism.[21] But because the particular element is itself a microcosm of the whole, every element is mediated by the whole. The construction obviates the distinction of thesis and argument.[22] Only to the extent that *Kierkegaard* fails could his early reviewers have succeeded at extracting the main points; every point is the main point. To call the style mannered hedges; it is pretentious. Although this is galling, it follows from the demands of the material, not from Adorno's supposed high-handedness. If the material is to have full autonomy, if it is not to be subordinated to anything, a coyness is required: unerringly Adorno seems to take up something else whenever one is finally settling into an issue. The result is hardly a harmonious flow, and it is not uncommon to find the jaggedness of Adorno's language censured as no longer German, or language at all. Adorno went so far as to displace the reflexive pronoun to the end of the sentence[23] to trip up its natural momentum. Related to his critique of the organic idiom of tonality, which achieves a gaplessness under a forward pressure that drives one note into the next with which it merges, the gesture of Adorno's language is an awkwardness to undo awkwardness: language that refuses to push.[24]

From Kracauer to Benjamin: The Problem of Truth

When Adorno was fifteen he studied Kant on Sundays with Siegfried Kracauer who was, if anyone, the origin of Adorno's idea of philosophy. Adorno wrote of these Sunday meetings: "I don't exaggerate in the slightest when I say that I owe

more to this reading than to my academic teachers. Extraordinarily talented ped-
agogically, Kracauer brought Kant to life for me. From the beginning, with his
guidance, I discovered that the work was not to be read as pure epistemology, as
an analysis of the conditions of scientifically valid judgments, but as a sort of
encipherment from which the historical situation of the mind could be read, with
the vague expectation that with it something of the truth itself was to be won."[25]
This "vague expectation" of truth directs the initial impulse of Adorno's study to
decipher the social content of Kierkegaard's thought. But this expectation would
never have sufficed for the writing of the *Construction of the Aesthetic*. With
characteristic generosity devoid of any desire to claim Adorno as his student, it
was Kracauer who pointed out in an affectionately careful and judicious review
of the book that its methodology derived from the concept of truth developed by
Benjamin in his studies of Goethe and the Baroque drama: "In the view of these
studies [i.e. Benjamin's] the truth-content of a work reveals itself only in its collapse. . . . The work's claim to totality, its systematic structure, as well as its
superficial intentions share the fate of everything transient; but as they pass away
with time the work brings characteristics and configurations to the fore that are
actually images of truth."[26] This process could be exemplified by a recurrent
dream: throughout its recurrences its images age, however imperceptibly; its historical truth takes shape as its thematic content dissolves. It is the truth-content
that gives the dream, the philosophical work, or the novel its resiliance. This idea
of historical truth is one of the most provocative rebuttals to historicism ever conceived: works are not studied in the interest of returning them to their own time
and period, documents of "how it really was," but rather according to the truth
they release in their own process of disintegration. Thus Adorno writes in *Kierkegaard*: "the innermost (and hence from Kierkegaard hidden) dialectical truth
could only be disclosed in the posthumous history of his work."[27] Interpretation
therefore depends on the historical configuration of the material.[28] The presentation of truth-content proceeds as a critique of the semblance of the organic, the
claim to totality. The first step of Adorno's work is therefore to challenge the
purported living autonomy of Kierkegaard's pseudonyms through a critique of his
poetic claim: "By rejecting his claim to be a poet . . . his pseudonyms are
excluded as the constitutive element of his philosophy. . . . They are not living
bodies in whose incomparable existence intention is densely embedded."[29]
Adorno shows the pseudonyms to be illustrations of philosophemes, and thus
breaks the shell of the philosophy; the imagery, however, rather than being
reduced to the intention of these philosophemes, pulls away from it: "What the
pseudonyms then turn out to say that is more than what the philosophical schematism had intended, their secret and concrete essence, falls, in the literalness of
the disclosure, into the hands of interpretation."[30] This is not a matter of sub-
tracting philosophical intention from imagery. Once interpretation has rejected
the compulsion of identity[31] the relation of the philosophemes to the imagery that

illustrates them is reversed. The philosophemes become metaphors of the imagery which, taken literally, hold the keys to the philosophy. In *Construction of the Aesthetic* the bourgeois *intérieur* of the nineteenth century emerges as the central image of Kierkegaard's philosophy: this image is a peculiar interweaving of nature and history and it pulls all of his thought into its perspective.

Between Neo-Kantianism and Marxism

Studies of Adorno's early writings have stuck to the facts and thus distorted them. They embrace Adorno's stated allegiance to neo-Kantian idealism in his dissertation and find a break from this position mid-way through his Kant/Freud study. This break is said to mark a transition from Kant to Marx; the first mature work of this Marxist was *Kierkegaard*.[32] But Adorno no more started off as a neo-Kantian—as is clear from his reminiscences of Kracauer—than he matured in any simple sense as a Marxist. *Kierkegaard*, in fact, itself places Marx in the idealist tradition by taking cognizance of Marx's effort in *Capital* to deduce society from the principle of exchange (a critique Adorno reiterated throughout his life). Adorno's positions in his early works did indeed become increasingly Marxist, but once Marx is recognized as part of the idealist tradition it is no longer possible to suppose that, as Adorno became a Marxist, a complete break from idealism was made. While there are points of complete opposition, philosophies are not mutually exclusive; it is possible, even necessary, to have Marxian thoughts as a neo-Kantian, and the reverse. When Adorno's works are not simply sorted according to the old saw of pre-and post-Marxist, a more concrete figure emerges. In his dissertation, *The Transcendent Thing and Noema in Husserl's Phenomenology*, Adorno criticizes the claim of phenomenology to having secured the mind as a sphere of directly experiential, absolute origins. This sphere of immediacy—Adorno shows—is predicated on a subterfuge. Husserl excluded the structural aspect of the object—which would have introduced synthetic, mediating mental functions—by positing a transcendental object, which was then placed by methodological caveat beyond the bounds of investigation.[33] This critique of a spurious immediacy is fundamental to all critique of ideology. In Adorno's work, however, this critique becomes more emphatic by drawing on the cognate critique of a false nature, as becomes more apparent in the Kant/Freud study. In this work, Adorno employed neo-Kantian transcendental psychology to justify the psychoanalytic concept of the unconscious in opposition to the organic ideal of vitalism. An unconscious that is rationally investigable is defended against one conceived as incommensurable with reason and available only to intuition. Adorno then gives a social analysis of the motivation of the vitalist doctrine: it is an effort to establish "islands . . . for the individual to which the person need only withdraw from the flood of the economic struggle in order in contemplation or pleasure to rest from the pressure of economic forces as at a summer camp for consciousness.'' But the separateness of these islands is illusory: ''Freedom from the economy is nothing else than economic freedom and remains restricted to a small circle of people as a luxury.''[34] The island beyond is dead center. Neither this Marxian analysis nor the psychoanalytic unconscious could finally be justified in neo-Kantian terms: both ultimately spring the unity of transcendental apperception; both reject the claim of consciousness that all its contents are ''mine.'' It is not a surprise that Cornelius rejected the study. But however antagonistic these positions may be, Adorno was carrying out a related reflection as a neo-Kantian and as a Marxist: a realm of immediacy is shown to be established on the basis of a sort of dualism, which is itself shown to be merely tactical; once criticized, the claim to immediacy collapses. A great deal is implied here, much of which becomes apparent only in Adorno's later writings: the critique of a false immediacy, a false nature, has as its intention a true immediacy, a new nature, but dialectically through the greatest distance from it. The idea of the reversal of mediation into a second immediacy, a second nature, has its source in the romantic rejection of the antithesis of nature and technic, and can be traced from Rousseau and Kant through Schiller, Hegel, and Marx, alternately functioning—as throughout Adorno's work—in socio-political and aesthetic contexts. In his aesthetics, Adorno follows this idea in every possible direction. In an early critique of the sound motion picture he writes that its effort to achieve a perfect organicity composed of image and voice actually tends toward stiltedness: ''There is even reason to believe that the more closely pictures and words are co-ordinated, the more emphatically their intrinsic contradiction and the actual muteness of those who seem to be speaking are felt by the spectators.'' Although the effort to mimetically achieve organicity ultimately leads to stiltedness, which it is the role of film music to obscure, a true organicity can be achieved only by way of a principle of dissonant composition: ''The relation between music and picture is antithetic at the very moment when the deepest unity is achieved.''[35] Adorno pursues this same dialectic throughout his later writings, here characteristically: ''Only the aesthetically completely articulated art work offers an image of a non-mutilated reality, and thus of freedom. The art work that has been completely articulated through the most extreme mastery of the material, a work that by means of that mastery escapes most completely from simple organic existence, is once again closest to the organic.''[36]

Idealism versus Idealism

Kierkegaard's critique of idealism, particularly in the *Concluding Unscientific Postscript* was devastating, to the point that the major works of objective idealism were hardly read.[37] Benjamin's unfamiliarity with most of these works, for

example, was probably part of Kierkegaard's legacy. Important is Adorno's critique of Kierkegaard, which situates him within the idealist tradition, taking the
side of idealism against Kierkegaard. Enlightenment is bound to the problem of
the recuperation of idealism because idealism holds the fate of the principle of
identity. If reason is to be rescued from the vitalist critique, or the Kierkegaardian—in which thought attempts to repent for its claim to absoluteness by
sacrificing itself in the paradox—then identity must become the force of non-
identity in such a way as to fulfill the claim to knowledge. The *Construction of
the Aesthetic* is in the first place a "construction," a concept with a long tradition
in objective idealism. Although Adorno's work does not deduce the object from
the principle of identity, it remains allied with idealism in the ambiguity of its
title as to whether the book is a presentation of Kierkegaard's construction or is
itself the construction of the aesthetic; this ambiguity is actually a claim to know
the object from within. Central to Adorno's construction is a reappropriation of
Hegelian mediation. Mediation is usually understood as a going between, a third
element that reconciles opposites, conceived on the model of communication and
compromise. In Hegel, on the contrary, mediation is by way of the extremes;
exaggeration is the route of truth. At its extreme, and by way of its own process,
a concept becomes its opposite.[38] What it excludes prevails. Where Helmut
Kuhn felt that the failure of Adorno's work was that no fixed concepts emerged,
he put his finger on the book's achievement. Every fragment of Kierkegaard's
work can be treated micrologically because it includes in itself its opposite as its
own essence, and this opposite is the whole.[39] Just as in Adorno's aesthetics the
art work is socially interpretable not because its represents society but because it
acquires its social content through resistance to society and is thus the unconscious writing of history, so Kierkegaardian inwardness, the spiritual *intérieur*,
gains its determinations through negation. In opposition to the privations of early
high-capitalism, the Kierkegaardian *intérieur* was to encompass "a lost immediacy"[40] and function "as a romantic island where the individual undertakes
to shelter his 'meaning' from the historical flood."[41] But precisely "by denying
the social question Kierkegaard falls to the mercy of his own historical situation,
that of the *rentier* in the first half of the nineteenth century."[42] The imagery of
the *intérieur* reveals social contents: a class based asceticism is sedimented in it.
By the effort to overcome the body, this sociological spiritualism reverses on
itself. Kierkegaard's imagery uses the living body exclusively as an allegory of
truth and untruth:[43] "This, to be sure, indicates the crucial reversal. If the body
only appears under the sign of the 'meaning' of the truth and untruth of spirit,
then in return spirit remains bound to the body as its expression." The more
spirit eviscerates the body, the more it depends on what it excludes: ultimately,
"nature takes possession of it [spirit] where it occurs most historically in objectless interiority."[44] In the spirit's will to autonomy it falls to the mercy of nature:
"My soul is so heavy that thought can no more sustain it, no wingbeat lift

it up into the ether."[45] Autonomous spirit is necessarily melancholic: "Bodiless spirit for him [Kierkegaard] becomes a burden that drags him into despair."[46]

Allegory

In the setting of the sun, the Baroque allegorists pictured the fall of the king. This allegorical image bears "the seal of the all too earthly": history, the king, "has physically merged into the setting,"[47] nature. The unpuzzling of such natural-historical figures is the primary interest of Benjamin's study of the Baroque, *The Origin of the German Play of Lamentation*. In his study of Kierkegaard's imagery, Adorno obviously followed Benjamin's lead. Since Benjamin's theory of allegory stands at the center of *Kierkegaard*, as it does at the center of Adorno's philosophy altogether, its introduction would be useful here. This, however, would be more difficult by drawing directly on Benjamin's work rather than on the work that he was translating while he was preparing his study of the Baroque and that may have given him his own critical insight into allegory, *La recherche du temps perdu*. In *Combray*, Marcel tries to understand the allegorical character of a servant girl, "a sickly creature far 'gone' in pregnancy."[48] What strikes Marcel about her is that her face shows no spiritual trace of the symbol born by her body: "The figure of this girl had been enlarged by the additional symbol that she carried in her body, without appearing to understand what it meant, without any rendering in her facial expression of all its beauty and spiritual significance, but carried as if it were an ordinary and rather heavy burden."[49] Here significance is not meaningful, but a physical burden and in this transformation of meaning into nature Marcel recognizes the servant girl's relation to other allegorical characters. Like the pregnancy of the servant, a portrait of "Envy" bears a serpent on her tongue. But, rather than the serpent being expressed in her face as "envy," Envy herself looked like "a plate in some medical book, illustrating the compression of the glottis or uvula by a tumour in the tongue."[50] Marcel sums up his observations and the entire fascination of allegory in a single parenthesis that distinguishes it from symbol: allegories are not symbols "(for the thought symbolised was nowhere expressed)."[51] This, however, does not mean that they are inexpressive; their expression, rather, is by way of nonexpression: the collapse of meaning into nature. In a talk Adorno gave just before the final revisions of *Kierkegaard*, "The Idea of Natural History," he presented the methodological idea of Kierkegaard (though not by name) as that of allegory: "Whenever 'second nature' appears, when the world of convention approaches, it can be deciphered in that its meaning is shown to be precisely its transience."[52] Paraphrasing Adorno, nature appears at the greatest extreme of second nature.[53] Although this thought is drawn from Benjamin, its form is Hegelian. The Hegelian dialectic, passed through Benjamin's idea of allegory, became in Adorno's work the form for the interpretation of all culture. No longer a dialectic of progress, the Hegelian dialectic, as the critique of any first, continually transforms meaning into the expression of transience. For Adorno, as he once said in a lecture, "the aim of philosophy is to say by way of concepts precisely what is is that cannot be said, to say the unsayable."[54] He clarified this at another point: "One could almost say that the aim of philosophy is to translate pain into the concept."[55] This would be the aim of a Hegelian dialectic that has become the presentation of allegory.

Revisions

In a letter of September 20, 1932, written from the home of his fiancée, Adorno apologized to the composer Ernst Krenek for having been unable to respond sooner: "I have been here for two months and living under the most extreme pressure. November 1st I must deliver the final manuscript for my book on Kierkegaard to Mohr, the publisher. Initially the revisions were only to trim the manuscript for publication; once I got into it, however, I found that I had to rewrite it altogether; certainly every stone of the original has been maintained, but not one remains where it once stood, every sentence has been reformulated, the whole has now for the first time been truly worked-through . . . and large and precisely central sections have been completely rethought. And all this has been compressed into the period between September 8th and November 1st. I must tell you, I am really in the harness: in three weeks I've dragged eighty pages out of myself, and I may say of the most rigorous sort."[56] Adorno did not exaggerate the intensity with which the material was at once maintained and completely transformed. Here is a juxtaposition of the manuscript's first few lines followed by the corresponding lines of the revision:

> All attempts to comprehend the writings of philosophers as poetry have missed their truth content. The object of philosophy is reality, which is interpreted by philosophy. Only by comprehending reality does the subjectivity of the philosopher stand the test. Neither the communication of this subjectivity, however profound, nor the degree of the work's internal coherence, decide its philosophical quality, but only the claim and the justice of the claim to state the truth about the real.[57]

> All attempts to comprehend the writings of philosophers as poetry have missed their truth content. Philosophical form requires the interpretation of the real as a binding nexus of concepts. Neither the manifestation of the thinker's subjectivity nor the pure coherence of the work determines its character as philosophy. This is, rather, determined in the first place by the degree to which the real has entered into concepts, manifests itself in these concepts and comprehensibly justifies them."[58]

Adorno's excitement in his letter was not only over his productivity, but over the unexpected emergence of what became his mature style. Characteristic of the revisions was that the language becomes more self-assuredly Hegelian; the best lines—among which the first line of this passage—were maintained, while the rest [though this is not true of this passage] underwent extreme condensation. By the time Adorno delivered the manuscript to Mohr a month later, he had cut it by half. Structurally, the basic order of the chapters remained intact; Chapters 1, 4, and 6 were least revised, and many headings and subheadings were maintained throughout. Yet much was changed, most important: Chapter 1 lost a section entitled "The Aesthetic as a Category of Knowledge"; the title of Chapter 2 changed from "Subject and Ontology" to "Constitution of Inwardness"; the title of Chapter 4 changed from "Analysis of the Existential" to "Concept of Existence"; Chapter 5 lost three major sections—"Excursus on Constellation," "Excursus on Goethe," and "Abstraction and Concretion"; Chapter 6 lost sections on the "Mythical Character of Kierkegaard's Christentum" and "Demythologization"; the title of Chapter 7 changed from "Rescuing the Aesthetic" to the title of the book, "Construction of the Aesthetic," its first section from "Apology of Melancholy" to "Transformation of Melancholy," the second from "Semblance and Reconciliation" to "Disappearance of Existence," and the last from "Outline of the Ontological in the Fragment" to "Transcendence of Longing." Without trying to find a common denominator for all these revisions, what is evident is a trimming back of ontological efforts, though not to the point demanded by his later philosophy. In *Kierkegaard* Adorno is still concerned with the possibility of a rescue of ontology. Along with the reduction of passages on ontology, theological motives are also dropped at many points. This, however, is more of a sublimation than excision, for theology is always moving right under the surface of all of Adorno's writings. This theological context is so dense that one can easily fail to be struck by the peculiarity that, for example, Adorno dated the published notice of an edition of *Kierkegaard* "Easter, 1963." The degree to which theology penetrates every word of his writings can be measured by the most misfired sentence he ever wrote, one that points far beyond biographical attachments: in his introduction to Benjamin's writings he compared Benjamin's fascination to that of the reflected light of a Christmas tree.[59] Opaque ideas in Adorno (as in Benjamin) often become immediately comprehensible when grasped in this context of theological interests. The idea of "truth-content" for example, which has remained so obscure, is a work's content of hope. Kierkegaard itself is the research of hope in Kierkegaard's oeuvre. It is not hard to sympathize with this effort in any year, certainly not 1933. Still, as the research of hope, *Kierkegaard* wants to take hope under its wing; when it does, it becomes ministerial and damages itself. On the last page of the book, Adorno writes of the "inconspicuous hope" sedimented in Kierkegaard's imagery; lists of similar passages could be given, including a passage in which he writes: "No truer image of hope can be imagined than that of ciphers, readable as traces, dissolving in history, disappearing in front of overflowing eyes, indeed confirmed in lamentation."[60] The passage is beautiful, but the mistakenness of this beauty is betrayed by its coziness, which brings it to the edge of rationalization.[61] Kafka's quoted-to-death "Hope, but not for us" is soberly optimistic in comparison with these passages. The best that can be done for them is to translate them back into the helplessness that motivates them. In the revisions of *Kierkegaard*, particularly in the sublimation of the theological, the distance to his later works was already being covered. The notice to the 1966 edition of *Kierkegaard* drops "Easter." In *Aesthetic Theory* (1969), his last work, the idea of hope no longer sails through the window: rather the work follows out the idea of allegory. In the sparseness of the late Adorno, the air may be thin, but it is what can be breathed: it carried out the revision of the earlier image of the reading of the palimpsest: "Authentic art knows the expression of the expressionless, a crying from which the tears are missing."[62]

* * *

Limitations to Adorno's study highlight those of this translation. Adorno cracks the surface of Kierkegaard's work by the literal interpretation of the imagery of his writings. His access to this literal level, however, was restricted by an at best rudimentary knowledge of Danish.[63] Adorno relied exclusively on Christian Schrempf's flawed, perhaps mangled,[64] German translation of Kierkegaard's collected work, an edition now largely superseded. Although a full estimation of the implications of Adorno's reliance on Schrempf must await critical commentaries, it is clear that this dependence resulted in occasional serious errors of detail, and details are almost the least of what goes wrong in translation. The translation into English of a book that itself hovers awkwardly between two languages poses special problems that are compounded by the condition of the current English translations of Kierkegaard, themselves of mixed quality and under revision. Where a choice had to be made between maintaining the coherence of Adorno's text and the extant translation of Kierkegaard, Kierkegaard was adjusted to Adorno. In general the differences were not of obviously great significance, but, as mentioned, further research may well show the contrary. Footnotes could have signaled these adjustments, but since anyone seriously interested in the fissures between these texts must know the languages involved in the first place, such notes would have been out of place here. Only the several greatest discrepancies have been marked.

A further limitation of this translation must be mentioned. German philosophical language has two sets of terms, deriving from the classical and the Germanic roots. Thus for "melancholy," German (like Danish) has two words:

Melancholie and *Schwermut*. When it makes sense to say that one language has several words for a single word in another language, the one word to some degree carries the meanings of the other two, though it is less able to distinguish them in certain contexts. This is the situation with a central concept of this translation: the English ''existence,'' on one hand, faces the German *Existenz* and *Dasein*, on the other. One could hardly begin to sum up what these concepts hold, but on the bluntest level the English concept is used either in the sense of specifically human existence or empirical existence in space and time. *Existenz* and *Dasein* can each carry either of these senses. But because German has two distinct, yet often synonymous terms, it is able to play off the different aspects found in the English concept in a way that is hard for English to reproduce. Translation of the German terms is of course further complicated by what they have undergone in the writings of Kierkegaard and Heidegger, who have made them terminological to the point that, in certain circles, *Existenz* effectively means Kierkegaard and *Dasein* means Heidegger. In Adorno's book, *Dasein* and *Existenz* occur in all possible ways, including the specifically Heideggerian and Kierkegaardian, and as synonyms. It has turned out to be impossible to use any device to mark the many jugglings of these concepts. If the German concepts were given in parenthesis, their great frequency would have clotted the text; special typefaces or capitalizations would have been incompatible with Adorno's style as well as made it impossible to understand the concepts when they are synonymous, overlapping, or ambiguous. This translation has therefore had to rely on ''existence'' for all the various instances of *Existenz* and *Dasein* in the original. The English concept is indeed able to hold them all. The reader, however, must develop an eye for its differentiations comparable to the way that the color-blind distinguish traffic lights by position; the distinction is that in this translation the colors really are missing.

Adorno has been much more widely and dependably translated into European languages than into English. The failings of the English translations are the result of anything but ill will or indifference: rather, they are due to the fact that Adorno has not yet been even rudimentarily understood in this country. Once this begins, better translations will become possible. *Kierkegaard* has to date been well translated into Italian, Spanish, and Swedish. If the original cannot be read alongside this translation, any of these others would help considerably. Getting a line at a slightly different rhythm or angle often makes the difference between obscurity and comprehension. This translation is not shy about its deficiencies and looks forward to going the way of Schrempf's and all those other mistaken first translations. I would not claim to have pulled the sword out of the stone; I hope I did not just pull off the handle.

Kierkegaard:
Construction of
the Aesthetic

Chapter 1
Exposition of the Aesthetic

Poetry and Dialectical Concept

All attempts to comprehend the writings of philosophers as poetry have missed
their truth content. Philosophical form requires the interpretation of the real as a
binding nexus of concepts. Neither the manifestation of the thinker's subjectivity
nor the pure coherence of the work determines its character as philosophy. This
is, rather, determined in the first place by the degree to which the real has entered
into concepts, manifests itself in these concepts, and comprehensibly justifies
them. The interpretation of philosophy as poetry is opposed to this. By tearing
philosophy away from the standard of the real, it deprives it of the possibility of
adequate criticism. Only in communication with critical thought may philosophy
be tested historically. That almost all — in the proper sense of the word — "subjective" thinkers had the rank of poet allotted to them can be accounted for by the
equation of philosophy and science that the nineteenth century effected. Everything in philosophy that could not be integrated into the ideal of science was
dragged along behind as a stunted appendage under the title of poetry. It was a
requirement of scientific philosophy that its concepts be constituted as the distinctive characteristics of the objects subsumed by them. If, however, the Kantian
conception of philosophy as science was first comprehensively formulated by
Hegel in the sentence "that now is the time for philosophy to be raised to the
status of a science,"[1] still his demand for scientific conceptualization does not
coincide with that for the unambiguous givenness of concepts as unities of distinctive characteristics. The dialectical method, to which, despite all his opposi-

tion to Hegel, Kierkegaard's work entirely subscribes, has its essence rather in the recognition that the clarification of particular concepts, as their complete definition, can be accomplished only through the totality of the fully developed system and not through the analysis of the isolated particular concept. In the preface to the *Phenomenology*, which expounds this, Hegel explicitly had in mind the aura of the poetic that surrounds every philosophical beginning. Consciousness "misses in the newly emerging form the range and specificity of content, and even more the articulation of form, whereby distinctions are given a fixed definition and are arranged in their firm relations. Without such articulation, science lacks universal intelligibility and gives the appearance of being the esoteric possession of a few individuals—an esoteric possession since it is as yet present only in its concept or in its inwardness; and of a few individuals, since its undiffused manifestation makes its existence something singular."[2] The revealing power of the newly emerging, however, is maintained beyond the scope of the definition of characteristic traits even in a model of thought that is no longer encompassed by a rigid system. Thus does a contemporary materialist interpreter of Hegel answer "the question of the determination of concept and terminology. It is of the essence of dialectical method that concepts which are false in their abstract onesidedness are later transcended. The process of transcendence makes it inevitable that these one-sided, abstract, false concepts be constantly employed; that the concepts be brought to their correct meaning less through a definition than through the function that they acquire as sublated elements of totality."[3] Not even "totality" is required to confer on dialectical concepts the ability to reveal the content of phenomena. If, however, philosophy as "subjective" thought has renounced totality altogether, it is the newly emerging that is most likely to confer on it the questionable reputation of being poetic. Yet dialectical concepts are indeed the proper instrument of philosophy. Philosophy is distinguished from science not so much as the supreme science that systematically unifies the most universal propositions of subordinated sciences. Rather, it constructs ideas that illuminate and apportion the mass of the simply existing; ideas around which the elements of the existing crystalize as knowledge. These ideas present themselves in dialectical concepts. As soon as this type of philosophy is tolerantly accepted as poetry, the strangeness of its ideas, in which its power over reality manifests itself, is neutralized along with the seriousness of its claim. Its dialectical concepts then serve as metaphorical decorative additions that may be arbitrarily dismissed by scientific rigor. Philosophy is thereby depreciated: poetry in philosophy means everything that is not strictly relevant. The same goes for the concurring praise of philosophical poetry. Gottsched, one of Kierkegaard's translators, finds not only that in *Repetition* "the aesthetic element is most brilliantly represented in both playful and earnest sections,"[4] but also that "this essentially dry philosopher, although he left behind no single verse of poetry, is at the same time not only a poet who played on his beloved mother tongue as on a fine instrument, setting free the greatest variety of tones; he is at the same time a poet with a lyre strung with the loftiest and most delicate, the gloomiest and most brilliant cords."[5] This praise dishonors the poetry as well as the philosophy. As opposed to the sheer possibility for confoundment, like that of Gottsched's, the first concern of the construction of the aesthetic in Kierkegaard's philosophy is to distinguish it from poetry.

The Claim to Poetry

The relation of Kierkegaard's work to the claim of being poetry is ambiguous. It is cunningly organized to take into account every misunderstanding that in the reader inaugurates the process of appropriating the content of the work. The dialectic in the material is for Kierkegaard at the same time a dialectic of communication. In this dialectic his work deceptively claims the title of the poetic just as often as it again disavows it. In the posthumous *The Point of View for My Work as an Author* he has an imaginary poet uncontestedly call him a "genius in a provincial town."[6] This formula was still effective in the work of Theodor Haecker, who in an early study of Kierkegaard's pseudonymous production writes that it is to be considered "a compendium written not by various scholars, but by various geniuses."[7] On the other hand, Kierkegaard, in the work whose external form could best be called poetic, grasps the status of the poet problematically: "He who wrote it" — the *Journal of a Seducer* — "was of a poetic nature, and as such, we might say was not rich enough, or perhaps, not poor enough, to distinguish poetry and reality. . . . First he enjoyed the aesthetic personally, and then his personality aesthetically. . . . Thus the poetic was constantly present in the ambiguity in which he passed his life."[8] The ambiguous image distorts that of the philosopher of the extremes, a philosopher such as Kierkegaard considered himself to be. At other points he sternly rejects the status of poet: "I am no poet and I go at things only dialectically."[9] Insight into the specific function of the claim to the poetic in his own works elucidates Kierkegaard's vacillation. He considers all those theses of his theology poetic, insofar as they are not apodictically derived from Christian doctrine: "As a writer I am a peculiar sort of genius, neither more nor less — absolutely without authority and therefore continually dependent on his own liquidation so as never to become, for anyone, an authority."[10] As a "genius," he preempts the title of poet primarily in order to avoid usurping, in his own and others' eyes, the name of apostle. In this respect, the "Ethico-Religious Treatises," the stereotypical opening formula of the *Religious Orations*, the carefully calculated publication of the essay on the actress, leave no room for doubt. Without "mission," he attempts to extract the concept of faith from a recalcitrant reason, to produce it from that recalcitrance. The poetic stance of "speaking without authority" moves him into the realm of religio-philosophical speculation of the kind that he opposed in Hegel and Schelling—from which, however, it is obviously distinguished by the irony of a method that claims to be able to prove nothing but what is already secretely inherent in it as faith. For Kierkegaard, poetry is the mark of the deception borne by all metaphysics in the presence of positive revelation. — In less formal language he calls himself a poet when he undertakes to recapitulate the poetic existence that constitutes, according to his hierarchy of the spheres of spiritual life, the location of depravity in human life. Without exception, the origin of the name poetry in Kierkegaard's work is transparently philosophical.

Poetry as Illustration

Anonymously, of course, it is the structure of the work itself that to a great extent announces the claim to be poetry. The various writings, *Either/Or, Fear and Trembling, Repetition, Stages on Life's Way*, contain novels, novellas, lyrical fragments; from the dense surface of the *Journal of a Seducer* to conceptually transparent works like *In Vino Veritas* and the passion narrative *Guilty/Not-Guilty*. But precisely these writings that would like to fulfill aesthetic criteria prove conclusively that the concept of the artist cannot possibly be applied to Kierkegaard. It is not the "impurity" of their self-reflective form that excludes them from art. This impurity established itself in the works of Friedrich Schlegel, Hoffmann, and Jean Paul, the models of Kierkegaard the novelist, as a binding law that is not confuted by Kierkegaard's having often opposed to it, as aesthetic theoretician, a reactionary classicism that his literary efforts themselves had left behind. Nowhere, however, in these writings of Kierkegaard is the electrifying clash of perceived reality and reflexive subjectivity to be found, which constitutes the formal principle of German romantic prose. Kierkegaard repeats this rhythm only externally. In every instance, intuition, as well as thought, is reducible to subjective intention. This is nowhere more drastically evident than where this intention so imperiously appears in the *Journal*, which down to the last fortuitous coincidence can be deduced from the predetermined model of the seducer. He who as a philosopher steadfastly challenged the identity of thought and being, casually lets existence be governed by thought in the aesthetic object. Only Lukács provides a full understanding of this in an early essay on Kierkegaard and Regine Olson: "An incorporeal sensuality and a plodding, programmatic ruthlessness are the predominant features of these writings" in the *Journal of a Seducer*. "The erotic life, the beautiful life, life culminating in pleasure, occurs in them as a world-view — and as no more than that."[11] Even Vetter, who senses the dubiousness of Kierkegaard's artistic results, seeks their origins in romantic aestheticism, which the *Journal* programmatically presents, without noticing that the immanent claim of the *Journal* is in no way fulfilled in them: "Kierkegaard's literary reputation was established by the *Journal of a Seducer*, which bewitched with its voluptuously ornate presentation of moods. The second literary triumph is less daring: *In Vino Veritas*. . . . In both cases an ostentatious eloquence has dangerously hollowed out the content; they are also evidence of a decadent, over-refined and exhausted creative force."[12] The "bewitchment" of the *Journal*, however, was only possible in the literary situation of a country that in Kierke-gaard's earlier work barely matched the literary sensation of *Lucinde*; the Pla-tonic symposium of pseudonyms, in its bare antithetic of worldviews, as whose mouthpieces the interlocutors function, is anything but a *"tour de force,"* or per-haps merely a *tour de force*; finally, in regard to Kierkegaard's eager aestheti-cism, there can be no question of "a decadent, overrefined and exhausted cre-ative force." The philosophy of the *Journal* may be extracted from its romantic husk without losing anything in the process, but also without any remnant of the husk being left behind. Even the alternation of presentational and reflective sec-tions, through which this worldview would like to assert itself in the *Journal*, is produced by a dialectic to which Johannes, a subject/object of romantic aesthet-icism, is subordinated, so that in accord with the Hegelian schema of triplicity, all immediacy in him can be transcended. This dialectic distinguishes itself from the Hegelian only by the—in Hegel's terms—"bad" infinity of the process, which is precisely to condemn reflection as depravedly aesthetic. This holds true for the entire dynamic of the plot, the entire psychology of the individual picto-rial consciousness right down to the last detail: the seduction itself. Intentionally or not, the seduction turns out to be a parody of Kierkegaard's concept of the instant. In spite of its intended demonic content, the seduction is constructed according to the same logic as the "point at which time and eternity touch"; the seducer possesses the beloved once, in order to abandon her at once forever.— Kierkegaard's aesthetic figures are strictly illustrations of his philosophical cate-gories, which they exemplify in primitive simplicity before they have been ade-quately articulated conceptually. As anyone today would recognize, all are marked by that peculiar characteristic of semblance typical of many illustrations of the first half of the nineteenth century. In their coloration, waning in their bourgeois miniature format, the great intention of allegory is hidden; although it acquires a lofty dignity in his philosophical works, it is incommensurable with the psychological novel that tempted Kierkegaard early on. If, in his last novel-istic effort, the passion narrative, even the external structure manifests the alter-nation of immediacy and reflection; if he hardly any longer bothers to anecdot-ally cover the skeleton of conceptuality and in the postscript to Taciturnus altogether reveals it, this may have been motivated—along with the bluntly emerging philosophical intention—by the recognition of the insufficiency of his fictional, aesthetic technique. The conceptual skeleton is identical in the three studies of erotic life: the *Journal*, *Repetition*, and the passion narrative. And indeed he presents it differently from how his concept of repetition would literally have it. Three times, with allegorical rigidity, he presents the enigmatic empty image of his disintegrating love. Its collapse degrades the entire phenomenal world to mere semblance. In its presence people are transformed into masks, while speech comes to sound like opera dialogue: "He who lays his head on a fairy hillock sees the image of a fairy in his dreams. I do not know if that is true. But I do know this: When I rest my head on your breast and do not close my eyes but look up at you, I see an angel's face."[13] Or, similarly, the Platonic banquet of pseudonyms helplessly conjures up the scenery of Don Giovanni: "The exalted mood of the participants, the noise of the festivities, the foaming delight of the champagne, are recollected best in a place which is quiet, remote and forgotten."[14] Finally, the catastrophe in nuce: "As soon as they were together the French doors were thrown open. The effect of the radiant illumination, of the coolness which encountered them, of the infatuating fragrance of perfume, of the elegance of the table-arrangement, overwhelmed for an instant the guests who were on the point of entering the room; they were transfixed and for an instant stood still as if in reverence before an invisible spirit encompassed them."[15] —It is not accidental that Kierkegaard's artistic insufficiency most prefers art and the artistic as its object. One of the central motives of semblance in the nineteenth century is announced here. As an artist, he was not involved with giving form to the contents of experience, but with the reflection of the aesthetic process and of the artistic individual in himself. The consequence, that art becomes its own object, is prefigured in the aesthetic idealism of the early Schelling and in Schopenhauer and finally brought to its destructive completion in Wagner and Nietzsche. Under the influence of German romanticism, Kierkegaard's writings prepare the transition of this intention from philosophical systematics—which he critically breaks through—to an artistic praxis of which he was not yet capable. At the same time he gives testimony to the isolation of an intellectual, living on private income, shut in on himself; an isolation that, in this period of late German romanticism and late idealism, was expressed in philosophy only by Schopenhauer. Kierkegaard was well aware of his affinity to Schopenhauer and shortly before his own death noted: "A.S. —strange, my initials are S.A.; we also comport ourselves as contraries—he is undeniably a major writer and has interested me considerably. It is disconcerting to find a writer who in spite of the total divergence of our positions resembles me so closely."[16] Close affinity through "deportment" is an idea not limited to Kierkegaard's radical Protestantism. For even though Kierkegaard's criticism of Schopenhauer extends to the latter's private life,[17] the primary characteristic of both is the private. Schopenhauer's experienced thought mourns a bad reality; Kierkegaard's loneliness never reached it. For this reason, his artistic failure can no more be adequately explained in exclusively aesthetic terms than it can be meaningfully criticized. Because the world of objects recedes before the gaze of his melancholy, for him the writing of poetry becomes the determination of the poet's comportment. The emblems of his self-election as poet surround him like stage props, unmoved by his language, ominous decorations of his monologue.

Aestheticism

For the aesthetic Kierkegaard, no poet himself, the figure of the "aesthete," passively driven between philosophical knowledge and the artistic demand for form was ready-made. This is how he characterized himself in an often quoted and obviously very early diary entry: "Here I stand like Hercules, but not at the crossroads—no, here there is a much greater multiplicity of roads, and so much the harder it is to choose the correct one. It is perhaps precisely the bad luck of my life, that I am interested in too many things without being able to decide on any one; my interests are not all subordinate to one, but are co-ordinate with one another."[18] Most recent studies of Kierkegaard have taken up the question of Kierkegaard the "writer." Its position is central is Schrempf's exhaustive biography and penetrates, as Przywara has correctly noted, the entire oeuvre, including Kierkegaard's theology of sacrifice: "If he wanted to be the sacrifice, which he *nolens volens* was as 'poet,' so the disproportion was overcome without however helping him, humanly (*kat anthropon*) as a person. That which was to be communicated to humanity through him as a chosen vehicle of the divine, consecrated as such to ruin, was indeed the idea for which he wanted to live and die. Were not these notions of the 'poet' the longed-for idea that would allow him to transcend the ever-present irony of life? Were they not the revelation that he was to deliver to humanity?"[19] In Schrempf's study, the question of Kierkegaard's literary aestheticism, as a question of "deportment," is removed from his work and becomes a psychological discussion of the person. The question appears as a strictly psychological problem in Vetter's "interpretation." Even the Catholic analysis of Erich Przywara has taken up the thesis of a romantic, aesthete *litterateur* as its psychological-dialectical infrastructure.[20] Apart from the attitude of the earlier pseudonymous writings and the assurances of the diaries of the same period, this interpretation can above all draw on the use of the word "writer." In Kierkegaard's work it is repeated like a magic spell; in the *Diary* it is at one point developed as the express conception of the whole of life as writing.[21] Only philosophical analyses can penetrate its formulaic character, which is on no account to be taken at face value. But even the secular imagination from which Kierkegaard distinguishes himself seems to be that of the literary aesthete, though less that of late German romanticism than of Baudelaire. Vetter, to whom this discovery is owed, gathers an abundance of proof from the latter's *Journaux intimes*, which attest to startling correspondances between the aestheticism of "A's Papers" or the "Symposium" and Kierkegaard's unrecognized Parisian exemplum.[22] The analogy may reach deeper, into more determinate historical figures than even

Vetter realized. Kierkegaard, in fact, reminiscing on the period of *Either/Or*, referred to himself as a *flaneur* and thereby fostered a corporeal similarity of his own image to that of the Baudelairian dandy.[23] But it is precisely in the dense nexus of these similarities that the differences make themselves sharply apparent. Aestheticism is no "deportment," to be assumed at will. It has both its hour and place: the early history of the metropolis. It is there, like artificial street lighting, in the twilight of incipient despair, that this strange, dangerous, and imperious form emits its beam to eternalize, garishly, life as it slips away. Kierkegaard's writings never attained this arena. The noisy earnestness of a narrow private life that accompanies the promulgation of Kierkegaard's aestheticism; the lack of any evident experience of the social landscape, the terrain of the *flaneur* and the dandy; the confines of a small town in which a seduction must search out its victim in a cooking school[24] — this ensemble results in a parody of an intended dandyism. To take it at face value would obscure the true seriousness of his philosophy. Schrempf's down-to-earth wisdom is incontrovertible; with less inhibition than any of the well-versed Kierkegaard critics, he recognized the "affected, coquettish and even silly aestheticism" of the first part of *Either/Or*, whose "aesthetic earnestness" could not protect "it in any way from the childish and trifling."[25] The seducer confesses, harmlessly enough: "I am an aesthete, an eroticist, one who has understood the nature and meaning of love and knows it from the ground up, and only makes the private reservation that no love affair should last more than six months at the most and that every erotic relationship should cease as soon as one has had the ultimate enjoyment."[26] Or, more bluntly, in *In vino veritas*: "Since at a banquet the essential business is to eat and drink, woman ought not to be included in the company, for she cannot acquit herself properly, and if she does, it is exceedingly unaesthetic."[27] Even as allegories of aestheticism such as the one presented by the cipher of "Aesthete A," these formulas unmask him as harboring the absurd ambition of *laisser faire laisser aller*. The same is true of the category of the "interesting." It is expressed subordinately as "deportment": "To be in love: how beautiful! To know that one is in love: how interesting!"[28] The philosophical correlative of the "interesting," of "aesthetic concupiscence," presents, as the dividing line between two spheres of Kierkegaard's existential logic, their precise, if objectively dubious, meaning: "The category I shall consider in more detail is the *interesting*, a category that especially now — since the age lives *in discrimine rerum* [at a turning point in history] — has become very important, for it is actually the category of the turning point. . . . The interesting is a border category, a *confinium* [border territory] between aesthetics and ethics. Accordingly, this examination must constantly wander into the territory of ethics, while in order to be of consequence it must seize the problem with aesthetic fervor and concupiscence."[29] The thinker is able to formulate as a "problem" what the aesthete nowhere proves in his "deportment."

Masks and Methods

That all this talk of Kierkegaard the aesthete, of Kierkegaard the poet, could ever take hold, can only be understood as an effect of the fascination of a rigid litany of tightly maintained aesthetic formulas, to which he — for better and for worse — does not correspond. Fascination is the most dangerous power in his work. Whoever succumbs to it by taking up one of the imposing and inflexible categories he inexhaustibly displays; whoever bows to its grandeur without comparing it with concretion, without ever investigating if it is adequate to concretion, has fallen under its dominion and become the servant of a mythical realm. Just as this realm is ruled by magical incantation, Kierkegaard's realm is ruled by logical immanence in which everything must find its place, come what may. The highest concept of his purported aestheticism, geniality, is itself of magical provenance. Although it was originally intended to conjure away the apostolic claim, Schrempf, Gottsched, and even Haecker successively fall under its spell. This explains Haecker's supposition of "various geniuses." It is as such that he regards the pseudonyms, like the force of "geniality," as powers of fascination on the Kierkegaardian landscape. By rejecting his claim to be a poet, however, his pseudonyms are excluded as the constitutive element of his philosophy. The possibility of a method fundamentally oriented to them is therefore precluded. Kierkegaard's fruitless attempt to compose self-animating poets confuses creator with artist and corresponds better to his idealist origins than to his theological goal. Every interpretive effort that unreflectively accepts the claim of the particular pseudonyms and measures itself by this claim misses the mark. They are not living bodies in whose incomparable existence intention is densely embedded. They are altogether abstract representational figures. This is not to say that criticism can ever disregard their function and take their opinion as Kierkegaard's own. Criticism has, rather, to confront the abstract figures of the pseudonyms as a group with the concrete motives encompassed by the framework of pseudonymity and to determine the coherence of the organization accordingly. Under this pressure the deceptive consistency of the pseudonyms may crumble; as it is, the superficial coherence of the philosophical doctrine inevitably blocks the way to any real insight. Criticism must first understand the assertions of the pseudonyms in terms of their philosophical construction; it must understand how this construction may be demonstrated in every instance as a dominating schema. What the pseudonyms then turn out to say that is more than what the philosophical schematism had intended, their secret and concrete essence, falls, in the literalness of the disclosure, into the hands of interpretation. No writer is more cunning in his choice of words than Kierkegaard or aims at concealing more through his language than he who inexhaustibly denounced himself as a "spy in a higher service,"[30] part of the secret police, a dialectical seducer. There is no way to meet up with him in the fox kennel of infinitely reflected interiority other than to take him at his word; he is to be caught in the traps set by his own hand. The choice of words, whose stereotypical (if not always planned) repetition indicates contents that even the deepest intention of dialectical procedure would rather conceal than reveal. Thus, the interpretation of Kierkegaard's pseudonymous writings must break down the superficially simulated poetic coherence into the polarities of his own speculative intention and a traitorous literalness. The impulse for the literal examination of Kierkegaard's language does not have to be imported psychoanalytically into his work, although there is more than enough occasion and temptation. It has its precedent in the work itself, in the theological Christian exegesis. Like the edifying writings, the pseudonymous *Training in Christianity* is exegetical; and all the pseudonymous writings are interwoven with exegetical sections. No meaningful exegesis can be conceived, however, that is not obligatorily bound to the vocabulary of the text. In Kierkegaard's work, the model of the exegesis is the canonical explication of the doctrine of the Parousia. According to the *Training*, "the whole existence of the Church here on earth is a parenthesis, a parenthesis in Christ's life; the content of this parenthesis begins with Christ's ascension, and with His second coming it ends."[31] It would do injustice to Kierkegaard's exegetical seriousness if one destroyed the dignity of his language through a psychological treatment of the pseudonyms. For at every point Kierkegaard's statements refer to texts that he held to be holy. The individual pseudonymously written statements are to be taken literally, according to the logic by which they are positioned in the construction of the spheres; that is, as explications of the aesthetical, ethical, and religious forms of existence that at the same time have their borders in literalness. In contrast to Kierkegaard's exegesis, the exegetical method must be concerned primarily with metaphor. Whereas metaphorically intended objects are to be clarified according to the logic of his "spheres," the literal metaphors gain their own autonomy. It is at this point that the mythical contents of his philosophy become evident, contents that the transparent logical architecture of the spheres vainly sought to ban. Their force is most evident precisely in his loftiest conceptions, where substance and statement are most deeply intertwined. A line from *The Sickness unto Death* reads: "As according to the report of superstition the troll disappears through a crack that no one can perceive, so it is for one who despairs all the more important to dwell in an exterior semblance behind which it ordinarily would never occur to anyone to look for it."[32] The metaphor, besides exposing the disjunction between a superficial context and a hidden content, intends with the fairy-tale figure of the disappearing troll to express the hiddenness of despair: "as indeed an exterior corresponding to concealedness would be a contradiction in terms; for if it is corresponding, it is then of course revealing."[33] At the same time, however, the word "troll" is the mythical-corporeal announcement of what indeed remains effective in general conceptual form as the category of the demonic in *The Sick-*

ness unto Death, yet only as incarnate constitutes the true object of Kierkegaard's demonology. The objective images, whose interpretation is the aim of his writing, are volatilized into such metaphors under the pressure of his subjectivism. They are to be called back out of the imagery to their authentic reality. However near this method seems to border on the psychoanalytic in its approach to Kierkegaard's demonic concealment, it must be distinguished from it as a philosophical method to the same degree so that it does not capitulate to the demonic. For to date psychoanalysis conceives of the person in complete immanence and grounds every impulse in the total nexus of the life of consciousness. Kierkegaard uses the doctrine of existence and radical personalism to make alluring the composition of individual immanence as autonomous and self-enclosed as psychoanalysis would like to pry the same immanence away, as knowledge, from the antagonistic struggle of the instincts. Immanence is for Kierkegaard the sovereign realm of the demonic; psychoanalysis subordinates itself to it *ab initio* by deducing itself from this very immanence that Kierkegaard's formulas conjure. Criticism, however, questions precisely the prerogative of the *argumentatio ad hominem*, even in the most inward theology; the prerogative of the identity of person and object, the thesis of the *Concluding Unscientific Postscript* that subjectivity is truth. Granting this thesis to Kierkegaard amounts to subordination to his regime. For this reason Schrempf's bold biography, starting with the thesis of the subjective thinker, argues despairingly with Kierkegaard over every sentence of his oeuvre and every decision in his life, and is a struggle with specters. Its arena is the cave of subjective immanence, hopeless from the beginning. Superior to all the other works on Kierkegaard, though not simply because of the much acclaimed "passion" (which is the inevitable topic wherever critical ability is insufficient) but rather because of the close dialectical contact with its object, this book is yet ultimately unable to make its insights fruitful: the casuistry of the postulate of the subjectivity of truth knocks the wind out of them. Blinded, it pursues the tracks of its opponent, whose figure remains ungraspable so long as it nebulously envelops its pursuer. Schrempf saves himself by surrendering the tracks that he faithfully pursued; he retains the empty hands of the secularized, ethical free thinker while whatever truth, sedimented in Kierkegaard's work, better than that of the dubious postulate of identity, escapes him. The closeness to the object, which Schrempf was the first to achieve, is to be maintained: every insight into Kierkegaard is to be wrung out of his own context. This insight, however, first becomes truth when its own spell is broken and singularly maintained. Indeed, Kierkegaard the person cannot simply be banished from his work in the style of an objective philosophy, which Kierkegaard unrelentingly, and not without good cause, fought. But the person is only to be cited in the content of the work, a content that is no more identical with the person than the person with the work.

Equivocations

By the same token, the aesthete cannot serve as a starting point for the construction of the aesthetic in Kierkegaard. The category of the aesthetic is, in contrast to the position of the aesthete, one of knowledge. Little as the aesthetic may be anticipatorily defined, it is equally clear that it must be freed from all muddlement. Even with respect to an ultimate convergence of art and philosophy, all attempts to aestheticize philosophical method are to be rebuffed. On the contrary, the more exclusively philosophical form is crystallized as such, the more firmly it excludes all metaphor that externally approximates it to art, so much the better is art able to survive as art by the strength of its own law of form. To begin with, the equivocations of the term "aesthetic" in Kierkegaard must be sought out. The synthesis of its various meanings is not to be found in Kierkegaard's art or in his deportment but only through the construction of elements that have been adequately differentiated. Although they are always mutually implicating, three of these elements should be distinguished. In Kierkegaard "aesthetic" means, first of all—as it does in common usage—the realm of art works and the theory of art.[34] This is its sense in many sections of the first volume of *Either/Or*, in the large essay on Don Juan, in the brief and important treatise "The Ancient Tragical Motive as Reflected in the Modern," in the "Shadowgraphs" of *dramatis personae*, and in Scribe's interpretation of "The First Love." They refer to Kierkegaard's second and central employment of the term by their choice of objects: the aesthetic as deportment or, in his later terminology, as "sphere." The sensual seducer constitutes the dialectical thesis to the antithesis of the reflected Johannes; the voices of Marie Beaumarchais, Elvira, and Gretchen reply sadly to the call of seduction; in Scribe's comedy, love based exclusively on memory is fully illusory. But at the same time the essays, as aesthetic theory, can be taken as largely self-sufficient and independent from the intention of the pseudonymous Erimita or the anonymous A. In particular the essay on the tragic contains motives that recur unchanged in Kierkegaard's theology. Similarly, the essay on the actress is not fully absorbed by the Machiavellian plans of its publication. The essay can be sensed distinctly in Kierkegaard's "ethical" theory whereby marriage protects love from time; and it contradicts the formulation of the aesthetic as the mere present and immediate, just as it develops this thesis more consistently in the presentation of the "sphere." For the mature Kierkegaard, the aesthetic as the artistic may have fused with the formula of the "poetic" through which he wanted to secure the position of speaking without authority. It is otherwise impossible to understand Kierkegaard's declaration of his total pseudonymous work prior to the *Fragments*, even the manifestly theological writings like *Fear and Trembling* and *The Concept of Anxiety*, as aesthetic.—The second manner in which he developed the concept of the aesthetic was already expressly defined in *Either/Or*: "The aesthetical in a man is that by which he is immediately what he is; the ethical is that whereby he becomes what he becomes. He who lives in and by and of and for the aesthetical in him lives aesthetically."[35] Aesthetic deportment appears as an absence of decisiveness from the perspective of the "ethical." The ethical recedes behind his doctrine of the paradoxical-religious. In the face of the "leap" of faith, the aesthetic is deprecatorily transformed from a level in the dialectical process—that of the failure of decisiveness—into simple creaturely immediacy. For it is precisely this immediacy that should be broken by paradox and that constitutes the absolute contrary of decisiveness. Thus, the aesthetic finally falls, with whatever proviso, subject to the verdict that at least dialectically asserts its legitimacy in the early writings. The attacks on art, beginning in the *Training*, correspond to the terminological shift and have little in common with the early rebuff of aesthetic existence. —The third sense of "aesthetic" is somewhat peripheral to Kierkegaard's usual use of language. It is found only in the *Concluding Unscientific Postscript*. Here "aesthetic" refers to the form of subjective communication and justifies itself on the basis of Kierkegaard's concept of existence. "The subjective thinker is an existing individual essentially interested in his own thinking, existing as he does in his thought. His thinking has therefore a different type of reflection, namely the reflection of inwardness, of possession, by virtue of which it belongs to the thinking subject and to no one else."[36] The "double reflection" of subjective thought, that is, the reflection on the "matter at hand" and the "inwardness" of thought, must "also express itself in the form of communication. That is to say, the subjective thinker will from the beginning have his attention called to the requirement that this form should embody artistically as much of reflection as he himself has when existing in his thought. In an artistic manner, please note; for the secret does not lie in a direct assertion of the double reflection; such a direct expression of it is precisely a contradiction."[37] Accordingly, aesthetic means precisely the manner in which inwardness—as the mode of subjective communication—is manifested, since it cannot, according to his doctrine, become "objective." Thus: "Wherever the subjective is of importance in knowledge, and where appropriation thus constitutes the crux of the matter, the process of communication is a work of art;"[38] or, even more briefly: "the greater the artistry, the greater the inwardness."[39]—Kierkegaard's category of the aesthetic encompasses disparate usages. However, it can no more be added up out of them than won from their abstract contradictoriness. Nor does Przywara's supposition of a disparate psychology suffice: "The Kierkegaard of contemporary philosophy of existence" is "a foreground that may be passed through into the Kierkegaard of *Either/Or* between psychoanalysis and rigorous religion."[40] This would amount to a shadow play of competing concepts in the gigantic mass of which the definite colors and form of the objects would disappear. The pompous conflicts of the universal never attain the real issue. It is to be reached only in the concrete cells of the dialectic, just as Kierkegaard's work itself develops them. The obscurity of the category of the aesthetic cannot be dissolved by a more inclusive method, but only through the critical inspection of individual phenomena.

Classicist Material Aesthetics

The category seems to offer itself most readily to such inspection where it communicates with historical linguistic usage: in the doctrine of the beautiful, the explicit aesthetic in the first volume of *Either/Or*. Yet to suppose that the key to the category is located here would obfuscate its specific contents. The aesthetic stands isolated in the entirety of his thought. It maintains rudimentarily a phase of his philosophy of which the polemic against Anderson is perhaps a remnant. The latter, however, distinguishes itself from the authentic Kierkegaard by the neutrality with which it regards art and the demands of art without seriously posing the question of art's fundamental legitimacy. Even if the neutrality is included in the dialectic as the dialectic of "aesthetic deportment," in itself this neutrality proves to be only fragmentarily related to the dialectic. In the first volume of *Either/Or* the pseudonymous mask is the most minimal disguise that nowhere adequately conceals the features of naive aesthetic speculation and positive Christian doctrine. Schrempf rightly notes that "even in the first part A. always employs Christian thought in such a fashion that to one's amazement one notices that this frivolous person in fact thinks remarkably like a Christian."[41] Or—it should be added—as an aesthete he thinks with the concepts of Kantian and post-Kantian idealist aesthetics: the finite, the infinite, and contradiction. These concepts undergo no substantial correction by Kierkegaard's dialectic. With its loose weave they spin a web over the aesthetic object. The definitions of the tragic and the comic are developed out of them. Both are constructed according to the formal principle of contradiction, unchallenged by Kierkegaard's Hegelian criticism of Hegel: "The comical rests as such throughout on contradictory contrasts both between aims in themselves and also between their objects and the accidents of character and external circumstances, and therefore the comic action requires a solution almost more stringently than a tragic one does. In a comic action the contradiction between what is absolutely true and its realization in individuals is posed more profoundly."[42] The tragic and the comic, which coincide according to the formal conditions of contradiction, are distinguished by Kierkegaard according to the relation in which finitude and infinitude—the contradictory elements—respectively stand to each other. For Kierkegaard, the tragic is the finite that comes into conflict with the infinite and, measured according to it, is judged by the measure of the infinite; the comic is the infinite that is entangled in the finite and falls to the mercy of the determinations of finitude. This is explained by Taciturnus in the commentary to the "Passion Narrative" with an example from the erotic: "The tragedy is that two lovers do not understand one another, the comedy is that two who do not understand one another should love one another.''[43] The dialectic of these fundamental distinctions never gets beyond their formal "resolution." For this reason, Kierkegaard maintains a definition of the beautiful that is an equivalent of the Kantian;William presents it as the thesis of his opponent A, the official representative of Kierkegaards' aesthetic: "The beautiful according to your definition is that which has its teleology in itself.''[44] The emptiness of the concept of contradiction becomes evident in the shallow and arbitrary characterization of the tragic and comic: "The matter is quite simple. The comical is present in every stage of life (only that the relative positions are different), for wherever there is life, there is contradiction, and wherever there is contradiction, the comical is present. The tragic and the comic are the same, in so far as both are based on contradiction; but the tragic is the suffering contradiction, the comical, the painless contradiction.''[45] It did not, however, escape Kierkegaard that the dialectical key concept of contradiction is at the same time not fully unifiable with the formal-idealistic definition of beauty. He wanted to play off Hegel's material aesthetics against the formal aesthetic tradition: "It has often seemed strange to me that these aestheticians attached themselves without question to the Hegelian philosophy, since a general knowledge of Hegel, as well as a special acquaintance with his aesthetics, makes it clear that he strongly emphasizes, with regard to the aesthetic, the significance of the content.''[46] The vain and empty lyric is appropriate to formal aesthetics: "God only knows what books the present generation of young versifiers is reading! Their study probably consists of learning rhymes by heart. God knows what importance they have in this world! At this moment, I know of no benefit from them other than that they provide an edifying proof of the immortality of the soul, since of them one may safely say to oneself what Baggesen says about the local poet Kildevalle: 'If he becomes immortal, then all of us will.' ''[47] Yet in his material aesthetics, Kierkegaard only apparently succeeds in correcting formalism. For wherever aesthetics is established on the basis of a dualism of content and form, without the clarification of the production of one through the other in the full analysis of forms and contents, formalism prevails. Kierkegaard maintains this dualism unconditionally and at the same time reveals his own classicism: "The good fortune" of aesthetic success "has two factors: it is fortunate that the most distinguished epic subject fell to the lot of Homer; here the accent falls as much on Homer as on the material. It is this profound harmony which reverberates through every work of art we call classic. And so it is with Mozart; it is fortunate that the subject, which is perhaps the only strictly musical subject, in the deeper sense, that life affords, fell to— Mozart.''[48] The rigid divergence of forms and contents is mastered only by the primacy of form, and it is this primacy that immediately cancels the acknowledged independence of the contents. And it does so by a principle of selection. Kierkegaard distinguishes between aesthetic and nonaesthetic contents. This cancels the specific substance of the contents; through selection, subjectivity becomes the dominant factor by its prerogative over the material, and those contents are omitted that would challenge this rule. In spite of the supposedly dialectical procedure, Kierkegaard in fact falls behind Kant and Schiller. According to their unrestricted principle of form, all objects have the potential to become aesthetic material insofar as they are penetrated by form; and so little as the principle of form is able to awaken its own substance, just so little does it obstruct the access of the substance. This explains why in Hebbel, Flaubert, and Ibsen realistic impulses were able to break through under the mantel of formalism. Kierkegaard, however, does indeed grant autonomy to the material but manages it in such a fashion that the most urgent—that of social experience—is excluded on its own account from treatment. Confronted with the nascent realism of the 1840s, all he has to say is: "Poetry makes one attempt after the other to play the role of reality, which is entirely unpoetical. Speculative thought repeatedly attempts to reach reality within its own domain."[49] The consequences are drastic in the *Stages*; they are condemned by Kierdegaard as "aesthetic posture," yet unchallenged in their intra-aesthetic legitimacy: "Aesthetics replies proudly and quite consistently, 'Sickness is no poetic motive, poetry must not become a hospital.' That is quite right, so it must be, and it is only a bungler who would attempt to treat such subjects aesthetically. 'Health alone is lovable' according to Friedrich Schiller. And from the standpoint of aesthetics he is perfectly right. Poetry must have a similar attitude towards poverty. To keep off the moaning and groaning it must decree that 'Wealth alone is lovable.' It has no use for the truly poor. Even the idyll makes no real exception here."[50] Accordingly, even the possibility of the psychological in art is narrowed and deprived of its true object: "The reason why the aesthetic consistently treats all self-torment as comic can be easily perceived, just because it is logical. Aesthetics keeps the hero in an undamaged state by reason of the direct proportion between strength and suffering (the one within, the other from without). It therefore regards every inward direction of thought as desertion, and not being able to have the deserter shot it makes him ridiculous."[51] Thus, with regard to content, Kierkekgaard's aesthetics becomes "aesthetic deportment"; since aesthetic existence is for him that of mere immediacy, immediacy constitutes the exclusive object of poetry: "Poetry deals with immediacy and cannot therefore think an ambiguous situation. If for a single instant it is put in doubt whether the lovers are absolutely faithful as lovers, are absolutely ready within themselves for the union of love—a single doubt of this sort, and with that poetry turns away from the guilty one and says, 'To me this is an indication that thou dost not love, hence I cannot have anything to do with thee.' And in this poetry does well, if it would not become a ludicrous power, as in these latter times it often enough has been through a mistaken choice of its task."[52] For Kierkegaard, the aesthetic has, as art and as deportment, "nothing to do with the inward."[53] This alone fully determines the scurrilous figure of his aesthetics. If autonomous, selective subjectivity usurps the right of its objects, it must pay for this with its own self. Subjectivity cannot form itself in its concreteness as an art object: it only finds itself again in the objects as a schema of predetermined and conventional ideas that no more originate in subjectivity than subjectivity really puts itself to the test in them. Kierkegaard relies on Hegel who corrected "the expression of the undisciplined subject in its equally undisciplined emptiness"[54] by giving "the theme, the idea, its due."[55] Yet in truth he reads eighteenth-century theses out of Hegel. The identification of "theme" and "idea" echoes a natural-rational, predialectical ontology of the arts. This is apparent in his static delimitation of the arts, which he undertakes even though — with reference to Schelling[56] — he wanted to pursue "the development of the aesthetically beautiful dialectically and historically":[57] "Music has time as its element, but it gains no permanent place in it; as notes are struck they fade away, existing only in the instant that they originate and dissipate. Of all the arts poetry knows best how to set off to advantage the significance of time and is precisely for this reason the highest of all arts."[58] This taxonomy of the arts is as antiquated as it is inadequate to musical form. For time is precisely one of the constitutive conditions of music. In its formal organization, in the alternation of the repeated and the new, in the concept of motivic and thematic labor and all of their "tectonics," its temporal course produces relations that give objective duration to the ephemeral sounding of the note, the isolated individual musical element. His assertion that music "*is* merely because it is constantly repeated, existing merely in the instant of execution"[59] is completely absurd. In the musical text, readable just like a literary work, music has an existence independent from its punctual performance. — In spite of his insight into its failings,[60] Kierkegaard succumbs to the classification of the arts according to their subject matter. The idealism of his selection of material constantly verges on reversing into a barbaric faith in material. Many artworks are exalted simply because of their subject matter, regardless of their form. In any case, William — who in general readily affects a complete aesthetic naïveté — says: "There is a picture representing Romeo and Juliet — an eternal picture. Whether in an artistic sense it is remarkable, I leave undecided, whether the forms are beautiful, I do not presume to judge, I lack the requisite taste and competence. The eternal quality of the picture consists in the fact that it represents them by an essential expression. . . . Juliet has sunk down admiringly at the beautiful situation of love."[61] The aesthetics of emotion that was appropriate to the major works of the eighteenth century, here manages only to produce apologia for paltry genre-images. It is, of course, Hegel himself who pointed the way: "Real art works — e.g. Raphael's Madonnas — do not enjoy distinguished veneration, or elicit a multitude of offerings; on the contrary, it is the inferior pictures that seem to be especial favorites and to be made the object of the warmest devotion and the most generous liberality. Piety passes by real art for this very reason, that were it to linger in their vicinity it would feel an inward stimulus and attraction; an excitement of a kind that cannot but be felt to be alien, whereas what is desired is a sense of mental bondage in which self is lost—the stupor of abject dependence.—Thus art in its very nature transcended the principle of the Church.[62] It is not by accident that in Hegel the theological motive resounds that alone makes understandable the coarseness of the excesses of Kierkegaard's material aesthetics. It is the representation of the sacred image, more precisely the "symbol," whose theme predominates as truth content and fractures the immanent form, just as the later Kierkegaard presented it in the narration of the image of the crucified. This motive turns against the aesthetic itself.

Formalism

Where Kierkegaard clings to the dualism of form and content, this dualism retains its idealistic character. The material aesthetics becomes formalistic under the sign of the "greatness" of its objects: "The aestheticians particularly, who have one-sidedly emphasized poetic activity, have so enlarged this concept, the pantheon of the exemplary became so enriched, aye, so overloaded with classical gimcracks and bagatelles, that the natural conception of a cool hall containing individually distinguished and imposing figures completely disappeared, and this pantheon became rather a lumber-room. Every neat little bit of perfect artistry is, according to this aesthetic verdict, a classical work, assured of absolute immortality; indeed, in this hocus-pocus, such little trifles were admitted most of all. Although otherwise one hated paradoxes, still one did not fear the paradox that the smallest was really the greatest art. The falsity lay in one-sidedly emphasizing the formal. Such an aesthetic could therefore flourish only temporarily, only so long as no one noticed that time made it and its classic works absurd. This tendency in the aesthetic sphere was a form of that radicalism, which, in a corresponding manner, has expressed itself in so many different spheres."[63] In this passage the "greatness" of the object is measured by what the transcendental subject first stamped on it as "idea" and "totality." The Hegelian school—to which Kierkegaard owed his material aesthetics as well as the category of totality—was able to give a better account of the centers of aesthetic intuition. In the *Aesthetic of the Ugly*, which appeared ten years after *Either/Or*, Kierkegaard's highly esteemed Rosenkrantz writes that "there is nothing at all automatically sublime in greatness or magnitude (*magnitudo*); twenty million dollars is a vast estate whose possession is probably very enjoyable, but there is certainly nothing sublime in it. Similarly, there is nothing at all mean about smallness (*parvitas*). An estate of only ten dollars is very small but it is still funds in which there is nothing to despise. A Lord's Prayer written on a cherry pit is not for that reason ugly; it is only written minutely. Smallness, at the right time and place, can be as aesthetically necessary as magnitude. Even the undersized, like the oversized, can be legitimate in the right situation."[64] Kierkegaard evades this insight by clinging to the traditional concept of perfection: "All classic productions stand equally high, because each one stands infinitely high."[65] Immortality is the only criterion of the classical he knows: "With his *Don Juan* Mozart enters the little immortal circle of those whose names, whose works, time will not forget, because eternity remembers them."[66] Under the heading of immortality he volatilizes eternity in the same fashion as he had previously accused Hegel of having done. For Kierkegaard, eternity is in art bound to abstractness: "I believe, on the other hand, that the following considerations may open the way for a classification that will have validity, precisely because it is altogether accidental. The more abstract and hence the more void of content the idea is, and the more abstract and hence the more poverty-stricken the medium is" — i.e., aesthetic material such as tone and language — "the greater the probability that a repetition will be impossible, and the greater the probability that when the idea has once obtained its expression, then it has found it once for all";[67] the greater the probability, in other words, that the work is immortal. The abstract is defined as the temporally invariant, the concrete as the historically conditioned.[68] Aesthetic ideas are for Kierkegaard *universalia post rem*, achieved through the exclusion of historically specific elements. His aesthetics thereby becomes ensnared in a nominalism that ultimately robs it of its object. What truly endures in artworks is not that from which time has been abstracted; in its emptiness it falls most completely to the mercy of time. Those motives assert themselves whose hidden eternity is most deeply embedded in the constellation of the temporal and is most faithfully maintained in their ciphers. Artworks do not obey the power of the universality of ideas. Their center is the temporal and the particular, whose figuration they are; what they mean that is more than this, they mean exclusively through this figure. Every division of the arts into the abstract and concrete remains, along with the hierarchy of their "eternity," inessential because concretion is required in every artwork and on no account limited to language. Once again, music contradicts Kierkegaard's definitions. Kierkegaard does indeed take music to be language in a certain sense: "The kingdom known to me, to whose utmost boundaries I intend to go in order to discover music, is language. If one wished to arrange the different media according to their appointed developmental process, one would have to place music and language next to one another, for which reason it has often been said that music is a language, which is something more than a genial remark."[69] But he conceives the relation of music and language as a mere analogy founded exclusively on the character of the receptive organ: "Aside from language, music is the only medium that addresses itself to the ear."[70] Their difference is equated with that of the abstract and the concrete: "But what does it mean to say that the medium is more or less concrete, other than to say it more or less approximates language, or is seen in approximation to language."[71] And the reverse: "What is the most abstract idea? The most abstract idea conceivable is sensuous geniality. But in what medium is this idea expressible? Solely in music."[72] Regardless of the justification for naming sensuous geniality the most abstract idea, the definition of music as its most abstract material leads to absurd conclusions. *Don Juan* is deduced from it as the single and exclusive musical masterpiece, just as in Hegel the Prussian state is deduced as the realization of historical reason: "The perfect unity of this idea" — of sensuous geniality — "and the corresponding form we have in Mozart's *Don Juan*. But precisely because the idea is so tremendously abstract, because the medium is also abstract, so it is not probable that Mozart will ever have a rival. It was Mozart's good fortune to have found a subject that is absolutely musical, and if some future composer should try to emulate Mozart, there would be nothing else for him to do than to compose *Don Juan* over again. . . . *Don Juan* . . . will always stand alone by itself, in the same sense that the Greek sculptures are classics. But since the idea in *Don Juan* is even more abstract than that underlying sculpture, it is easy to see that while sculpture includes several works, in music there can be only one. There can, of course, be a number of classical musical works, but there will never be more than the one work of which it is possible to say that the idea is absolutely musical, so that the music does not appear as an accompaniment, but reveals its own inner-most essence in revealing the idea. It is for this reason that Mozart stands highest among the immortals through his *Don Juan*."[73] Aesthetic idealism cannot be driven any further; in the face of the unity of the "idea," the contentless univer-sal concept of "sensuous geniality," all qualitative differences—in which art has its existence—shrivel up. The masterpiece is the canonically defined residue, mournfully alone, a closed and conclusive totality. Music is arbitrarily consigned to the abstractly demonic, and "absolute" music is, as in the George circle, con-demned: "By saying that when language ceases, music begins, and by saying, as people do, that everything becomes musical, we do not advance but go back-wards. This is the reason why I never had any sympathy—and in this perhaps even the experts will agree with me—with that sublime music which believes it can dispense with words. As a rule it thinks itself higher than words, although it is inferior."[74] The same Kierkegaard who often enough seems to perceive in the image of Mozart the contours of the future course of music; who detects in Don Giovanni the demonic reign of a mere natural power that was only to be set free musically in Wagner, and who interprets the *opera buffa* according to a romantic-hermeneutical schema that in fact took just this course; this same Kierkegaard would have been unable—according to his aesthetics—to have approved of a single phrase of Beethoven. His musical intuitions, like the description of the *Don Juan* overture, that found their counterpart only in Nietzsche's comments on the prelude to the *Meistersinger*, fell to him despite his own theory. The hierar-chy of the arts provides him with sufficient theoretical insights only in the realm of language. His dualistic form/content aesthetics therefore finds its most compelling expression in the philosophy of language; that is, in the doctrine of "communication" that incorporates in itself the third sense of the term "aesthetic." Here the idealism of Kierkegaard's aesthetic reaches its philosophical foundation: "The reduplication of the content in the form is essential to all artistry, and it is particularly important to refrain from referring to the same content in an inadequate form."[75] As mere reduplication, however, "the aesthetic" is detachable from the content and supererogatory; it is simply the addition of subjectivity to a being which remains foreign to subjectivity and which subjectivity is unable to gain in any other way except in that it, through communication, stamps being with its merely external seal. Against any claim of "inwardness," an unmediated unity with its object is not granted to it in the aesthetic object. The misconstrual of Kierkegaard's commentators, that his artistry lies in the embellishment and not in the matter itself, is promoted by his theoretical aesthetics. It originates in the constellation in which the fundamental elements of all idealistic and accordingly of Kierkegaard's philosophy appear: subject and object. He sees art where something objective, the "content," formed by the subject, "is expressed in existence." As an element of the "existential," form is for him subjective. He conceives the concretion of the artwork, like all concretion, as a mere product of two abstract elements: the abstract self and the abstract idea; at least by analogy to the elements of subject and object, of form and content. Without further ado he applies this polarity—and that of "existential statement"—to the concrete aesthetic region. Kierkegaard's aesthetic is more than the schema of this transposition. In it one is unable to grasp the meaning of his category of the aesthetic. It is only to be constructed out of the subject/object relation itself and therefore out of the obscure depths of a philosophy that his doctrine of art touches upon only in momentary shudders.

Chapter 2
Constitution of Inwardness

"Scripture"

Kierkegaard stipulates that the truth and untruth of thought be determined solely by reference to the thinker's existence. That this requirement, however, constitutes no epistemological *a priori* is made evident by the fundamental intention of Kierkegaard's own philosophy. For it aims not at the determination of subjectivity but of ontology, and subjectivity appears not as the content of ontology but as its stage. In "A First and Last Declaration," the principal investigation into pseudonymity and candor, Kierkegaard states that the meaning of the pseudonyms—which indeed guarantee the radical subjectivity of "communication"—does not lie "in making any new proposal, any unheard-of discovery, or in forming a new party, or wanting to go further, but, precisely on the contrary, consists in wanting to have no importance, in wanting (at a distance which is the remoteness of double reflection) to read solo the original text of the individual, human existence-relationship, the old text, well known, handed down from the fathers—to read it through once more, if possible in a more heartfelt way."[1] The archaic image of scripture, in which human existence is supposedly recorded, expresses more than the merely existing person. Kierkegaard's countless metaphors derived from the image of scripture refer to the writer of scripture; but this writer is also the reader of scripture, indeed including his own. The coquettishness of "A First and Last Declaration" hides yet does not ultimately destroy its earnestness: "From the beginning I perceived very clearly and do still perceive that my personal reality is an embarrassment which the pseudonyms with pathetic self-as-

24

sertion might wish to be rid of, the sooner the better, or to have reduced to the least possible significance, and yet again with ironic courtesy might wish to have in their company as a repellent contrast."[2] In the theology of the *Instant* the image of scripture is finally torn away from the subject: "The New Testament therefore, regarded as a guide for Christians, becomes . . . a historical curiosity, pretty much like a guidebook to a particular country when everything in that country has been totally changed. Such a guidebook no longer serves the serious purpose of being useful to travelers in that country, but at the most it is worth reading for amusement. While one is making the journey easily by railway, one reads in the guidebook, 'Here is Woolf's Gullet where one plunges 70,000 fathoms down under the earth'; while one sits and smokes one's cigar in the snug cafe, one reads in the guidebook, 'Here a band of robbers has its stronghold, from which it issues to assault the travelers and maltreat them.' "[3] The passage polemicizes not so much against the "text," against the guidebook itself, as against its historical deterioration. This is what makes the text a cipher. Implicit in Kierkegaard's metaphor of scripture is: the unalterable givenness of the text itself as well as its unreadableness as that of a "cryptogram" composed of "ciphers" whose origin is historical.—The invariable givenness of the text is founded on his theology. God's unchangeableness and that of truth is a theme of the religious discourses. Hence in the *Training*, where "edifying" and philosophical contents interweave, one reads: "Now this 'something higher' may be something very various; but if it is to be truly capable of drawing the person towards it, and at every instant, it must not itself be subject to 'variableness or the shadow of turning,' but must have passed triumphantly through every change and become transfigured like the transfigured life of a dead man."[4] As for the creator, so for the created: "Whatever one generation learns from another, no generation learns the essentially human from a previous one."[5]—The invariable meaning of the invariable text is, however, in Kierkegaard, incomprehensible: the fullness of divine truth is hidden from the creature. Kierkegaard speaks of this in parables comparable to those perfected by his student of a much later generation, Kafka: "If one were to offer me ten dollars I would not undertake to explain the riddle of existence. And why should I? If life is a riddle, in the end the author of the riddle will doubtless explain it. I have not invented the temporal life, but I have noticed that in the periodicals which make a custom of printing riddles, the solution is generally offered in the next number. To be sure, it does happen that some old maid or pensioner is mentioned with honor as having solved the riddle, i.e. has known the solution a day in advance—that difference is certainly not very considerable."[6] Kierkegaard is more closely allied with the opinion of such a "humorist" than he would like to admit in the *Postscript*. The same goes for the "moralist" of the second volume of *Either/Or*: "The man who lives ethically may do exactly the same things as the man who lives aesthetically, so that for a time this may create a deception, but finally there comes an instant when it is evident that he who lives ethically has a limit which the other does not recognize. This is the only way in which the ethical can become manifest; according to its positive meaning it remains hidden in the deepest layer of the soul."[7]—Paradoxically, the absolutely hidden is communicated by the cipher. It is, as is all allegory according to Benjamin, not merely a sign but expression.[8] The cipher no more belongs to ontological archetypes than it could be reduced to immanently human determinations. It is rather a middle realm that presents itself in the "affects," which Kierkegaard treated under the heading of psychology, particularly in *The Concept of Anxiety* and *The Sickness unto Death*. Haecker is right to separate sharply Kierkegaard's psychology from traditional scientific psychology. Yet it is also not to be equated—as Haecker in his early work still thought possible[9]—with current phenomenological philosophy. For phenomenology attempts to constitute ontology directly, on the basis of the autonomous *ratio*. Kierkegaard's psychology, however, is aware that ontology is blocked by the *ratio*. It attempts only to gain the reflections of ontology in the affects. This psychology depends on theology; it is not a self-sufficient anthropology. In *The Concept of Anxiety* Kierkegaard does not simply use the relation of anxiety and sin to imply that the affects are ciphers of a positive-theological object; he expressly defines them as such: "The mood of psychology is that of a discovering anxiety, and in its anxiety psychology portrays sin, while it worries and torments itself over the portrayal that it itself develops."[10] In *The Sickness unto Death*, despair is likewise a cipher of damnation: "By the aid of conscience things are so arranged that the judicial report follows at once upon every fault, and that the guilty one himself must write it. But it is written in sympathetic hues and therefore only becomes thoroughly clear when in eternity it is held up to the light, while eternity holds audit over the consciences."[11]—Obstructed ontology and cipher, however, are not simply conditions of the natural individual. They are not even adequately accounted for as a prehistorical result of the Fall. History engraved the fissure between the unreadable cipher and truth. What William asserts of the "exception," and therefore of Kierkegaard's person, contains at the same time fragments of Kierkegaard's conception of the history of spirit: "For in the face of the desolateness into which he has ventured and where there is more to lose than merely one's life, every person, who is still a humanly responsive person, recoils. He is quit with everything fundamental to human existence and thus these fundaments, which should have been his support through life, have become for him hostile powers."[12] The fissure stands not only between individual and text. If in his theology the two do not confront each other directly, but reciprocally refer to one another, decay necessarily attacks the text itself. Whereas according to every undiminished theological doctrine the signifying and the signified are unified in the symbolic word, in Kierkegaard the "meaning" separates from the cipher in the text. The affects, as ciphers, draw the fullness of immanence into themselves; the "meaning" remains frozen as an abstract desideratum: "I do it in the interest of its idea, its meaning; for I cannot live exclusive of the idea; I cannot endure that my life should have no meaning at all. The nothing that I do does after all give a little meaning to it."[13] For Kierkegaard, meaning was not always estranged from man, but became so historically: "The individuals of the contemporary generation are fearful of existence, because it is God-forsaken; only in great masses do they dare to live, and they cluster together *en masse* in order to feel that they amount to something."[14] Hence the retrograde direction of his philosophy: "In one word the direction of my writings is, 'Back!' And although it is all done without 'authority,' there is, nevertheless, something in the accent which recalls a policeman when he faces a riot and says, 'Back!' "[15] Kierkegaard's psychology of emotion wants to use the eternally, authentically human to conjure up historically lost meaning.

Objectless Inwardness

What Kierkegaard describes as "being quit with everything fundamental to human existence" was called, in the philosophical language of his age, the alienation of subject and object. Any critical interpretation of Kierkegaard must take this alienation as its starting point. Not that such interpretation would want to conceive the structure of existence as one of "subject" and "object" within the framework of an ontological "project." The categories of subject and object themselves originate historically. But it is precisely in these categories that interpretation is able to secure Kierkegaard's historical figure, a figure that dissolves into general anthropological considerations when the question becomes that of a "project of existence." If subject and object are historical concepts, they constitute at the same time the concrete conditions of Kierkegaard's description of human existence. This description conceals an antinomy in his thought that becomes evident in the subject/object relation, to which his "being quit" may be traced. This is an antinomy in the conception of the relation to ontological "meaning." Kierkegaard conceives of such meaning, contradictorily, as radically devolved upon the "I," as purely immanent to the subject and, at the same time, as renounced and unreachable transcendence. — Free, active subjectivity is for Kierkegaard the bearer of all reality. In his youth he accepted Fichte's criticism of Kant, and although he scarcely ever again formulated the problems that are the legacy of the history of idealism from its origins to Hegel, there is still no doubt that the dissertation expresses what is silently presupposed by all "existential communication": "Indeed, the more the ego became absorbed in scrutinizing the ego in the Critical philosophy, the more emaciated the ego became, until it ended by becoming a spector, as immortal as the husband of Aurora. The ego was like the crow, which, deceived by the fox's praise of its person, lost the cheese. Thought had gone astray in that reflection continually reflected upon reflection, and every step forward naturally led further and further away from all content. Here it became apparent, and it will ever be so, that when one begins to speculate it is essential to be pointed in the right direction. It failed to notice that what it sought for was in the search itself, and since it refused to look for it there, it was not in all eternity to be found. Philosophy was like a man who has his spectacles on but goes on searching for them; he searches for what is right in front of his nose, but he never looks there and so never finds them. Now that which is external to experience, that which collided with the experiencing subject like a solid body, after which each recoiled from the force of the impact in its own direction; the thing-in-itself, which constantly persisted in tempting the experiencing subject (as a certain school in the middle ages believed the visible emblems in the Eucharist were present in order to tempt the believer); this externality, this thing in itself was what constituted the weakness in Kant's system. It even became a problem whether the ego itself was not a thing in itself. This problem was raised and resolved by Fichte. He removed the difficulty connected with this 'in-itself' by placing it within thought, that is, he rendered the ego infinite as I = I. The producing ego is the same as the produced ego; I = I is the abstract identity. With this he infinitely emancipated thought.''[16] A phrase from the *Unscientific Postscript* corresponds to this thesis where Fichte is played off theologically against Hegel at the same time that the relocation of all "meaning" in pure subjectivity is affirmed: "Instead of conceding the contention of idealism, but in such a manner as to dismiss as a temptation the entire problem of a reality in the sense of a thing-in-itself eluding thought, which like other temptations cannot be vanquished by giving way to it; instead of putting an end to Kant's misleading reflection which brings reality into connection with thought; instead of relegating reality to the ethical — Hegel scored a veritable advance; for he became fantastic and vanquished idealistic scepticism by means of pure thought, which is merely an hypothesis, and even if it does not so declare itself, a fantastic hypothesis."[17] Here, however, the countervaling tendency is already apparent. The question of the thing-in-itself is no longer answered in the affirmative with the postulate of identity and absolute subjectivity; instead it is repulsed as "temptation" and held in abeyance. For the absolute "I," the reality of the thing-in-itself must become problematical along with the reality of the "meaning" that is indeed to be situated in the spontaneity of the "I." This insight can also be traced to the dissertation: "But this infinity of thought in Fichte is like every other Fichtian infinity (his ethical infinity is incessant striving for striving's own sake, his aesthetic infinity is perpetual production for production's own sake, God's infinity is continual development for development's own sake), that is, a negative infinity, an infinity without finitude, an infinity void of all content. Hence when Fichte rendered the ego infinite he asserted an idealism in relation to which all actuality became pale, an acosmism in relation to which his idealism became actuality, notwithstanding the fact that it was docetism. With Fichte thought was rendered infinite, and subjectivity became infinite absolute negativity, infinite tension and longing. Fichte hereby acquired a significance for knowing. His *Theory of Science* rendered knowledge infinite. But that which he rendered infinite was the negative, hence in place of truth he acquired certainty, not positive but negative infinity in the infinite identity of the ego with itself. Instead of positive endeavor, i.e. happiness, he obtained negative endeavor, i.e. an *ought.*"[18] Absolute subjectivity is denied "meaning" along with happiness. The idealist who conceived of "relegating reality to the ethical," that is, to subjectivity, is at the same time the archenemy of any assertion of the identity of the external and the internal. The pathos of his philosophy is directed against this assertion from the very first sentence of his pseudonymous works: "Dear Reader: I wonder if you may not sometimes have felt inclined to doubt a little the correctness of the familiar philosophic maxim that the external is the internal, and the internal the external. Perhaps you have cherished in your heart a secret which you felt in all its joy or pain was too precious for you to share with another. . . . Perhaps neither of these presuppositions applies to you and your life, and yet you are not a stranger to this doubt; it flits across your mind now and then like a passing shadow."[19] Every line of Kierkegaard's work makes this presupposition.—The contradictory elements in Kierkegaard's formulation of meaning, subject, and object are not simply disparate. They are interwoven with one another. Their figure is called inwardness. In *The Sickness unto Death*, inwardness is deduced as the substantiality of the subject directly from its disproportionateness to the outer world: "Well, there is no 'corresponding' external mark, for in fact an outward expression corresponding to close reserve is a contradiction in terms; for if it is corresponding, it is then of course revealing. On the contrary," here—in the moment of despair—"outwardness is the entirely indifferent factor in this case where introversion, or what one might call inwardness with a jammed lock, is so much the predominant factor."[20] Where Fichte's idealism springs and develops out of the center of subjective spontaneity, in Kierkegaard the "I" is thrown back onto itself by the superior power of otherness. He is not a philosopher of identity; nor does he recognize any positive being that transcends consciousness. The world of things is for him neither part of the subject nor independent of it. Rather, this world is omitted. It supplies the subject with the mere "occasion" for the deed, with mere resistance to the act of faith. In itself, this world remains random and totally indeterminate. Participation in "meaning" is not one of its potentials. In Kierkegaard there is so little of a subject/object in the Hegelian sense as there are given objects; there is only an isolated subjectivity, surrounded by a dark otherness. Indeed, only by crossing over this abyss would subjectivity be able to participate in "meaning" that otherwise denies itself to subjectivity's solitude. In the effort to achieve a transcendental ontology, inwardness takes up the "struggle with itself," on which Kierkegaard the "psychologist" reports. Yet no psychology is required to explain this struggle; not even the supposition—in which

Schremf, Przywara, and Vetter agree–of sexual inversion, whether characterizing the work or the person. Mourning can be shown, pragmatically, to be Kierkegaard's central affect in the foundational nexus of his philosophy. Whereas the psychological factors under which Kierkegaard's philosophy developed are scarcely to be denied, his character expresses a historical constellation. From a historico-philosophical perspective, Kierkegaard, the psychologically solitary, is least solitary. He himself vouches for a situation of which he never tires of asseverating that he has lost reality. Even the extreme of solipsism falls within the boundaries of his philosophical landscape: "This that inhers in the individual is the only reality that does not become a mere possibility through being known, and which can be known only through being thought; for it is the individual's own reality."[21] In the image of the concrete individual, subjectivity rescues only the rubble of the existent. Subjectivity, in the form of objectless inwardness, mourns in its painful affects for the world of things as for "meaning."

Immanent Dialectic

Kierkegaard bestows the term "dialectics" on the movement that subjectivity completes both out of itself and in itself to regain "meaning." This cannot be conceived as a subject/object dialectic since material objectivity nowhere becomes commensurable with inwardness. This dialectic transpires between subjectivity and its "meaning," which the dialectic contains without being merged with it, and which does not merge with the immanence of "inwardness." The affinity between this dialectic and the mystical dialectic does not escape Kierkegaard . He uses the "moralist" William—who in the overall plan of the oeuvre represents the figure that does justice to reality—to carry out the critique of mysticism; this undoubtedly serves at the same time to free Kierkegaard from any suspicion of mysticism. True, like the "moralist" who has perfected inwardness, the mystic "has chosen himself absolutely."[22] But, whereas for the "ethical character" prayer becomes "more deliberate,"[23] for the mystic prayer takes on an "erotic character" as an "intrusiveness in his relation to God."[24] The mystic impatiently disdains "the reality of existence to which God has assigned him"[25] and commits "a deceit against the world."[26] Through the negation of reality, however, the content of mystical faith itself becomes dubious: "The mystic is never consistent. If he has no respect for reality in general it is not obvious why he does not regard with equal distrust that moment in reality when, as he believes, he was affected by the higher experience. That too is indeed a moment of reality!"[27] This thought could easily enough turn against Kierkegaard himself. But his arguments do not crystalize. The mystic is judged not according to the measure of a reality that he fails, but according to the measure of his own inwardness: "The failing of the mystic is that by his choice he does not become concrete for himself, nor for God either; he chooses himself abstractly and therefore lacks transparentness."[28] Transparentness, however, is itself exclusively determined inwardly: by repentance.[29] Ethical concretion therefore remains as abstract as the mystical act, as the mere "choice of choice." This choosing constitutes the schema of all of Kierkegaard's dialectics. Bound to no positive ontic content, transforming all being into an "occasion" for its own activity, Kierkegaard's dialectic exempts itself form material definition. It is immanent and in its immanence infinite. Indeed he hopes to protect the dialectic from the bad infinity of the simply unlimited: "When a mystification, a dialectical reduplication, is used in the service of a serious purpose, it will be so used as merely to obviate a misunderstanding, or an over-hasty understanding, whereas all the while the true explanation is at hand and ready to be found by him who honestly seeks it."[30] Or in the act of "choice": "The self that one chooses in so far as one chooses oneself, is assumed to be in existence prior to the choice; and likewise, one can only choose the beloved that is indeed already the beloved. To choose the beloved can only mean her acceptance."[31] Yet the origin of this immanent dialectic presents itself at the same time as functional: "Am I just suffering from an excess, morbid reflectiveness? I can give evidence that this is not the case. For there is a leading thought in this whole matter that is as clear to me as day, namely to do everything to work her loose and to keep my soul upon the apex of the wish."[32] Maintaining the self at the apex of the wish is nothing other than dialectical movement within the enigmatic-unreal figure that Kierkegaard's philosophy of immanence confers upon this movement. This is the proper place for the question that Theodor Haecker poses in his important treatise on Kierkegaard's concept of truth. He reproaches Kierkegaard for a subjective dynamic that, beyond its own tension, assumes no autonomous being given to man. Kierkegaard's "terrible error" is "that the starting point and ultimately everything is 'how.' For the individual commences with the 'what,' in a still weak, and just as distant 'how' the enduring, the dogmatic 'what' of faith, the supernatural seed, the content, that can only be just that, which alone corresponds to the supernatural faith of the person and which no human passion, however intense, can gain by coercion."[33] Kierkegaard is—Haecker continues—a "philosopher of becoming . . . a spiritualist, that is, one who according to expectation and nature would be a philosopher of being."[34] However pointedly this takes issue with the basic organization of the philosophy, it does not do justice to the historical depth of its foundation. Kierkegaard did not, in neo-Kantian fashion, reconceive being as pure becoming. Being is supposed to inher in becoming as its content, one that is of course concealed from the individual. Concealed being, enciphered "meaning," produces dialectical movement, not blind subjective coercion. This raises Kierkegaard above romantic efforts of reconstruction that claim to be able to recreate ontology whole, phenomenologically. He prefers to let consciousness circle about in the self's own dark labyrinth and communicating passageways, without beginning or aim, hopelessly expecting hope to flair up at the end of the most distant tunnel as the distant light of escape, rather than deluding himself with the *fata morgana* of static ontology in which the promises of an autonomous *ratio* are left unfulfilled. This explains the preponderance of becoming over being in spite of the ontological question of origin. — The qualitative multiplicity of the being of ideas is transposed into the unity of immanent becoming. Croce's thesis that Hegel "only recognized contradictions and denied validity to differences"[35] also holds good for Kierkegaard. The objectless dialectic subsumes all qualitative determinations under the formal category of "negation." According to Kierkegaard's philosophy, dialectic is to be conceived as the movement of individual human consciousness through contradictions. Its "intellectualized," essentially rational structure does not in truth conflict with its content. Geismar, drawing on Hirsch, has shown that Kierkegaard's "intellectualism" in the dialectical centerpiece, the doctrine of Christian paradox, is of a part "with the energy with which Kierkegaard wants to isolate Christ's revelation from that of any other religiosity."[36] The same evidence can be used to philosophically deduce the "intellectualism" from the condition of objectless inwardness, to which the theology of sacrifice itself belongs. Where the intuition of things is repudiated as temptation, thought holds the field and its monologue articulates itself exclusively through contradictions that thought itself produces. Reality finds expression only in the internally contradictory temporal course of the monologue, that is, as history. Kierkegaard conceives the choice of choice itself as historical, and its historicity is to guard against mysticism: "For man's eternal dignity consists in the fact that he can have a history, the divine element in him consists in the fact that he himself, if he will, can impart to this history continuity."[37] — The doctrine of a "real dialectic," which contemporary Protestantism reads out of Kierkegaard and opposes to the idealist dialectic, remains unconvincing. Kierkegaard did not "overcome" Hegel's system of identity; Hegel is inverted, interiorized, and Kierkegaard comes closest to reality where he holds to Hegel's historical dialectic. Indeed, Kierkegaard himself conceives the dialectic exclusively according to the schema of internality. But in this schema he is continually confronted by history as it in truth is.

Philosophy of History

As an opponent of Hegel's doctrine of objective spirit, Kierkegaard developed no philosophy of history. He wanted to use the category of the "person" and the person's inner history to exclude external history from the context of his thought. But the inner history of the person is bound anthropologically to external history through the unity of the "race": "At every moment, the individual is both himself and the race. This is the individual's perfection viewed as a state. It is also a contradiction. A contradiction, however, is always the expression of a task; a task, however, is a movement; but a movement that as a task is the same as that to which the task is directed is an historical movement. Hence the individual has a history. But if the individual has a history, then the race also has a history."[38] Race and individual are to substantiate each other reciprocally and indissoluably. Kierkegaard takes the "person" to be the point of indifferentiation between them. This point of indifferentiation must both maintain the exclusive unity of the subjective dialectic and assign it an appropriate position in reality. The indifferentiation, however, cannot be stabilized. Objectless inwardness strictly excludes objective history; history relentlessly drags into itself the enclaves of isolated inwardness. Therefore Kierkegaard's construction of indifferentiation becomes mere ambiguousness. This can be shown concisely in *The Concept of Anxiety*, whose definition of hereditary sin as an anthropological and equally as a historical constant is supposed to illuminate the essence of historicity itself. Kierkegaard hesitates to recognize hereditary sin as a historical constant: "In traditional terms, the difference between Adam's first sin and the first sin of every other man is this: Adam's sin conditions sinfulness as a consequence, every other first sin presupposes sinfulness as its condition. Were this so, Adam would actually stand outside the race, and the race would not have begun with him but would have had a beginning outside itself, which is contrary to the terms of the discussion."[39] The recommencement in each individual that is required, so that Adam is not situated "outside the race," negates any authentic history as the constitutive transformation of the individual. Yet certain doubts are stirred up that oppose this: What "the presence of sinfulness" — of hereditary sin, in any case — "in a man, the power of the example, etc . . . otherwise means in the history of the race or as preliminary runs to the leap, without being able to explain the leap, is something else."[40] It is precisely the "something else," however, that is under consideration. It is the dependence of the person on external history. As soon as Kierkegaard admits this, he arrives at the opposite thesis of his initial assertion: "Since the race does not begin anew with every individual, the sinfulness of the race does indeed acquire a history."[41] The contradiction is not correctable as a mere inexactness in the logic of the presentation. It originates in two different concepts of history. — On one hand, history is conceived as "historicity": the abstract possibility of existence in time. As such, history is an element of philosophical anthropology. It is therefore exemplified by a prototypical phenomenon, which as prototypical is therefore an extrahistorical phenomenon: Adam. He is not able to "condition sinfulness as a consequence" because he would otherwise stand "outside the race," which would contradict the concept, that is, the general concept of the historical individual altogether. Precisely what constitutes authentic history, the irreversible and irreducible uniqueness of the historical fact, is emphatically rejected by Kierkegaard. According to his doctrine, this is simply because this uniqueness itself excludes the fact — on account of its uniqueness — from history; more important, however, the unique is excluded from history because uniqueness is contrary to the ahistorical, general determination of the race; contrary, that is, to the determination of the individual by the natural quality of the possibility of history. Indeed, Kierkegaard attempts to rescue the content of real historical uniqueness through the categories of the leap and the beginning. He speaks impressively of the "secret of the first."[42] Precisely as the "leap," however, the appearance of the first is abstractly set apart from historical continuity; it becomes a mere means for the inauguration of a new "sphere," for which category the historical moment, the specific content of the emerging first, remains entirely insignificant. Its historical force continues to resound only in the act of "achieving" a new sphere. Hereditary sin itself, however, is bled of its historical substance: "That sin was not in the world before Adam's first sin is, in relation to sin itself, something entirely accidental and irrelevant. It is of no significance at all and cannot justify making Adam's sin greater or the first sin of every other man lesser."[43] In Kierkegaard's doctrine of hereditary sin, history is nothing else than the formal schema according to which the intrasubjective dialectic is to reverse into the dialectic of the "absolute." It establishes the borders against mere subjectivity, leaving, however, the historical fact in dark contingency. — On the other hand, real history prevails in his philosophy. Even the objectless "I" and its immanent history are bound to historical objectivity. Kierkegaard makes this plain with regard to language. For language is materially and qualitatively dependent on the objective historical dialectic and at the same time, according to Kierkegaard's doctrine, ontologically predetermined. He attests to the doctrine's ambivalence. Language is said to be ontological in *The Concept of Anxiety*: "If one were to say further that the issue then becomes a question of how the first man learned to speak, I would answer that this is very true, but also that the question lies beyond the scope of the present . . . psychologically pathbreaking . . . investigation. However, this must not be understood in the manner of modern philosophy as though my reply were evasive, suggesting that I *could* answer the question in another place. But this much is certain, that it will not do to represent man himself as the inventor of language."[44] In contrast, the *Stages* teaches the rudiments of a nominalistic theory of language that separates thoughts and words and surrenders language to the "accidental," in any case to the intrahistorical: "People generally believe that what makes a presentation of thought unpopular are the many technical terms of scientific phraseology. That however is an entirely extrinsic sort of unpopularity, which scientific speakers have in common with sea-captains, for example, who also are unpopular because they speak a jargon, and by no means because they speak profoundly. Therefore time and again the phraseology of a philosophy may penetrate even to the common man, proving that its unpopularity was only extrinsic. No, it is the thought and not the expression that makes a formulation essentially unpopular. A 'systematic' handicraftsman may be unpopular, but he is not intrinsically unpopular, because he does not attach much thought to the exceedingly strange things he says. . . . Socrates, on the other hand, was the most unpopular man in Greece, precisely because he said the same thing as the simplest man, but attached infinite thought to it."[45] The paradox of the interpretation of language as at once historical and extrahistorical has, however, as its consequence that the concept of sin, whose content for Kierkegaard varies only quantitatively in history while it is qualitatively assumed as prior to everything historical, is also determined qualitatively and historically through language. For the "innocence" of every later generation, which according to his theory enters the sphere of sin exclusively through the "qualitative leap," has at its disposal in language a concept of sin that the generations have bequeathed to language. Kierkegaard is able to escape from this dilemma only through the powerless, psychologistic assertion that this later innocence, when it speaks of sin, in truth has no idea of what is actually meant by it: "Nevertheless, his anxiety is not anxiety about sin, for the distinction between good and evil does not exist prior to the developing actuality of freedom. This distinction, to the degree that it exists, for example in language which even guiltlessness hears and speaks, is only a foreboding presentiment that through the history of the race may signify a more or a less."[46] Accordingly, intrahistorical persons would be situated at a level of consciousness that they do not find themselves in, even as children. Against Kierkegaard's intention, innocence and sin would constitute a continuum of various levels of consciousness without a "qualitative leap," and the genesis of language would be psychologically relativized. These aporia may have obliged Kierkegaard to let the paradox of language and history stand. Even in the positive-theological *Training*, concrete historical language is for him at the same time the seal of truth: "Believe me it is highly important that a man's speech be accurate and true, for so then will his thought be."[47] Precisely here Kierkegaard shows reverence for the historical scars on the creaturely body of language, the foreign words, for the sake of their function in history: "Life is—to use a foreign word (partly because it so exactly characterizes the situation, and partly because it so promptly and definitely reminds everyone of what one should remember)—it is an 'Examen' [examination]."[48]—If language is the form of the communication of pure subjectivity and at the same time paradoxically presents itself as historically objective, objectless inwardness is reached in language by the external dialectic. In spite of the thesis of the abstractness and contingency of the world of things, inwardness is not altogether able to escape from it: they collide in "expression" and in its historical figure. Inwardness attempts to still the external world that crowds in on it by anathematizing history. Thus originates Kierkegaard's struggle against history, prompted empirically by the events of 1848.— "Internal history is the only true history; but true history contends with that which is the life principle of history, i.e. with time. But when true history, that is, the individual, contends with time, then the temporal and therefore every little moment of it acquires its immense reality."[49] In this sentence, written in 1843, historical heteronomy still appears as a matter of indifference, worthy of neglect. Later, however, the image of history becomes that of radical evil, whose power he admits insofar as he rages against it: "Oh, that there were someone (like the heathen who burnt the libraries of Alexandrea) able to get these eighteen centuries out of the way—if no one can do that, then Christianity is abolished. Oh, that there were someone capable of making it clear to these many orators who prove the truth of Christianity by the 1,800 years—that there were someone who could make it clear to them (terrible as it is) that they are betraying, denying, abolishing Christianity—if no one can do that, then Christianity is abolished."[50] From the annihilation of historical reality by the absolute self, the motive of "contemporaneousness" emerges in which contemporary dialectical theology imagines it possesses the key to reality: "For in relation to the absolute there is only one tense: the present. For him who is not contemporary with the absolute—for him it has no existence."[51] The external world is lost in the face of "inner history"; but inner history can only transpire simultaneously as a "relation to the absolute." For its time has no binding unity of measure; it is exclusively the immanent form of the dialectical movement, unreal in the face of the "absolute." Thus history vanishes. The early Kierkegaard attempted to justify this epistemologically in one of the essays of "aesthete A," who invariably represents Kierkegaard's own doctrine. The doctrine is Platonizing, in contrast to the larger dialectical intention of the work, and therefore at the same time problematically expressed: "Should anyone feel called upon to say that the tragic always remains the tragic, I should in a sense have no objection to make, in so far as every historical evolution always remains within the range of the concept. On the supposition that his statement has meaning, and that the repetition of the word *tragic* is not to be regarded as constituting an empty meaningless parenthesis, then the meaning must be this, that the content of a concept does not dethrone the concept but enriches it. On the other hand, it can scarcely have escaped the attention of any observer . . . that there is an essential difference between ancient tragedy and modern tragedy. If, in turn, one were to emphasize this difference absolutely, and by its aid, first stealthily, then perhaps forcibly, to separate the conceptions of the ancient and modern tragical, his procedure would be no less absurd than that of the man who denied any essential difference; for he would thereby be cutting off the branch he sits on and would only prove that what he wanted to separate belongs together."[52] If here history is still mastered by the "range of the concept" in which, according to the Hegelian model, a historical dialectic transpires, history later evades the plan and appears simply as a threat to inwardness.—The horror in the face of every specifically historical content is finally concretized as a negative philosophy of history. Such a negative philosophy of history is found, in defiance of "simultaneity," in the *Instant*, and is notably reminiscent of neo-Platonic, gnostic doctrine: "In a totally opposite sense history is a process. The idea is introduced—and with that it enters into the process of history. But unfortunately this does not (as one ludicrously assumes) result in the purification of the idea, which never is purer than in its primary form. No, it results, with steadily increasing momentum, in garbling the idea, in making it hackneyed, trite, in wearing it out, in introducing the impure ingredients which originally were not present (the very opposite of filtering), until at last, by the enthusiastic cooperation and mutual approbation of a series of successive generations the point is reached where the idea is entirely extinguished and the opposite of the idea has become what they now call the idea, and this they maintain has been accomplished by the historical process in which the idea has been purified and refined.''[53] Kierkegaard thereby takes up in his final polemic the romantic thesis of a golden age. Already in *Either/Or*, William claims: "Our age reminds one vividly of the dissolution of the Greek city-state: everything goes on as usual, and yet there is no longer anyone who believes in it. The invisible spiritual bond which gives it validity no longer exists, and so the whole age is at once comic and tragic — tragic because it is perishing, comic because it goes on.''[54] This borders on insight into the historical origin of objectless inwardness: "Men have perceived that it avails nothing to be ever so distinguished an individual man, since no difference avails anything. A new difference has consequently been hit upon: the difference of being born in the nineteenth century.''[55] All that would be needed is the sequacious insight that in fact "no difference avails anything" for his own concept of absolute inwardness to appear in front of his own eyes as a romantic island where the individual undertakes to shelter his "meaning" from the historical flood. But it is at this point that Kierkegaard's thought breaks off, and he supposes himself protected on the island from the flood. The following sentence is perfectly characteristic: "It is not to be denied that the whole tendency of the age often makes such a marriage" — one "that has been rescued from reflection and its shipwreck" — "a dolorous necessity. As for this 'necessity,' however, it must be remembered that every generation, and each individual in the generation, begins life anew to a certain extent, and that for each one severally there is a possibility of escaping this maelstrom.''[56] The flood of history is similar to the devastating maelstrom; in it, however, the person asserts himself as free. Only at particular instants do person and history come into contact. At these moments of contact, however, the historical dimension shrivels. The concept of "situation," Kierkegaard's own present isolated from historical contingency, corresponds to the concept of "simultaneity," the revelation that has already occurred. It is true that the concept of "situation" contains historical, real elements in itself. These elements, however, are isolated and subordinated to the individual. "Situation," for Kierkegaard, is not — as is objective history for Hegel — graspable through the construction of the concept, but only by the spontaneous decisiveness of the autonomous individual. To put it in the language of idealism, in "situation" Kierkegaard pursues the indifferentiation of subject and object. He is able to do without it so long as inwardness — lacking any object—is withdrawn into itself. It becomes the refuge of the subject as soon as it is overwhelmed by objectivity.

"Situation"

Therefore the "situation" is not directly intuited; rather it is produced in advance by its concept; according to the schema in which he presents the movement of inwardness and which at the same time largely corresponds—in the category of reflection—to the Hegelian philosophy of history: "For in fact the people he addresses are already Christians. But if it is Christians he is addressing, what can be the sense of getting them to become Christians? If, on the contrary, they are not Christians, in his opinion, although they call themselves such, the very fact that they call themselves Christians shows that here we have to do with a situation that demands reflection, and with that the tactics must be entirely reversed."[57] The situation that "translates everything into terms of reflection"[58] is itself at the same time conceived as a "sphere of reflection." Situation thereby proves itself to be subjective-objective indifferentiation: on the basis of its objective-historical derivation, it gives cause for reflection and at the same time roots itself in the element of subjective reflectedness that, according to Kierkegaard, "has transcended all immediacy." In Kierkegaard's "situation," historical actuality appears as reflection. Indeed, it appears re-flected, literally thrown back. The harder subjectivity rebounds back into itself from the heteronomous, indeterminate, or simply mean world, the more clearly the external world expresses itself, mediatedly, in subjectivity. The course of this process is the same as that of Kierkegaard's own development. Only when its immanent dialectic is repelled by external reality—where it is still tolerated as aesthetic immediacy and as the "middle reality" of the ethical—does reality enter into the dialectic and the dialectic plastically reproduce the contours of the external world. The polemical character, which characterizes all of Kierkegaard's statements on the "situation," originates not from the pathos of a "prophetic attack" occasionally arrogated by his tone. On the offensive, his philosophy responds to the painful intrusion of reality into the objectless interior, marked by the recessive movement of the self. This accounts for Kierkegaard's political opinions. However consistently they fail to grasp the circumstances, they are more deeply formed by them than the blatantly reactionary, provincial, and individualistic thesis (particularly in the *Diaries*) would ever lead one to imagine. This ultimately becomes evident. For the later Kierkegaard, situation is "what subsists." In the *Training* and *For Self-Examination*, the subsistent is still spoken of with a timidity that would happily give unto Caesar what is his, because in truth a Caesar no more exists for it than does property. In the final essays, however, the concept of the "subsistent" obtains its true force insofar as it absorbs the actual social condition: "Might there in these shrewd times be found even a youth who does not easily understand that, if the state got the notion, for example, of wanting to introduce the religion that the moon is made out of a green cheese, and to that end were to arrange for 1000 jobs for a man with family, steadily promoted, the consequence would be — if only the state held to its purpose — that after a few generations a statistician would be able to affirm that this religion (the moon is made out of a green cheese) is the prevailing religion in the land?"[59] For Kierkegaard, the relation of church and state stands in the foreground. Yet his attack takes him far enough to allow him to see through the socioeconomic bases of this relation: "Of course it will cost money, for without money one gets nothing in this world, not even a certificate of eternal blessedness in the other world; no, without money one gets nothing in this world."[60] This sort of comment, whose applicability could easily enough spring from the bearers of religion to religion itself, can be found in Georg Buechner. The economic motive of society is formulated with perfect clarity in the antithesis: "By seeing the glorious ones, the witnesses to the truth, venture everything for Christianity, one is led to the conclusion: Christianity must be truth. By considering the priest one is led to the conclusion: Christianity is hardly the truth, but profit is the truth."[61] — For Kierkegaard, the external world becomes effectively real only in its depravity. It is therefore in the "situation" that his dialectic makes its way out of a closed immanence. The situation confronts immanence with the depraved present as its own origin; in protest, the situation is forced toward "reflection." Kierkegaard gladly played off left-Hegelian materialist authors, such as Boerne and Feuerbach, against an empty idealist philosophy of identity — against a church he thought less knowledgeable of the essence of Christianity than precisely Feuerbach;[62] behind his ironic-dialectical intention, a secret affinity may be hidden. There is enough materialist explosive present in the *Instant*, and the either/or of inwardness must, once shaken by the impact of the subsistent, reverse as fundamentally into its antithesis as Kierkegaard asserts the thesis. The efficient cause, however, hidden in the "subsistent," which the "situation" reveals, is none other than the knowledge of the reification of social life, the alienation of the individual from a world that comes into focus as a mere commodity. This clarifies Kierkegaard's formulation of the relation of subject and object. In his philosophy the knowing subject can no more reach its objective correlative than, in a society dominated by exchange-value, things are "immediately" accessible to the person. Kierkegaard recognized the distress of incipient high-capitalism. He opposed its privations in the name of a lost immediacy that he sheltered in subjectivity. He analyzed neither the necessity and legitimacy of reification nor the possibility of its correction. But he did nevertheless — even if he was more foreign to the social order than any other idealistic thinker — note the relation of reification and the commodity form in a metaphor that need only be taken literally to correspond with Marxist theories. According to the *Training* (1850): "To reflect means, in one sense of the word, to come quite close to something which one would look at, whereas in another sense it implies an attitude of remoteness, of infinite remoteness so far as the personality is concerned. When a painting is pointed out to one and he is asked to regard it, or when in a shop one looks at a piece of cloth, for example, he steps up quite close to the object, in the latter instance he even takes it in his hands and feels it, in short, he gets as close to the object as possible. But in another sense, by this very movement he goes quite out of himself, gets away from himself, forgets himself, and there is nothing to remind him that it is he that is looking at the picture or the cloth, and not the picture or the cloth that is looking at him. That is to say, by reflection I enter into the object (I become objective), but I go out of or away from myself (I cease to be subjective)."[63] Christianity, however, brings rescue from the extremity of reification: "For Christian truth, if I may say so, has itself eyes to see with, yea, is all eye."[64] Truth does not have the character of a thing. It is the divine glance, which falls like the *intellectus archetypus* on alienated things and releases them from their enchantment. — Along with the things, human relations and humanity itself are enchanted: "Some reflections! You can perceive that in the speaker: his glance is drawn back into the eye, he resembles not so much a man as one of those figures carved in stone that has no eyes. . . . So it is that the 'I,' who was the speaker, dropped out; the speaker is not an 'I,' he is the thing at issue, the reflection. And as the 'I' failed, so also the 'thou' was done away with, thou the hearer, the fact that thou who sittest there art the person to whom the discourse is addressed. Indeed, it has almost gone so far that to talk in this personal fashion to other people is regarded as 'getting personal.' By 'getting personal' one understands unseemly and rude behavior — and so it will not do for the speaker, 'I,' to talk personally, and to persons, the hearer, 'thou.' "[65] Inwardness takes hold of the reified person and breaks its own spell: "When the castle door of inwardness has long been shut and is finally opened, it does not move noiselessly like an apartment door which swings on hinges."[66] Admittedly, this door opens only for the instant. For "in the external world, everything belongs to the possessor. It is subject to the law of indifference" — of reification — "and the spirit of the ring obeys the one who has the ring, whether he is an Aladdin or a Noureddin, and he who has the wealth of the world has it regardless of how he got it. It is different in the world of the spirit."[67] Thus shallow idealism consoles itself over the "situation"; it comfortably divides up its objects into internal and external, spirit and nature, freedom and necessity.

Intérieur

The fitting name of the "situation," as the powerless-momentary indifferentiation of subject and object, is not the castle, with which Kierkegaard romantically compares inwardness. Nor need the name be established sociologically by mere "coordination" with Kierkegaard; rather, it is pragmatically implicit in his work. And, indeed, it is to be found in the imagery of the apartment interior, which, while it discloses itself only to interpretation, demands interpretation by its striking independence. It is the bourgeois *intérieur* of the nineteenth century, before which all talk of subject, object, indifferentiation, and situation pales to an abstract metaphor, even though for Kierkegaard the image of the *intérieur* itself serves only as a metaphor for the nexus of his fundamental concepts. The relation is reversed as soon as interpretation gives up the compulsion of identity that is exerted even by Kierkegaard's idea of situation, which indeed exclusively occurs as the actual site of inward decisiveness. — Philosophically schooled authors have not yet given any attention to Kierkegaard's *intérieur*. Only Monrad's innocuous biography betrays — in a single passage — knowledge of the true state of affairs: "How his fantasy developed, aided by the arts of disguise and imagery, during promenades in the parlor, how it ran wild! — In the parlor! Everywhere one looks in Kierkegaard, one finds something undeniably shut-in; and out of his prodigious oeuvre there comes to us the smell of the hothouse."[68] From Kierkegaard's youthful writings Geismar quotes the description of those "promenades in the parlor" that importantly illuminate the work of the isolated individual. There the report is of a "Johannes Climacus" (the pseudonym with which Kierkegaard later cloaked his own position): "When Johannes on occasion asked for permission to go out, he was most often denied; as an alternative, the father occasionally offered his hand for a walk up and down the hall. At first sight this was a meager ersatz, and yet . . . something totally out of the ordinary was hidden in it. The suggestion would be accepted, and it would be left entirely up to Johannes where they would go. Then they went out the front door to a nearby garden house, or to the beach, just as Johannes desired; for the father was capable of everything. As they now went up and down the hall, the father pointed out everything they saw; they greeted others passing by, cars noisily crossed their way, drowning out the father's voice; the cakes in the bakery window were more inviting than ever."[69] Thus the *flaneur* promenades in his room; the world only appears to him reflected by pure inwardness. Images of interiors are at the center of the early Kierkegaard's philosophical constructions. These images are indeed produced by the philosophy, by the stratum of the subject-object relation in the work, but they point beyond this stratum by the strength of the things that they record. Just as in the metaphorical *intérieur* the intentions of Kierkegaard's philosophy intertwine, so the *intérieur* is also the real space that sets free the categories of the philosophy. The central motive of reflection belongs to the *intérieur*. The "seducer" begins a note: "Why can you not be quiet and well behaved? You have done nothing the entire morning except to shake my awning, pull at my window mirror, play with the bell-rope from the third story, rattle the windowpanes, in short, in every possible way tried to get my attention!"[70] Kierkegaard may have introduced the "window mirror" as a "symbol" for the reflected seducer with intentional casualness. But it defines an image in which—against Kierkegaard's intention—social and historical material is sedimented. The window mirror is a characteristic furnishing of the spacious nineteenth-century apartment; that such an apartment is under discussion is evident from the mention of the "bell-rope from the third story" that must be occupied by another family for him to have a separate bell-rope. The function of the window mirror is to project the endless row of apartment buildings into the isolated bourgeois living room; by the mirror, the living room dominates the reflected row at the same time that is is delimited by it—just as in Kierkegaard's philosophy the "situation" is subordinated to subjectivity and yet is defined by it. In their time, the nineteenth century, window mirrors were commonly called "spies"—which is how Kierkegaard refers to himself in his final self-account: "I am, that is, like a spy in a higher service, in the service of the idea and as such must keep watch on the intellectual and the religious and spy out how 'existence' matches up with knowledge and 'Christendom' with Christianity."[71] He who looks into the window mirror, however, is the private person, solitary, inactive, and separated from the economic process of production. The window mirror testifies to objectlessness—it casts into the apartment only the semblance of things—and isolated privacy. Mirror and mourning hence belong together. It is thus that Kierkegaard himself used the metaphor of the mirror in the *Stages*: "There was once a father and a son. A son is like a mirror in which the father beholds himself, and for the son the father too is like a mirror in which he beholds himself as he will someday be. However, they rarely regarded one another in this way, for their daily intercourse was characterized by the cheerfulness of gay and lively conversation. It happened only a few times that the father came to a stop, stood before the son with a sorrowful countenance, looked at him steadily and said: 'Poor child, you live in silent despair.' "[72] Melancholy appears in the symbol of the mirror, in the archaic and the modern, as the imprisonment of mere spirit in itself. This imprisonment is, however, at the same time imprisonment in a natural relation; in the ambiguous bond between father and son. The image of the *intérieur* therefore draws all of Kierkegaard's philosophy into its perspective, because in this image the doctrine's elements of ancient and unchanging nature present themselves directly as the elements of the historical constellation that governs the image. Thus the key to Kierkegaard's entire oeuvre may indeed be sought in a passage from the "Diary of a Seducer": "Environment and setting still have a great influence upon one; there is something about them which stamps itself firmly and deeply in memory, or rather upon the whole soul, and which is therefore never forgotten. However old I may become, it will always be impossible for me to think of Cordelia amid surroundings different from this little room. When I come to visit her, the maid admits me to the hall; Cordelia herself comes in from her room, and, just as I open the door to enter the living room, she opens her door, so that our eyes meet exactly in the doorway. The living room is small, comfortable, little more than a cabinet. Although I have now seen it from many different viewpoints, the one dearest to me is the view from the sofa. She sits there by my side; in front of us stands a round tea table, over which is draped a rich tablecloth. On the table stands a lamp shaped like a flower, which shoots up vigorously to bear its crown, over which a delicately cut paper shade hangs down so lightly that it is never still. The form of the lamp reminds one of oriental lands, the movement of the shade of the mild oriental breezes. The floor is concealed by a carpet woven from a certain kind of osier, which immediately betrays its foreign origin. For the moment I let the lamp become the keynote of my landscape. I am sitting there with her outstretched on the ground, under this wonderful flower. At other times I let the osier rug evoke ideas about a ship, about an officer's cabin—we sail out into the middle of the great ocean. When we sit at a distance from the window, we gaze directly into heaven's vast horizon. . . . Cordelia's environment must have no foreground, but only the infinite boldness of far horizons. She must not be of the earth, but ethereal, not walking but flying, not forward and back, but everlastingly forward.''[73] In this description Kierkegaard's philosophical intention encounters, without any effort on his part, objective, historical contents in those of the *intérieur*. The "illustration" takes on a life of its own that ignites in the text of his thoughts, and consumes the text with its images. The text was concerned with a vague-erotic "mood,"which is only deciphered in the outline of the illustration; and concerned as well with the category of the infinite that, through contrast, binds the dialectic of the seducer to the intimacy of the personal-private. But the force of the material goes beyond the intention of the metaphor. The *intérieur* is accentuated in contrast to the horizon, not just as the finite self in contrast to the supposedly erotic-aesthetic infinitude, but rather as an objectless interior vis-à-vis space. Space does not enter the *intérieur*; it is only its boundary. The *intérieur* is polemically posited on the boundary of space as the sole determinate being; it is polemically the equivalent of Kierkegaard's "subjective thinker." Just as external history is "reflected" in internal history, in the *intérieur* space is semblance. Kierkegaard no more discerned the element of semblance in all merely reflected and reflecting intrasubjective reality, than he sees through the semblance of the spatial in the image of the *intérieur*. But here he is exposed by the material. It is not by accident that he readily compares inwardness with a fortress. Under the sign of the fortress as that of the primordial past, and under the sign of the *intérieur* as that of the incalculably distant, which are stamped upon the present and the nearest, semblance gains its power. The contents of the *intérieur* are mere decoration, alienated from the purposes they represent, deprived of their own use-value, engendered solely by the isolated apartment that is created in the first place by their juxtaposition. The "lamp shaped like a flower"; the dream orient, fit together out of a cut paper lampshade hung over its crown and a rug made of osier; the room an officer's cabin, full of precious decorations greedily collected across the seas—the complete *fata morgana* of decadent ornaments receives its meaning not from the material of which they are made, but from the *intérieur* that unifies the imposture of things in the form of a still life. Here, in the image, lost objects are conjured. The self is overwhelmed in its own domain by commodities and their historical essence. Their illusory quality is historically-economically produced by the alienation of thing from use-value. But in the *intérieur* things do not remain alien. It draws meaning out of them. Foreignness transforms itself from alienated things into expression; mute things speak as "symbols." The ordering of things in the apartment is called arrangement. Historically illusory objects are arranged in it as the semblance of unchangeable nature. In the *intérieur* archaic images unfold: the image of the flower as that of organic life; the image of the orient as specifically the homeland of yearning; the image of the sea as that of eternity itself. For the semblance to which the historical hour condemns things is eternal. God-abandoned creation presents itself marked by the ambiguity of semblance until it is rescued by the actuality of judgment. The semblance of the eternity of creation in the image of the *intérieur* is the eternity of the transcience of all semblance.—This alone gives the doctrine of "situation" as indifferentiation its concrete meaning. Indifferentiation is not simply, as it is conceived in Kierkegaard's philosophy, that of the subjective and objective, but of the historical and the natural. The *intérieur* is the incarnate imago of Kierkegaard's philosophical "point": everything truly external has shrunken to the point. The same spacelessness can be recognized in the structure of his philosophy. It is not developed successively, but in a complete simultaneity of all moments in a single point, that of "existence." This explains the peculiar difficulty for every presentation of Kierkegaard that must arduously analyze the spatial and temporal instant of his thought into the extensive and sequential. Kierkegaard intimates this himself in the ironic afterword to the *Stages*: "enthralled by the one thought I have not budged from the spot."[74] The world, however, cannot spread itself out in the point, but can appear only as an optical illusion, as through a peephole. In semblance, however, the historical world presents itself as nature.—That in Kierkegaard the "situation"—i.e., of Christianity—and the "modern" apartment belong together is evident in a passage of the preparative, polemical work *For Self-Examination*: "No, just as in a well-appointed house one is not obliged to go downstairs to fetch water, but by pressure already has it on the upper floors merely by turning the tap, so too is with the real Christian orator, who, just because Christianity is his life, has eloquence, and precisely the right eloquence, close at hand."[75] A metaphor of technical life as the temporal present stands in for the eternal preparedness of the Christian condition, and in the apartment eternity and history merge. In the most noteworthy fashion the images of demonic, nature-bound defiance in *The Sickness unto Death* are derived from mechanics, even though the sickness is supposed to be that of the creature and not of the historical individual. They devour the historical motive of reification with an archaic motive that is summoned up out of it: "No, this puffing and the onrush which succeeds it is really not the thing that has to be considered, but rather the even momentum with which the locomotive proceeds and which occasions the puffing. And so it is with sin."[76]—Elsewhere Kierkegaard combines sorcery and machine, unintentionally revealing the demonic character of subjective-autonomous existence more through the image than through the thought: "The least inconsistency is a prodigious loss, for with that a man . . . [and] existence which is under the rubric of spirit . . . in fact loses consistency; that same instant the spell is perhaps broken, the mysterious power which bound all powers in harmony is enfeebled, the spring loses its tension, the whole machinery is a chaos where the forces fight in rebellion against one another, to the injury of the self, and therein there is no accord with oneself, no momentum, no impetus. The prodigious machine which in consistency was so compliant with its iron strength, so pliable with all its power, is in disorder."[77] He goes even further with the "secret of the first," the most obscure image of the mechanics of his day: "As one who ascends in a balloon rises by casting weights from him, so does the despairing man sink by casting from him the good."[78] The final metaphor of the train irradiates like a flare in a thoroughly magical metaphysics such as Kierkegaard otherwise disdained: "The case of the guilty man who journeys through life to eternity is like that of the murderer who with the speed of the railway train fled from the place where he perpetrated his crime. Alas, just under the railway coach where he sat ran the electric telegraph with its signal and the order for his apprehension at the next station. When he reached the station and alighted from the coach he was arrested. In a way he had himself brought the denunciation with him."[79] Thus Kierkegaard himself turns over the key to all civilizatory metaphors: in the assumption of the actuality of judgment, the semblance of sudden historical figures is at once destroyed and fulfilled. They revolve around the bourgeois apartment as the locus of their historical fulfillment and as their powerful cipher. Thus is to be understood the most memorable passage that Kierkegaard dedicated to the *intérieur* from the multiply important *Repetition*: "One climbs the stairs to the first floor in a gas-illuminated building, opens a little door, and stands in the entry. To the left is a glass door leading to a room. One continues directly ahead into an anteroom. Beyond are two entirely identical rooms, identically furnished, as if one were the reflection of the other. The farther room is tastefully illuminated. A candelabra stands on a writing table; a gracefully designed armchair upholstered in red velvet stands before the desk. The nearer room is not illuminated. Here the pale light of the moon blends with the strong light from the inner room. One takes a seat by the window and looks out on the great square, sees the shadows of passersby hurrying along the walls; everything is transformed into theatrical decoration. A dream world glimmers in the background of the soul. . . . Having smoked a cigar, one retires to the further room and begins to work.—It is past midnight. One extinguishes the candles and lights a little night candle. Unmingled, the light of the moon is victorious. A single shadow appears even blacker; the echo of a single footstep takes a long time to disappear. The cloudless arch of heaven has a sad and pensive look as if the end of the world had already come and heaven, unperturbed, were occupied with itself."[80] The idea of judgment, as otherworldly as the moonlit scenery beyond the *intérieur* and mere inwardness, softly echoes in the image of the apocalypse. Gas lighting and red plush armchair are the historical traces in the image; with the false comfort of singing flames, with their diffuse light, with the cheap imitation of crimson, they are at the same time the refuge of semblance. The gaslight flees from the moon back into itself, just as does Cordelia's room from the open horizon, and suffers the street only as a reflection, "a dream world glimmers in the background of the soul." The duplication of the room is unfathomable, seeming to be a reflection, without being so: like these rooms, all semblance perhaps resembles itself, so long as it itself, obedient to nature, persists as semblance. With the word "decoration" the image of the apartment calls itself by name, as if it wanted to awaken. But in the *intérieur* melancholy dreams on; "as if the end of the world had already come," it begins and remains in the apartment. Later Kierkegaard once again brought together illumination and melancholy—which, being objective, he could not comprehend: "Silence! Silence! Silence is not a definite something, for it does not consist simply in not speaking. No, silence is like the subdued light in the cozy room, like friendliness in the humble chamber"[81]—in the *intérieur* as the prototypical cell of abandoned inwardness. Even the solace of this light is semblance, "more beneficial than the subdued light of evening to weak eyes."[82] Out of the half-light of such melancholy emerge the contours of "domesticity," which for Kierkegaard constitutes the arena of existence.[83] It therefore constitutes the contours of his doctrine of existence itself. Inwardness and melancholy, the semblance of nature and the actuality of judgment; his ideal of concrete individual human life and his dream of a hell that the despairing inhabits for his lifetime exactly like a house—the models of all of his concepts are sworn to a silent tableau in the deceptive light of crepuscular rooms in which escape is the issue if one wants to separate what is true in them from what is deceptive. In the *intérieur* the historical dialectic and the eternal power of nature pose their peculiar puzzle. It must be solved by philosophical criticism, which seeks the real origin of his idealistic inwardness in the historical, as in the prehistorical.

Chapter 3
Explication of Inwardness

Sociology

A sociology of inwardness would be necessary to historically explain the image of the *intérieur*. The idea of such a sociology is only apparently paradoxical. Inwardness presents itself as the restriction of human existence to a private sphere free from the power of reification. Yet as a private sphere it itself belongs, if only polemically, to the social structure. — With ironic modesty and some arrogance, Kierkegaard occasionally lays claim to the title of a man of private means: "An insignificant thinker, an intellectual with a private income, a speculative melancholic, occupying like a poverty-stricken lodger a garret at the top of a vast building, sits there in his little refuge, held captive in what seemed to him difficult thoughts."[1] Kierkegaard disclosed something of the character of the social relation between the outer world and the privately supported thinker: "A truly great ethical personality would seek to realize his life in the following manner. He would strive to develop himself with the utmost exertion of his powers; in so doing he would perhaps produce great effects in the external world. But this would not seriously engage his attention, for he would know that the external result is not in his power, and hence that it has no significance for him, either *pro* or *contra*."[2] But how would the moral person have to conduct himself if the outer world were indeed in his power or if he could gain control of this power? Does not Kierkegaard recognize the external as distinct from the internal and as material of ethical conduct; would not, in that case, morality itself be dependent on the historical condition of this material as its proper object? By denying the social question, Kierkegaard falls to the mercy of his own historical situation, that of the *rentier* in the first half of the nineteenth century. Within commodious limits the *rentier* is economically independent, more so than the owner of the same amount of productive capital in the age of high-capitalism in which a comparable amount of wealth lost all independence as a result of the concentration of finance capital and the division of stock in public corporations. Yet the limits of this economic position are evident: excluded from economic production, the *rentier* does not accumulate capital, or in any case incomparably less than an industrialist with a similar estate; nor is he able to exploit economically the intellectual labor of isolated "literary work," as he mentions in the *First and Last Declaration*: "the honorarium has, to say the least, been rather Socratic."[3] He stands in opposition to the progress of economic competition that made his type almost extinct. Only an agrarian, economically underdeveloped country could initially guarantee him security and make possible his particular style of life. According to Geismar, Kierkegaard spurned—on the basis of religious scruple—any interest-bearing investment of his small estate and instead consumed it in installments. Neither the *rentier* nor its counterpart, the "philistine"—which Kierkegaard constantly criticized—are to be understood in the sense of the modern antithesis of industrial- and petty-bourgeoisie. Not dependent on borrowed capital, not required to sell his labor power, the *rentier* maintains an "open view." His knowledge goes beyond the pure immediacy of his "milieu," in which the "philistine" is immured; the necessities of his own social position do not block an overview of the whole and the "essential"; hence the vain self-irony of the tone with which he refers to himself as a simple pensioner, whereas it is precisely his economic position as *rentier* that guarantees a totality to which classical German idealism laid claim with less ceremony.—What today appear as Kierkegaard's petty-bourgeois characteristics correspond to his exclusion from economic production, the "accidents" to which he is indeed ultimately subject. One such characteristic is the powerless hatred of reification in which only the powerful capitalist—in the words of Karl Marx—feels "at ease and strengthened" for he understands "self-estrangement" as his "own power," and in it possesses "the semblance of a human existence,"[4] a semblance that alienation grants only conditionally to the *rentier*. Even cautious interpretation that does not derive philosophical contents directly from the economic circumstance of the philosopher must take as confirmation of Kierkegaard's "external powerlessness" that he sustained major losses in the market fluctuations of 1848 and thought he had fallen into such difficult straits as to be obliged to look for employment. The influence of his effort to obtain a position through Mynster on his later relation to the bishop is certainly not to be judged as any less important than his piousness toward the "confessor of his father." It would have been impossible during Mynster's life to attack him as a representative of a hypocritical ministry when he himself had tried to use him to gain a paid seminarial position in the established church. As a rule, philosophical criticism may hardly deduce its arguments from economic circumstances, yet they are not to be overlooked in the case of Kierkegaard's claim of the identity of truth and person. Whatever the mediation of private existence and theoretical thought, the philosophy itself cannot disclaim the characteristic features of the *rentier*. The lack of any developed concept of praxis, in contrast to idealist philosophy since Kant and Fichte; the polemical-retrospective attitude toward an overwhelming capitalist external world is, in terms of its impulse, private. The external world, which at least gives the person some prerogative, is for this very reason condemned in general as the "external world," and not as a specifically capitalist world. The economic context becomes apparent when objectless inwardness must understand itself in social existence: in Kierkegaard's ethics.—His moral rigorism derives from the absolute claim of the isolated person. He criticizes all eudaemonism as heteronomous for the objectless self: "He who says that he wants to enjoy life always posits a condition which either lies outside the individual or is in the individual in such a way that it is not posited by the individual himself."[5] The material contents of the autonomous ethic of the absolute person, however, give evidence of its dependency on bourgeois society. The concrete self is for Kierkegaard identical with the bourgeois self: "This self is not merely a personal self but a social, a bourgeois self."[6] For this reason the self posits precisely those "distinctions" that the universality of the moral law should have excluded. The basis of these distinctions is class consciousness. Blacks and female singers fall outside the limits of Kierkegaard's ethical universality; in the *Stages* he says of Othello: "a colored man, dear boon companions . . . cannot be supposed to represent *esprit*"[7]; and he writes in a letter to Boesen, justly quoted by Schrempf: "The death of a female vocalist does not count for much."[8] In *Fear and Trembling* he occasionally defends the crassest social immorality and irrationality with the naïveté of a class perspective that refuses to comprehend socioeconomic interrelationships: "Once when the price of spices in Holland fell, the merchants had a few cargoes sunk in the sea in order to jack up the price. This was an excusable, perhaps even necessary, deception."[9] Wherever the "moralist" happens to speak of those conflicts that can occur between inwardness (represented by marriage) and the material situation (poverty), he justifies inwardness with the cozy cynicism of the petty-bourgeois *rentier*: "When, for example, poverty is proposed as a difficulty with which marriage may have to contend, I would answer: 'Work—then all obstacles give way.' Since we are now relying on our imaginations, you will perhaps take advantage of your poetic license and make answer: 'They couldn't get any work. The decline in business and in the shipping trade has left a great many people without bread.' Or you permit them to get a little work, but it is not sufficient. In my opinion, by wise economy they surely could have been able to make both ends meet."[10] The logic of the argument bears witness against itself. And still it goes too far for Kierkegaard. While he recognizes the influence of business cycles

on the possibility of savings, he extracts the entire crisis as an "arbitrary invention of poetic license"[11] from a period in which, at the same time that *Either/Or*
was being written, the most terrible impoverishment of the English industrial
proletariat was taking place. If the ethics of absolute inwardness cannot always
defend its puritanical demands unrelentingly enough, it in this case makes it easy
for itself: "Luther says somewhere in one of his sermons where he is talking of
poverty and want: 'One has never heard of a Christian man dying of hunger.'
Therewith Luther has disposed of the matter and thinks, in my opinion correctly,
that he has spoken about it with much unction and to the genuine edification of
his hearers."[12] The individual uncritically submits to church tradition. — Moral
action, for Kierkegaard, exclusively concerns the "neighbor." He says of the
intended effect of his defense of marriage: "Through her [the wife] I am a man,
for only a married man is a genuine man, every other title to honor is as nothing
compared to this which in reality is the assumption underlying all titles. Through
her I am a father; every other dignity is merely a human invention, an artifice,
which is forgotten in a hundred years; through her I am head of the family,
through her I am defender of the home, its breadwinner, the children's protec-
tor. — When one has so many dignities, one does not become an author for the
sake of attaining a new dignity. I have not the least desire for a dignity I dare not
lay claim to, but I write in order that he who is as happy as I am, if he reads this,
may be reminded of his good fortune; that he who doubts, if he reads this, may
be won over, if it were only a single individual, I am glad even of that."[13]
Because such an ethical address limits itself to the Christian "neighbor," it supposes itself immune to objective criticism; William "wishes that the man who
might possibly profit by it may not be put out by deficiency in form, and refuses
to tolerate any criticism. For a married man who writes on marriage is surely the
last person to write for critical appreciation."[14] The pathos of the entreaty, however, is unable fully to stave off criticism. For the concept of the "neighbor," the
foundation of Kierkegaard's ethics, is a fiction. The concept is valid only in a
society of direct human relations, from which Kierkegaard well knows that he is
separated. Fleeing precisely from reification, he withdraws into "inwardness."
In this arena, however, he acts as if that immediacy still existed in the external
world, whose ersatz is inwardness itself. The possibility that a person, faultless
in terms of private ethics, could act infamously in his objective social function, a
function not reducible to inwardness, is a thought that Kierkegaard does not
allow to occur. In fact neither this immediacy nor its semblance exist in the
framework of common class interests; the rupture of immediacy is identical with
that between the classes. Kierkegaard's ethics of concrete-meaningful life is
therefore a poor and deceptive class moral. In theological terms: "And to honor
every man, absolutely every man, is the truth, and this is what it is to fear God
and love one's 'neighbor.' But from an ethico-religious point of view, to recognize the 'crowd' " — which for Kierkegaard, as a product of reification, is the

opposition of the concrete "neighbor" — "as the court of 'truth' is to deny God, and it certainly cannot mean to love the 'neighbor.' And the 'neighbor' is the absolutely true expression for human equality. If everyone were in truth to love his neighbor as himself, complete human equality would be attained."[15] This equality is not achieved when human relations are so preformed by the domination of exchange-value, the division and commodity form of labor that one "neighbor" can no more respond spontaneously to the other for more than an instant than the individual's kindness suffices to do him any good, let alone have an effect on the social structure. Thus Kierkegaard's ethics is contentless. — This ethics originates in his concept of freedom. Such a concept does not remain, as does the Kantian concept, in the realm of the intelligible, surrendering the empirical realm to necessity. It establishes itself in the empirical, and the empirical world is tolerated only insofar as it is the arena of freedom. Society contracts to the circumference of free "neighbors," while precisely its necessities are shunted aside as "accidental" from the gates of philosophy. Freedom determines the self, which Kierkegaard conceives exclusively in its freedom, just as it determines society. If the material necessities of society are denied in the name of freedom, the necessities and reality of the instincts vanish from the self according to the same scheme. Kierkegaard's absolute self is mere spirit. The individual is not the sensuously developed person, and no property is accorded him beyond the bare necessities. Inwardness does not consist in its fullness but is ruled over by an ascetic spiritualism.

The Spiritual Body

The thesis of spiritualism receives an extreme formulation in the *Philosophical Fragments*. The relation of truth and untruth is equated with that of being and nonbeing. Kierkegaard writes of the "disciple," the sinful man who is to be awaken by Christ: "In so far as he was in error, and now receives the truth and with it the condition for understanding it, a change takes place within him like the change from non-being to being."[16] The exclusively spiritual "rebirth" that he sees in this, that one "receives the truth and with it the condition for understanding it," is compared to natural birth as the transition from nonbeing to being. Thus birth itself is spiritualized: "When one who has experienced birth thinks of himself as born, he conceives this transition from non-being to being. The same principle must also hold in the case of re-birth."[17] True, Kierkegaard himself fleetingly raises the objection of spiritualism: "Or is the difficulty increased by the fact that the non-being which precedes the re-birth" — that is, the natural being that is here specifically at issue qua nonbeing — "contains more being than the non-being that preceded the first birth?"[18] But this objection is casuistically overruled. The spiritualistic thesis of the *Philosophical Fragments* is maintained through the entire oeuvre. Like the natural self, "the crowd" is for Kierkegaard "the untruth."[19] Without exception, living people appear as allegories of truth and untruth. This alone makes the artistic failure comprehensible. The bodily substratum of intuition is canceled by philosophy and endured only insofar as it presents truth and untruth. It is illuminating that genuine aesthetic achievements fall to Kierkegaard only where he presented the bewilderment of pure spirit; where, that is, spiritualism no longer interferes with poetic form because (as in the novella "A Possibility" in the *Stages*) spiritualism becomes the object of form. Everything sexual is excluded from the psychology of the erotic; even in his synopsis of others' novels, the sexual is prudishly avoided.[20] If spiritualism reigns over instinct, it so completely prevails in the philosophical dialectic that, even in *The Sickness unto Death*, it is not construed as a dialectic of spirit and nature; instead spirit itself has split into freedom and the demonic. This, to be sure, indicates the crucial reversal. If the body appears only under the sign of the "meaning" of the truth and untruth of spirit, spirit in return remains bound to the body as its expression, bound as to the semblance of the *intérieur*. Nature, excluded by history from an objectless inwardness, nevertheless prevails in it, and the historical spiritualism builds for itself a natural-anthropological organology. The images of pure spirit that Kierkegaard comes up with are consistently images of the human body. "My sould is so heavy that thought can no more sustain it, no wingbeat lift it up into the ether"[21]; so says the melancholic in *Either/Or*, the most spiritual of Kierkegaard's many masks. Bodiless spirit for him becomes a burden that drags him into despair. The ancient somatic doctrine of humours strangely returns in idealistic spiritualism. It perfectly complements Kierkegaard's psychology of emotions. Where every emotion, stripped of any right of its own, is a cipher of the disguised truth that "appears" in it, it must itself be an apparition and as such paradoxically perceptible. If the functions of the eye and ear are differentiated not so much by their function in the three-dimensional world as in the spiritual inner world, so, on the other hand, the inner world itself is at the same time divided up according to images of the natural organs. "Here I will break off this reflection. It perhaps does not satisfy you, your greedy eye devours it without being satisfied by it, but that is because the eye is the sense which is most insatiable, especially when like you one does not hunger but suffers from a lust of the eye which cannot be satisfied with seeing."[22] Accordingly, the eye is the organ of aesthetic "immediacy" and semblance; it alone sketches the images of things for inwardness. In this the usual distinction of an "inner" and an "outer" sense, temporal and spatial forms of intuition, perhaps plays a role. Ultimately, however, it may have remained hidden from Kierkegaard—who took the music of Don Giovanni as the most perfect expression of "sensual genius"—that the visual as well as the auditory faculty inbue sensual qualities. Nevertheless, for him the ear is the direct instrument of inwardness itself, a physical representative of the strictly bodiless. At the beginning of *Either/Or*, one of the most emphasized passages reads: "For just as the voice is the revelation of an inwardness incommensurable with the outer, so the ear is the instrument by which this inwardness is apprehended, hearing the sense by which it is appropriated."[23] This is by no means an exclusive attribute of the mask of aesthete A. The idea of the dialectical necessity of God's distance is maintained even in *The Sickness unto Death*: "So strangely constructed in an acoustic sense is the world of spirit, so strangely are the relationships of distance arranged."[24] — Kierkegaard's spiritualism is above all enmity toward nature. Spirit posits itself as free and autonomous in opposition to nature because it considers nature demonic as much in external reality as in itself. In that, however, autonomous spirit appears corporally, nature takes possession of it where it occurs most historically: in objectless interiority. Spirit's natural content must be investigated if in Kierkegaard the being of subjectivity itself is to be explicated. The natural content of mere spirit, "historical" in itself, may be called mythical.

Mythical Content

In his dissertation Kierkegaard introduces the concept of the mythical both as the counterconcept to historical movement and in unity with it. What he says there in regard to the Platonic myths leads to the mythical content of his own thought, which his mature philosophy conceals. — His excurse on "The Mythical in the earlier Platonic Dialogues" assumes a "disparity between the dialectical and the mythical,"[25] said to be apparent between the conceptual and pictorial form of presentation in Plato. Kierkegaard sets as his task the deduction of the necessity of this divergence from the object and its unity. For the mythical, according to Kierkegaard, is not a free creation of the author. It "has a much deeper significance, a fact which becomes evident when one observes that the mythical in Plato has a history."[26] This is not only a history in the development of Plato's work but a history in itself. Even in the early dialogues "it is present in connection with . . . its opposite, the abstract"—that is, the conceptual— "dialectic."[27] If Stallbaum and F. C. Bauer establish a relation between the Platonic myths and "folk-consciousness" or "underscore the significance of tradition in the mythical,"[28] they have indeed caught a glimpse of the historical in myth, but only tangentially, without comprehending the common origin of dialectical and mythical modes of presentation. In contrast, Kierkegaard formulates the idea of an "inner history of the mythical."[29] This idea tends toward the historical figure of the mythical in his own work; the form of complete immanence, whose image turns out to be the *intérieur*. He recognizes the unity of the dialectical and the mythical in Plato as an image: whereas the mythical "in the earlier dialogues appears in opposition to the dialectical, inasmuch as the mythical is only heard or, more correctly, seen when the dialectical is silent, in the later dialogues it exhibits a more amiable relation to the dialectical, that is, Plato has become master of it, which is to say, the mythical becomes image."[30] Produced in the immanence of thought and according to its own "inner history," the "mythical" is at the same time visibly embodied as an image, just as the dialectic of Kierkegaard's spiritualism requires the embodied organic image. The production of this unity is at once natural and organic; in it the characteristics of historical facticity and ontological truth are jointly destroyed: "The mythical representation of the existence of the soul after death is not brought into relation either with a historical reflection, namely, whether it is indeed the case that Aeacus, Minos, and Rhadamanthus sit in judgment, or with a philosophic reflection, namely, whether it is true. If one may characterize the dialectic corresponding to the mythical as longing and desire, as a glance that gazes upon the idea so as to desire it, then the mythical is the fruitful embrace of the Idea."[31] In spite of Kierkegaard's intention, the discussion of "longing and desire" and "fruitful embrace" does not, as a detachable metaphor, demonstrate the productivity of pure spirit. To the contrary, spirituality itself is named "mythical" and the productivity of spirit natural. This is shown by a sentence whose pragmatic elements bring Kierkegaard's philosophy closer to self-consciousness than anywhere else: "One may arrive at a similar consideration of the mythical by beginning with the image. When in an age of reflection one sees the image protrude ever so slightly and unobserved into a reflective representation, and, like an antediluvian fossil, suggest another species of existence washed away by doubt, one will perhaps be amazed that the image could ever have played such an important role."[32] Kierkegaard wards off the "amazement" with what follows. And yet this amazement announces the deepest insight into the relation of dialectic, myth, and image. For it is not as the continuously living and present that nature prevails in the dialectic. Dialectic comes to a stop in the image and cites the mythical in the historically most recent as the distant past: nature as proto-history. For this reason the images, which like those of the *intérieur* bring dialectic and myth to the point of indifferentiation, are truly "antediluvian fossils." They may be called dialectical images, to use Benjamin's expression, whose compelling definition of "allegory" also holds true for Kierkegaard's allegorical intention as a configuration of historical dialectic and mythical nature. According to this definition "in allegory the observer is confronted with the *facies hippocratica* of history, a petrified primordial landscape."[33] — In Kierkegaard nature is mythical as proto-history, cited in the image and concept of his historical moment. It is thus that he overtly employed the expression in the single passage, after the dissertation, in which it is still accentuated; in the interpretation of Mozart's *Figaro*. There he calls the page boy a "mythical figure."[34] The historical costume of the page is at the same time the disguise of an ambiguous natural creature; the undefined and puzzling depth of this disguise is closely allied with that of pure spirit, whose mythical constitution cannot be denied: "Although desire in this stage is not qualified as desire, although this intimating desire, so far as its object is concerned, is entirely undefined, still it has the characteristic of being infinitely deep. . . . It does not yet indicate a relation to the object but remains an infinite, vague longing. In harmony with the earlier description given here, we shall find it very significant that the page's part is so arranged musically that it always lies within the range of a female voice. In this contradiction, the contradictory of every stage is indicated: the desire is so indefinite, its object so minimally distinguished, that the object of desire rests androgynously within the desire, just as in plant life the male and female parts are both present in one blossom. Desire and the desired are joined in this unity, in which both parts are of neuter gender.''[35] In the androgynous costume the element of semblance is present that characterizes everything in the *intérieur*. It is this element that Kierkegaard, in his dissertation, perceived in the Platonic myths and described with words clearly reminiscent of the intimating, obscure desire of the page boy: "As soon as consciousness appears, however, it becomes evident that these mirages" — the myths — "were not the Idea. If, after consciousness is awaken, the imagination again desires to return to these dreams, the mythical exhibits itself in a new form, that is, as image. . . . The mythical may well contain traditional elements, for the traditional is the lullaby as it were comprising one element of the dream.''[36] Yet it is most authentically mythical not in that instant — as Kierkegaard spiritualistically supposes — "where the spirit steals away, and no one knows from whence it came nor whither it goes,''[37] but when the appearing image startles up what has been from the caverns of prehistory. Since, however, in the mythical image of the page "desire rests androgynously within the desire,'' the image also remains immanently spiritual. Immanent spirituality itself is mythical. As mythical, spirituality becomes incarnate. Thus the drastic metaphor of the seducer: "I will be your poet! I will not be a poet for others; I eat my own verse and that sustains me. Show yourself! I want to compose you.''[38] Thus the artist, pure spirit, is mythically raised up among the stars in the image of Saturn who eats his children. In Kierkegaard's philosophy, pure spirit therefore goes over into the ghostly, its primordial archetype. Of a "modern-tragic" figure — presumably Regine — it is said: "Her life does not unfold like that of the Greek Antigone; the direction of her development is inward, not outward; the scene is not external but internal; it is a ghostly scene.''[39] And the unendingly reflected seducer enters without a trace, as a phantom: "In the same way as one might say of him that his way through life left no trace (for his feet were so formed that they took their footprints with them, which is how I best picture to myself his infinite self-reflection), in that same sense one might say that his art of seduction demanded no victim.''[40] Where Kierkegaard recognizes the mythical character of mere spirit, he calls it demonic. This is above all true in *The Concept of Anxiety*. Here the immigration of mythical nature into spiritual inwardness is interpreted historically: "It is of no use to make an ogre out of the demonic, at which one first shudders but afterwards ignores, since, after all, it is several hundred years since it was found in the world. Such an assumption is a great stupidity, but it probably has never been as widespread as in our times, except that nowadays it manifests itself especially in the spiritual spheres."[41] The demonic, defined as "the enclosing reserve and the unfreely disclosed,"[42] originates in the delusion in which autonomous spirit imagines itself absolute: "The demonic does not close itself up with something, but it closes itself up within itself, and in this lies what is profound about existence, precisely that unfreedom makes itself a prisoner."[43] As mythic, the demonic shatters subjectivity and becomes ontological untruth in opposition to the ontological truth of God: "The devil's despair is the most intense despair, for the devil is sheer spirit, and therefore absolute consciousness and transparency; in the devil there is no obscurity that might serve as a mitigating excuse, his despair is therefore absolute defiance."[44] All this could just as well be said of objectless inwardness as it is said of the depraved, eviscerated self of the purely demonic. For only that language can lead beyond the demonic that is debarred from an inwardness that does not know a priori "whether other human beings" in the world "exist":[45] "Enclosing reserve is precisely muteness. Language, the word, is precisely what saves, what saves the individual from the empty abstraction of enclosing reserve. Let x signify the demonic, the relation of freedom to it something outside x. The law for the manifestation of the demonic is that against its will it 'comes out with it.' For language does indeed imply communication"[46] with the external world, which is expressly excluded, as contingent, from inwardness. Certainly, Kierkegaard rejects any equivalence of the demonic and mythical-natural; he warns against "forgetting that unfreedom"—which he conceives as the demonic—"is a phenomenon of freedom and thus cannot be explained by naturalistic categories."[47] He attributes the mythical interpretation of the demonic to "aesthetic-metaphysical" thought; "the phenomena will then come under the rubrics of misfortune, fate, etc. and can then be viewed as analogous to being mentally deranged at birth."[48] But he is only able to separate the ideas of the demonic and fate, immemorially kindred concepts, by means of the vehement protestation of a theology for which the demonic is "free" because it takes the primordial Fall itself for an act of freedom and which escapes entanglement in fate through the "leap." However, the theological protestation does not suffice other than through sheer assertion to separate the demonic from nature—inwardness from the "mythical."—The character of the mythical in conceptual form is thus attributed to Kierkegaard's absolute inwardness as to all forms of idealism of absolute spirit. In radical idealism, the mythical-historical image of the intérieur becomes evident through philosophical self-consciousness. Hence the crude discussion of Hegel's mythology of history has a more profound justification than it imagines, though not because reality is metaphysically recast, but on the basis of the mythical content itself. "At this point Hegel's philosophy is driven inexorably into the arms of mythology."[49] This is certainly true of the philosophies of Baader and Schelling. They did not simply absorb mythical "elements" as "material" into the philosophical structure. Rather, the origin of the structure is mythical: the tyranny of spirit, of the created that enthrones itself as creator and sinks so much deeper into nature the higher that spirit imagines itself towering above it. In the final products of the idealist spirit, the mythical content simply breaks through the cells of the systematically developed concept, where philosophical criticism has banished it, and takes possession of the old images. Along with the stability of the system, however, it destroys itself: pure spirit, called by its name, loses its power. Kierkegaard stands alongside the late idealists at this moment of historical reversal. As in their case, the crisis of the autarchic spirit is consummated as the emancipation of the mythical content. But this reversal does not lead Kierkegaard into mythological metaphysics and "positive" philosophy. The mythical content remains embedded in the immanent dialectic and is expelled by him only with the obliteration of subjectivity itself.

Dialectical Conjuration

Only the category of the mythical serves to clarify the relation of objectless inwardness to blocked ontology that, as truth, is the concern of Kierkegaard's thought. Through conjuration a mythically self-enclosed subjectivity undertakes to rescue "fundamental human relations" and their meaning, ontology. Even the seducer admits, in a mythical image, to being a sorcerer: "But you do not suspect what it is I rule over as a kingdom. It is over stormy moods. Like Aeolus . . ."[50] And conjuration is no more limited to the "aesthetic sphere" than to the poeticizing metaphor. Inwardness itself conjures. "Thus in the ethical view of life, it is the task of the individual to strip himself of the qualification of interiority and to express this in something external."[51] Thus for inwardness the external is a magical apparatus that quotes a hidden content as "expression." But the conjured content, however inward, is not inwardness itself: "The paradox of faith is that there is an interiority that is incommensurable with exteriority; an interiority that is not identical, please note, with the first but is a new interiority."[52] This second interiority, however, with which Kierkegaard's dialectic is altogether concerned, is conjured truth. — Kierkegaard does not conceptually clarify the intention of conjuration. Its demonic character would imperil the truth claim of dialectical inwardness. But this intention becomes evident in the form of his language, and more so in the diffusenesss of the aesthetic writings than in their conjuring metaphors. This diffuseness has often been noted; scarcely, however, has its relation to the philosophical content been explained. His well-known reference to the "vastness of affliction," the bad infinity of the monologue and the dialectic of pain, does not suffice. Even its explanation as Socratic love of speech supplies only his intention, not its origin; the same is true of his aversion to concise formulation in the system, to which the "Expression of Gratitude to Less-ing" gives negative proof by its praise: "This stylistic equanimity, which devel-ops a simile in minutest detail, as if the literary expression had a value in itself, as if peace and safety reigned; and that although perhaps the printer's devil and world-history, indeed all mankind stood waiting for him to have it finished."[53] All this cannot illuminate why a philosophy that—unlike Hegel's, or for that matter Lessing's—dispenses with all *realien*, and that is obliged to develop its determinations altogether out of the mere "point" of the person, still requires the most extensive spatial extension in the form of its presentation. The law of this form is repetition: the repetition of conjuring formulas. The changeless and hidden truth is invoked as the invariable with invariable phrases out of power-lessness to posit its content positively or to deduce it progressively, but also out of the hope that truth might spring forth if the correct number of conjurations is fulfilled. The formulaic brevity of the particular corresponds precisely to the mythical repetition of the whole, just as the densely compressed and oracular propositions of *The Concept of Anxiety* and the founding passages of existential philosophy in the first sections of *The Sickness unto Death* correspond to the end-less paraphrases of the "Passion Narrative" and the *Unscientific Postscript*. Ontology, however, conjured by a mythical, autonomous will obeys only the entreaty in the form of a phantasmagoria. Fate, fortune, and misfortune are the mythical constellations of a dialectical voyage whose course is ambiguous be-cause "on the sea of possibilities" of the mere self, "the compass itself is dialectical."[54] Kierkegaard's dialectic must be termed ambiguous in the more exact sense. For as the movement of an isolated individual consciousness, whose own origins are mythical and even in its turbulence remains within the proximity of the mythical, it has two meanings. They are to be distinguished according to the form of appearance that the mythical content takes on in them.—On one hand, Kierkegaard conceives of mere nature, of mythical semblance, as a peril to the individual, who, as a sinful creature, is part of it, yet in freedom exalts him-self above it. Here dialectic is a process of spiritualization or, in Kierkegaard's language, "a making transparent," that the self undertakes by the force of its own free spirit. This dialectic transpires between nature and spirit, mythical con-tent and consciousness, as qualitatively different, strictly contrary powers; it should lay bear the entryway to reconciliation, for mythical semblance collapses in the face of spiritual splendor. The dialectic predominates throughout Kierke-gaard's explicit doctrine according to which the true self, the "freedom" of the individual, emerges from the perceived unreality of self asserting nature. But this dialectic offers only the frontal view of a second and deeper concept of dialectic that, without having been theoretically developed in the philosophy, may be objectively demonstrated in it. This concept is that of a dialectic in the mythical fundament of nature itself. It necessarily becomes the center of an interpretation that would critically expose the mythical character of what appears on stage supranaturally in Kierkegaard as spirit and freedom, i.e., objectless inwardness. In the *Fragments*, Kierkegaard himself cast into doubt the supranatural essence of "spirit" through the theological doctrine of the absolute transcendence of God, a doctrine that shatters every claim of the individual's spiritual freedom: "Still less will he be able in his own strength to bring God anew over to his side."[55] In that case, however, the individual is not divided into the natural and the supranatural, which struggle between themselves; rather, his natural being is dialectical in itself, and what contributes in the individual to his rescue is equally attributable to his nature as to what will ruin him. Kierkegaard's effort to separate nature and the demonic from each other refers to the model of the dialectic of nature, an effort that obviously cannot be brought into the foreground of the predominating spiritualism. This effort is more evident in the imagery that describes the same process of becoming transparent, which consciousness is to achieve over a resisting nature, as a natural process: "My being was transparentness, like the deep thought of the sea, like the self-satisfied silence of the night, like the soliloquizing stillness of midday."[56] While Kierkegaard spiritualistically risks the sentence "that every individual who is born is by being born and becoming part of the race, a lost individual,"[57] he raises, in opposition to this thought, the possibility of rescue in the dialectic of nature with the question of *The Sickness unto Death*: "How far complete clarity about oneself, that one is in despair, may be united with being in despair, that is, if this clarity of knowledge and self-knowledge might not avail precisely to tear a man out of his despair, to make him so terrified about himself that he would cease to be in despair."[58] The clarity of the despondent, who as spirit becomes demonically entangled in his own nature, is, however, a clarity that the mythical dialectic itself produces. In the captivity of total immanence mythical ambiguous nature is divided since it does not endure inertly, but moves dialectically, and its movement takes hold of nature in the depths from which it originates in order to pull it up to safety.

Melancholy

Kierkegaard's psychology of emotions portrays this movement as that of melancholy. It belongs to the *intérieur* to which "mood," the constellation of the factual content, binds it. Just as in the *intérieur* the historical image presents itself as mythical, here mere nature—the melancholic temperament—presents itself as historical. Therefore it presents itself as dialectical and as the "possibility" of reconciliation.—The inner history of melancholy, just like that of subjectivity altogether, is conceived by Kierkegaard without any regard for external history. "My concern is *egoistic* or *sympathetic melancholy*. People have now been talking long enough about the frivolity of this age; I believe it is now high time to talk a little about its melancholy, and I hope that by this everything will be better clarified. Or is not melancholy the ailment of our age? Is it not this that resounds even in its frivolous laughter? Is it not melancholy that had deprived us of courage to command, of courage to obey, of power to act, of the confidence necessary to hope?"[59] As an "ailment of the age," melancholy is not accidental; rather, inwardness becomes melancholic through the specific struggle with historical *realien*, which Kierkegaard's elaborate metaphor adequately outlines: "But the strange ideas of my melancholy I do not give up; for these humours (as a third party would perhaps sympathetically name them) lead me to the eternal certainty of the infinite. — In my loneliness therefore these ideas are dear to me, even though they terrify me; they have the utmost importance for me and teach me, instead of congratulating myself for rendering mankind blissfully peerless discoveries in the religious field — instead of this they teach me to my own abasement to discover as it were, and with endless contentment to be satisfied with the very simplest things. . . . Why is it indeed that in remote places where half a mile separates the little huts there is more godly fear than in the noisy town, that sailors have more godly fear than the inhabitants of the market town — why indeed unless on the heath, on the turbulent sea, one experiences something, and experience it in such a way that there is no escape? When at night the tempest rages and the hungry cry of the wolf howls ominously, when in peril upon the sea a man has saved himself upon a plank, that is to say, must be rescued by a straw from certain destruction: when one can save the bother of screaming because there is no human ear to hear it — then one learns to possess one's soul in patience, relying upon something else besides night watchmen and the police, the fire department and the coast guard. In the great cities both men and buildings are crowded too close together. If one is to receive a primitive impression, there must either be an event, or one must have another way, as I have in my melancholy."[60] The two ways mentioned by Kierkegaard intersect in his psychology of melancholy and constitute a crossroads, which according to ancient beliefs was the spot most propitious for conjuration. The intention of the metaphor is ontological: the "primitive impression" of that which "the original scripture of human existence" leaves behind in the individual's experience. In the reified world of the metropolis, whose inhabitants qua police and night watchmen, "functionaries" of order, are themselves things and caricatures, the truth content of scripture has been historically lost because the objectivity of the social forms no longer permits the "primitive impression." Only the primordial nature of the ship, the hut dwellers, beyond reification, with the sea and field still hold up to the individual the "original scripture." In the reified world itself, however, by its history, mythical nature is driven back into the inwardness of the individual. Inwardness is the historical prison of primordial human nature. The emotion of the trapped is melancholy. In melancholy truth presents itself, and the movement of melancholy is one toward the deliverance of lost "meaning." A truly dialectical motion. For if truth presents itself in melancholy, it indeed presents itself to pure inwardness exclusively as semblance. Truth is, in the pure imagination of inwardness, comparable to the pleasure of the melancholic: "The essence of pleasure does not lie in pleasure itself, but in the accompanying consciousness."[61] As imagination, melancholy is related to insanity; in the novella *A Possibility*, melancholy, bewitched, becomes insanity. At the center of the novella is a magical *intérieur*: "This is what one saw in the street; but whosoever entered his room might marvel still more. One frequently gets an entirely different impression of a person seeing him in his home and in his chamber than when one sees him elsewhere. And this is not only true of magicians, alchemists and astrologers . . . mythical figures . . . like Dapsul von Zabelthau, who on the street looks like other people, but seated in his observatory has a high peaked cap on his head, a mantle of gray callimanco, a long white beard, and talks with a disguised voice so that his own daughter cannot recognize him but takes him for a bugaboo."[62] The insanity of the bookkeeper, who essays magically through recollection to conjure up out of his distant past the "possibility" that a child of his own exists, is such an *intérieur*. In the conjuration, however, contingent reality and inwardness are severed: "The outward pallor is, as it were, the parting salutation of the inner excitement; and imagination and thought hasten after the fugitive emotion to where it conceals itself in its secret hiding place."[63] This pallid light is that of semblance as it draws the isolated melancholic to his mythical origin. Thus Kierkegaard combines the isolation of inward, pure nature and semblance in the metaphor of the echo: "If you stand face to face with nothingness, your soul may be calmed, yea, attuned to sadness, by the sound of the echo of your sadness reverberating back to you. To hear an echo one must face emptiness."[64] And the illusory quality of melancholy does not remain merely metaphorical in his work. The theory itself testifies to this quality: "Thus it is in the nature of melancholy to be deceitful."[65] As semblance, however, mythical melancholy is not depraved but dialectical in itself. "Providence" is concealed in it. Providence "endows an individual with uncommon powers of dealing with reality. 'But then,' says providence, 'lest he occasion too much harm I have confined this power in melancholy and thereby hide it from him' " —just as "truth" itself, according to Kierkegaard, is hidden from inwardness. " 'What he is capable of he shall never learn to know, but I want to make use of him. He shall not be humbled by any reality, to that extent he is treated with more partiality than other men, but in himself he shall feel shattered such as has no other man. Then and only then shall he understand me, but then he shall also be certain that it is I he understands.' "[66] Thus truth subordinates itself to melancholic semblance through semblance's own dialectic. In its semblance melancholy is, dialectically, the image of an other. Precisely this is the origin of the allegorical character of Kierkegaard's melancholy. In the face of melancholy, nature becomes allegorical: "Who, unless it were a madman, has ever beheld a young girl without a certain sense of sadness, without being most poignantly reminded by her sweetness of the fragility of earthly life?''[67] So asks William, reminiscing perhaps on Matthias Claudius's allegory of death and the maiden. The image of the maiden in her youth signifies precisely transience. Melancholy itself, however, is the historical spirit in its natural depth and therefore, in the images of its corporeity, it is the central allegory. Like Hermes, who led the dead with his stave, "melancholy must have led" him who is imprisoned in inwardness "through the previous stages.''[68] And melancholy's saturnine lineage is cited in the discussion: "What is sickness? Melancholy. Where is the seat of this sickness? In the power of imagination: and it feeds on possibility.''[69] If in the absolute break between inner and outer that is sealed only in the physical depth of emotion the fault lines of Kierkegaard's philosophy are reminiscent of Descartes, the allegorical intention fully testifies to an objective affinity to the Baroque. This allegorical intention could better establish the similarities between Kierkegaard and Pascal than a philosophical attitude that hopes to be able to eavesdrop through the centuries on conversations between Augustin, the Jansenist Catholic and the idealist Protestant, the lonely believer.

Baroque

Kierkegaard occasionally refers to himself as "the Baroque thinker,''[70] obviously playing on a comment made about him by one of his contemporaries, without realizing how much in fact his pragmatic impulses correspond to those of the literary Baroque. With the literary Baroque, he shares the condition of closed immanence[71] no less than the allegorical conjuration of lost ontological contents. Like flotsam on an island, scraps of long forgotten figures of Baroque drama—known to him in the original only through Shakespeare, to the degree that he is counted among the Baroque—are washed up on his philosophical landscape. The constituent elements of Baroque drama, which Benjamin exposed through its idea in the *Origin of the German Play of Lamentation*, appear fully assembled in the cave of his philosophy. The tyrant makes his appearance as a mythical-historical person: now called Nero,[72] now Periander,[73] now Nebachanezer;[74] the last named being a fully remote allegorical motive of the melancholic person as beast, a figure found in the works of the Baroque German dramatist Hunold,[75] Kierkegaard himself identified with the dialectical counterimage of the tyrant, the martyr, whose concept so thoroughly rules his later theology that in his final polemic Martensen, with justice, accused Kierkegaard of simply equating the "witness of truth" with the "martyr." Baroque intrigues are to be found not only in the tales of seduction, but also in the separation of Quidam from his love with whom he, like Hamlet, plays the part of the fool. The dialectic of melancholy leads to a complex casuistry of and apology for intrigue in the presentations of the "indirect method" in the *Unscientific Postscript* and *The Point of View for*

My Work as an Author. As in the Baroque, melancholy and disguise are inseparable: "This proportion—the equally great magnitude of melancholy and the art
of disguise—indicates that I was relegated to myself and to a relation with
God";[76] and at the same time the isolation of objectless inwardness shows signs
of the Baroque isolation of the creature in worldly immanence. Kierkegaard's
philosophy is even invested with the dreaded insignia of the Baroque spirit: pom-
posity and cruelty. Allegorical images are amassed: "Every woman has her
share: the merry smile, the roguish glance, the wistful eye, the pensive head,
the exuberant spirits, the quiet sadness, the deep foreboding, brooding melancholy"—and the center point of the imagery—"the earthly homesickness;
the inexplicable emotions";[77] thus it continues on with ever fresh variations.
Baroque cruelty characterizes Kierkegaard in the "Diapsalmata" of the magician
Vigilius and the oven of Phalaris; in the presentation of the schizophrenic
Periander; but also in the character of the "Passion Narrative," whose name does
not accidently cite the Passion; here melancholy, as the self's spiritual body, is
harrowingly divided up into its affective impulses as though they were its limbs.
The only other arena besides the *intérieur* that is acceptable to Kierkegaard's
philosophy (the streets of the *flaneur* are unrecognizably foreshortened in the
mirror) is the Baroque graveyard. "Everyone is asleep; only the dead rise at this
hour from the grave revived. But I, I am not dead, and so I cannot be revived; and
if I were dead, I could not be revived for indeed I have never lived."[78] Or again,
exactly like the opening scene of a Baroque drama, copied—perhaps intentionally—right down to the details of its diction: "A Leper's Soliloquy. The scene is
among the graves at dawn, Simon Lebrosus is sitting on a tombstone, he has
fallen asleep, he wakes and cries out: Simon! . . . 'Yes.' . . . Simon! . . . 'Yes,
who is calling?' . . . Where are you, Simon? . . . 'Here. With whom are you
speaking?' . . . With you, Simon! You filth! You plague! You loathsome thing!
Out of my way! Fly! To your home, the tombs! . . . Why am I the only one
who is unable to speak thusly to myself?"[79] All of these characteristics, barely
appraised in their continuity, surround the image of the melancholic, the dead,
and the mourning. The evidence of literary influence does not lead far. Kierkegaard certainly knew nothing of Lohenstein and Gryphius, and whether even
Calderon was known to him seems questionable since, given the affinity of intentions in his—indeed Baroque—pleasure in cultured citations, he would doubt-
lessly have made mention of him. Kierkegaard, furthermore, accepted the conventional argument against allegory, as is evident in a critical excursus on the text
of the "Magic Flute": "The speeches, for which either Schikaneder or the
Danish translator is responsible, are in general so crazy and stupid that it is
almost inconceivable how Mozart has brought as much out of them as he has. To
let Papageno say of himself, 'I am a child of Nature,' and so in that very moment
make himself a liar, may be regarded as an example *instar ominum.*"[80] But Papageno, whom Kierkegaard called—as he did the page boy—mythical, is an alle-

gorical figure of the concept of unspoiled nature (in the Enlightenment sense), and the incriminated sentence is not so much an individual's inept expression as it is the interpretative caption under the image of a feather-cloaked bird catcher, which has endured to the present in the "entrance aria" of operettas. Kierkegaard never reflected theoretically on the profundity of allegory. Its power is to be assessed as all the greater in an oeuvre whose most hidden impulses consistently demonstrate the same intention that the oeuvre would have to condemn according to the categories of the idealist aesthetics that it proclaims in its manifest doctrine. This power must inhabit the very center of Kierkegaard's philosophy. If his philosophy, unintentionally and without any substantial knowledge of the appropriate literature, produces not only allegorical forms of meaning but allegorical material contents right down to the choice of personal names, then this may demonstrate that fundamental connections between historically emerging philosophies are not established by "mental structures" and categories, but by pragmatic elements that serve prototypically as the fundament of the conceptual expressions and once again burst forth as soon as the objective constellation of the thought draws them near, whether or not the thought corresponds with the philosophical intention. According to its cultural-historical genesis, Kierkegaard's Baroque is anachronistic; yet it is historically consistent according to the law of mythical inwardness, whose labyrinth the "solitary person" traverses; an inwardness that is inseparable from its historical-natural imagery. Through melancholy, inwardness conjures the semblance of truth to the point that melancholy itself becomes transparent as semblance; to the point, that is, that melancholy is wiped out and at the same time rescued; melancholy conjures images, and these stand ready for it in history as enigmatic figures. It is not by accident that these images are all attributable to the region of a long past aesthetic figurativeness. It is, however, toward this topography that all of the disparate definitions that Kierkegaard conceives under the name of the aesthetic are directed.

Paradoxies of the Aesthetic

"Carking care is my feudal castle. It is built like an eagle's nest upon the peak of a mountain lost in the clouds. No one can take it by storm. From this abode I dart down into the world of reality to seize my prey; but I do not remain down there, I bear my quarry aloft to my stronghold. My booty is images that I weave into the tapestries of my palace. There I live like one of the dead. I immerse everything I have experienced in a baptism of forgetfulness, consecrating it to an eternal remembrance. Everything temporal and contingent is cast-off and forgotten. Then I sit, an old man, grey-haired and thoughtful, and explain picture after picture in a voice as soft as a whisper; and at my side a child sits and listens, although he long knows everything that I have to say."[81] While this definition of the aesthetic, itself pictorial and certainly the most precise that Kierkegaard gave, attempts to derive the mythical pictorial content of his philosophy from an aesthetic worldview, it would be better to seek the origin of what he calls aesthetic in the mythical substrate itself. Inwardness indeed conjures up the images, but they are not simply identical with it, and nothing divulges the mythical character of his absolute spirituality more precisely than the pictorial character of its "booty." What Kierkegaard critically recognized in the modern reinterpretation of the idea of the tragic holds good for his own concept of aesthetic inwardness: "It is certainly a misunderstanding of the tragic, when our age strives to transubstantiate the whole tragic destiny into individuality and subjectivity."[82] It is precisely in this fashion that Kierkegaard's doctrine of subjective aesthetic deportment misunderstands its mythical content. The tragic, as an aesthetic category, is defined—according to Kierkegaard's own insight—by fate and establishes the counterimage to every subjective dynamic. This is, however, precisely the case with the objects encompassed by Kierkegaard's concept of the aesthetic. For this reason, aesthetic behavior is more legitimately defined by him as that of the viewer than it is located in his "ethical" view of the aesthetic: "And now for you own life. Has that its teleology in itself? Whether a man is justified in leading the life of mere spectator I will not decide. But let us assume that the significance of your life is to contemplate others, then after all you would not have your teleology in yourself. Only when every particular man is an element and at the same time the whole can he be regarded with a view to his beauty; but when he is regarded thus he is regarded ethically, and if he is regarded ethically, he is regarded in terms of his freedom."[83] For to objectless inwardness, as to a "spectator," truth appears as a strange and enigmatic drama even when he tries to assure himself of it through introspection. The fissure that separates truth from inwardness, to which truth appears as mere semblance, defines the shape of truth itself. Hence the friable ambiguousness of the term "aesthetic" in Kierkegaard; hence the discontinuity of the aesthetic itself, which he recognizes from the perspective of the "ethical": "For about that you could not enlighten him, precisely because you yourself are enmeshed in the aesthetic; only he can explain the aesthetic who stands on a higher level and lives ethically. . . . The reason why the man who lives aesthetically can give no satisfactory explanation of his life, is that he constantly lives in the moment, and therefore has only a relative, limited consciousness. . . . The intellectual gifts of the aesthete are enslaved; transparency is lacking to them. . . . You are constantly only in the moment, and therefore your life dissolves into arbitrary particular occurrence, and it is impossible for you to explain it."[84] With the historical break between inner and outer, with the collapse of "totality," the mythical essence of the aesthetic image expresses itself at the same time as discontinuity. The aesthetic region is ambiguous and no more knows the sharp distinction of the individual than the nexus of the whole. Faithless, the aesthetic has fallen to the mercy of nature, and drags in whomever it encounters: "Of all the branches of knowledge, aesthetics is the most faithless. Anyone who has really loved it becomes in one sense unhappy, but he who has never loved it is and remains a *pecus* [dumb brute]."[85] This defines the peculiar danger of the "poet" in the *Moment*: "Precisely for this reason is the poet, from a spiritual perspective, the most dangerous, because man loves the poet above all, because he is the most dangerous. For it is an ordinary accompaniment of illness to desire most vehemently, to love most of all, precisely that which is injurious to the sick man. But, spiritually understood, man in his natural condition is sick, he is in error, self-deluded, and therefore desires most of all to be deceived, so that he may be permitted not only to remain in error but to find himself thoroughly comfortable in his self-deceit."[86] The poet as the merely natural man: it is as such that absolute spirituality perceives its own mythical origin. The paradoxy is clearly evident in Kierkegaard's outline of the aesthetic: "the aesthetic" is indeed the sphere of mere immediacy; yet it should be dialectical in itself and lead to precisely that decisiveness that is denied only to aesthetic life: "The aesthetic is that in a man whereby he immediately is the man he is; the ethical is that whereby a man becomes what he becomes. . . . If, then, he has the aesthetic seriousness you talk about so often and a little worldly wisdom, he will easily see that all cannot possibly thrive equally; hence he will choose, and what determines his choice is a more or less, which is a relative difference."[87] Kierkegaard occasionally claimed the dialectic that originates here as the schema of his entire authorial project: "The movement from the 'poet' to religious existence is fundamentally the movement of my whole activity as an author, understood in its totality. One may compare *The Works of Love*, with regard to the use which again is made of 'the poet' as *terminus a quo* for Christian religious existence. The movement *away from* the philosophical, the systematic, to the simple, i.e. the existential, is essentially the same movement as from the poet to religious existence, only in different terms."[88] — As a dialectical "stage," therefore, the concept of the aesthetic is pushed into definitive opposition to "existence." The objective images and the subjective modes of behavior, whose mythical illusoriness is exposed by the plan of his own philosophy, are, for Kierkegaard, aesthetic. In his philosophy, however, this insight into the mythical origin does not apply to the form of objective inwardness itself. Thus, although the spell of the "aesthetic" in Kierkegaard indeed covers the ruins of the immediate external world, which is jettisoned from inwardness as contingent; and, although this spell covers as well the ruins of a transsubjective "meaning," which he fends off as a romantic, metaphorical fraud; it does not extend to the movements of the illusory internality that are unhesitatingly appealed to, even in the *Passion Narrative*, as movements toward positive religiosity. This exposes the central antinomy in Kierkegaard's concept of the aesthetic. Where his philosophy, in the self-consciousness of its mythical semblance, encounters "aesthetic" characteristics, it comes closest to reality: to the reality of its own condition of objectless inwardness as well as that of the estrangement of things in regard to itself. Kierkegaard nowhere saw social reality in sharper outline than in an ''aesthetic'' diapsalm that he measured not according to the objects that it indicates but according to a ''deportment'' and therefore, spurning it, ranged it among the fragments of semblance, even though it originates not so much from an indecisive consciousness as it portrays the semblance of the situation itself: ''In the last analysis, what is the significance of life? Mankind is divided into two great classes: one works for a living, the other does not need to. But working in order to live cannot be the significance of life. For it would be a contradiction to say that the production of the conditions of life somehow answers the question of the significance of what is conditioned. The lives of the other class have no other significance than that they consume the conditions of subsistence. And to say that the significance of life is death, seems again a contradiction.''[89] When his philosophy — in the name of existence — takes objectless inwardness and mythical conjuration as substantial reality, it capitulates to the semblance that it rejects in the depths of oblivion. Semblance, which illuminates thought from the remoteness of the images like the star of reconciliation, burns in the abyss of inwardness as an all-consuming fire. It is to be sought out and named in this abyss, if the hope that it radiates is not to be forfeited by knowledge.

Chapter 4
Concept of Existence

Existence and Truth

Of all of Kierkegaard's concepts, that of existence is currently the most prominent. If his struggle with "official Christianity" has lost its urgency for a mentality in which the established church and individual life long ago left behind the dialectic in which Kierkegaard found them linked, however antagonistically; if the abstract transcendence of the idea of God—which dialectical theology extracts from *Fear and Trembling* and the *Philosophical Fragments*—appears all too bound to positive dogmatics and at the same time all too wanting in any binding content to become a significant epochal concern beyond the boundaries of the intra-Protestant controversy; then Kierkegaard's formulation of the problem of truth is most compelling when, without dogmatic thesis and without speculative antithesis, it is addressed to existence in the form in which it defines the circumference of his philosophical experience: when it is addressed, that is, to individual existence. The ontological question, as the question of the "meaning of existence," is today read out of Kierkegaard more than any other.[1] To be sure, the doctrine of "meaning" is equivocal from the beginning. In Kierkegaard existence is not to be understood as a "manner of being," not even if it were one "laid open" to itself.[2] He is not concerned with a "fundamental ontology" that "must be sought in the existential analytic of existence."[3] For Kierkegaard, the question of the "meaning" of existence is not that of what existence properly is, but rather what gives existence—meaningless in itself—a meaning. Philosophy's concern is not the "being of beings," but ideas insofar as they occur within the

68

movement of existence without remaining in it. Existence does not interpret itself through "meaning"; rather, it separates itself from the meaningless, from contingency. This is acutely formulated not only by "aesthete A" but even more definitively by the "anonymous friend" in *Repetition*: "One sticks a finger into the ground to smell what country one is in; I stick my finger into existence—it has no smell. Where am I? What does it mean to say: the world? What is the meaning of that word? Who tricked me into this whole thing and leaves me standing here? Who am I? How did I get into the world? Why was I not asked about it, why was I not informed of the rules and regulations but just thrust into the ranks as if I had been bought from a peddling shanghaier of human beings? How did I get involved in this big enterprise called reality? Why should I be involved? Isn't it a matter of choice? And if I am compelled to be involved, where is the manager—I have something to say about this. Is there no manager? To whom shall I make my complaint?"[4]—Kierkegaard himself used the term ontology only polemically, as equivalent to metaphysics. If it is applied to truth, the figure of which his philosophy wants to produce, then, according to his intention, existence could not be termed ontological. "Existence is ontically distinctive in that it is ontological:"[5] Heidegger's thesis is incompatible with Kierkegaard's intention. True, for Kierkegaard ontology is bound to creaturely existence, from which it must be inseparable if it is not to dissolve in the uncertainties of speculation: "All essential knowledge relates to existence, or only such knowledge as has an essential relationship to existence is essential knowledge. All knowledge that does not inwardly relate itself to existence, in the reflection of inwardness, is, essentially viewed, accidental knowledge; its degree and scope is essentially indifferent."[6] But since ontology is sought within the field of existence, it is not at the same time the answer to the ontological "question," and "meaning" is much more than simply the structure of the possibility of existence. This is Kierkegaard's point: "It is only momentarily that the particular individual is able to realize existentially a unity of the infinite and the finite that transcends existence."[7] Accordingly, "meaning" is not designated as the intention of interpretive ontological questioning, but as the unquestionable "infinity" that transcends existence. It is conjured up out of existence; transcendence is sought in immanence; and it is the movement of individual human consciousness—as engrossment—that offers the form of the conjuration. Kierkegaard's concept of existence does not coincide with mere existence, but with an existence that, dynamic in itself, obtains a transcendent meaning that is supposedly qualitatively different from existence. Accordingly, it does not pose the question of existence as that of simple existence, but as that of historical existence. For the paradoxy of a "meaning" that is not self-identically posited by the subject as a "unity of the finite and the infinite," yet all the same exclusively situated in the "reflexion of inwardness"—this paradoxy is none other than the law of Kierkegaard's objectless inwardness itself, which can be located historically. Unlike current existential philosophy, Kierkegaard's unrelenting polemic against Hegel and speculative metaphysics does not want to hold a transcendent meaning at a distance from the interpretation of existence, a meaning of which he felt more assured than Hegel ever did. On the contrary, Kierkegaard wants to preserve immanent consciousness as an arena of a manifest transcendent meaning, whereas in Hegel this meaning is to be immanent in transcendent being. What is real is rational. This makes possible the misrepresentation that, in its restriction to subjective existence, the interest of Kierkegaard's philosophy is "existential-ontological," whereas actually his dialectic of engrossment merely binds existence and ontology in order ultimately to divide them. The ontological question of interpretation is anathematized as "objective": "the way of objective reflection makes the subject accidental and thereby transforms existence into something indifferent, something vanishing. The way to objective truth leads away from the subject, and while the subject and his subjectivity become indifferent, the truth also becomes indifferent, and this indifference is precisely its objective validity; for all interest, like all decisiveness, is rooted in subjectivity. The way of objective reflection leads to abstract thought, to mathematics, to historical knowledge of different kinds; and always it leads away from the subject, whose being or non-being from the objective point of view quite rightly becomes infinitely indifferent. Quite rightly, since as Hamlet says, being and non-being have only subjective significance. In its perfection this way will arrive at a contradiction, and in so far as the subject does not become wholly indifferent to himself, this merely constitutes a sign that his objective striving is not objective enough. At its maximum this way leads to the contradiction that only the objective has come into being, while the subjective has gone out; that is to say, the existing subjectivity has vanished, in that it has made an attempt to become what in the abstract sense is called subjectivity, the mere abstract form of an abstract objectivity. And yet, the objectivity which has thus come into being is, from the subjective point of view in its perfection, either an hypothesis or an approximation, because all eternal decisiveness is rooted in subjectivity."[8] This is a critique not only of the scientific comprehension of the objective world, but equally of the "objectifying" interpretation of subjectivity and, therefore, *a priori*, of the possibility of an "existential analytic of existence." Fichte's "I am I" and Hegel's "subject-object" are for Kierkegaard hypostatizations under the sign of identity and are rejected precisely to the extent that they set up a pure being of existence in opposition to the existing "particular individual": "Speculative philosophy will immediately transport us into the fantastic realism of the I-am-I, which modern speculative thought has not hesitated to use without explaining how a particular individual is related to it; and God knows, no human being is more than such a particular individual. If an existing individual were really able to transcend himself, the truth would be for him something final and complete; but where is the point at which he is outside himself? The I-am-I is a mathematical point which does not exist, and to this extent there is nothing to prevent everyone from occupying this standpoint; the one will not be in the way of the other."[9] And similarly in opposition to Hegel: "Or is the existing spirit himself the identity of subject and object, the subject-object? In that case I must press the question of where such an existing human being is, when he is thus at the same time also a subject-object?"[10] Because the existing thus takes the place of existence, ontology is removed further from existence the more that the question of the existing is directed toward the existing particular person. Individual existence is for Kierkegaard the arena of ontology only because it itself is not ontological. Hence the existence of the person is for Kierkegaard a process that mocks any objectivation; hence, with regard to inner-philosophical constitution, absolute spirituality is held to be dynamic-dialectical. Spirituality is not being whose meaning is to be released ontologically, but a function that locks meaning within itself. As such, spirituality is not accidentally named by a word reminiscent of subjugation to nature, passion. Through passion the existing person should participate in truth, without being ontologized; and at the same time, without truth, hypostatized, being withdrawn from the person: "It is the passion of the infinite that is the decisive factor and not its content, for its content is precisely itself. In this manner subjectivity and the subjective 'how' constitute the truth";[11] that is, in Kierkegaard's opinion, insofar as passion is not the decisive factor, but becomes itself through infinite negation of itself. Under the category of negativity, of "uncertainty," truth is separated from any ontological project of the person, to whom ontology belongs only paradoxically: "An objective uncertainty held fast in an appropriation-process of the most passionate inwardness is the truth, the highest truth attainable for an existing individual."[12] Kierkegaard's idea of truth is distinguished from one that is merely subjectivistic by the postulate of "infinity," with which the finite self is simply incommensurate; and it is distinguished from objectivity of whatever sort by the rejection of any positive transsubjective criterion: "When the question of truth is raised in an objective manner, reflection is directed objectively to the truth, as an object to which the knower is related. Reflection is not focused upon the relationship, however, but upon the question of whether it is the truth to which the knower is related. If only the object to which he is related is the truth, the subject is accounted to be in the truth. When the question of the truth is raised subjectively, reflection is directed subjectively to the nature of the individual's relationship; if only the mode, the 'how,' of this relationship is in the truth, the individual is in the truth even if he should happen to be thus related to what is not true."[13] Immanent and transcendent truth are no longer "mediated" by the hypostatization of subjective and objective "participation" in truth. The predication of truth, just as any predication of content, would "objectivate" the idea of truth and is therefore, for Kierkegaard, not permissible. Truth's transcendence is produced instead through the negation of immanent subjectivity, through the infinite contradiction. Subjectivity and truth intersect in paradoxy: "Inwardness in an existing subject culminates in passion; corresponding to passion in the subject the truth becomes a paradox."[14] Thus Kierkegaard's idea of the paradox—conceived this side of all theological paradoxy of the symbol—has its philosophical genesis in the relationship of objectless inwardness and ontology. In Kierkegaard, paradoxy is raised to the highest power of conjuration; a power that renounces aesthetic semblance; a power, that is, without images. The critique of his concept of existence is concerned with this paradoxy, and not with the meaning of the being of existence.

Paradoxy and Ambiguity

The movement of existence is for Kierkegaard one that is to lead objectless inwardness out of its mythical entanglement in "freedom" to the presence of truth itself. Kierkegaard does not expressly conclude that this truth in paradoxy destroys semblance: for him, semblance is not bound to mythical content, but to the subjective mode of behavior, and is therefore unable to constitute the antithetical idea to that of existence. But the conception of paradoxical truth as imageless inheres in his terminology. For Kierkegaard, truth is "transparentness," and the profound gaze that without any resistance penetrates the transparent seems to be the complete opposite of what is embodied in the mythical images in which it satiates itself but at the same time encounters its own impenetrable border.—The centrality of the category of transparentness in Kierkegaard's doctrine of existence has been recognized by Guardini: "To be 'transparent' to oneself. For Kierkegaard the word has the greatest significance. It means ingenuous, free of all obscurity, manifestly authentic."[15] Clearly, Guardini's commentary is a Catholic interpretation of Kierkegaard's "transparentness": for him, nature has been atoned for by the sacrifice of Christ, whereas for the Protestant, Kierkegaard, a sinful-ambiguous nature stands ever again in need of rescue. Guardini takes transparentness as "simplicity" in the Christian sense: "There, where Kierkegaard looks back on his work, in *The Point of View of My Work as an Author*, he names 'simplicity' the highest value of Christian perfection, as Christ's said: 'Except ye become as little children, ye shall not enter into the kindgom of heaven.' Matthew 18:3—, simplicity and transparentness belong together."[16] This misses the dialectical character, which for Kierkegaard the idea of transparentness itself preserves. Simplicity, the concrete condition of transparentness, is for him not identical with simple-correct "ethical" life. As the goal of infinite and "negative" movement, simplicity remains virtual; it is the "highest value of Christian perfection" not so much in life as in perfect contradiction to it, i.e. in sacrifice. To understand this it is not enough to suppose "that Kierkegaard was perhaps the most complicated person who ever wrote on religious matters."[17] For the dialectical conception of transparentness is not adequately grasped psychologically, but only in terms of the configuration of Kierkegaard's idea of truth. Transparentness is indeed conceived ontologically: "I could have called the good 'transparency.' "[18] But it is, according to the concept of knowledge, not so much an achieved level of being as dynamic in itself: "The ethical individual knows himself, but this knowledge is not a mere contemplation (for the individual would understand himself only as determined by necessity), it is a reflection upon himself that itself is an action, and therefore I have deliberately preferred to use the expression 'choose oneself' instead of know oneself."[19] But then transparentness is no longer paradoxical truth but ambiguous. Imageless truth, into which the movement of individual consciousness is to flow paradoxically, negating itself, is itself drawn into the movement without any possibility of differentiation: the ontological good is the ontical existence in the act of "choice," and ontology, previously wrenched away from subjective immanence by the strength of "infinity," threatens once again to sink back into itself as soon as the idea of truth itself—as "transparentness"—is subjected to the dialectic. This ambiguity of Kierkegaard's idea of truth is to be emphatically separated from the paradox. Truth appears paradoxical in the subjective—and not only subjective—dialectic that is extinguished in it; truth becomes ambiguous as the quintessence of dialectical movement without being its measure. It is easy to suppose, and it has been often enough asserted, that Kierkegaard's dialectic reaches its pinnacle when spirit emerges pure and undisguised from the dialectic in order to achieve transcendence as simplicity. Whether or not this is true of Kierkegaard's Christology, this schema does not hold good for the doctrine of truth and the corresponding dialectic of existence. For truth, metamorphosed as fear, does not absorb into itself the rising sap of the dialectic, instead it is conceded to the aimless growth of the tree.

The Abstract Self

For Kierkegaard, ontological "meaning" is not one in which a self-interpretive existence could know its own being; rather, existence must conjure meaning; conjure it without imagery in order to gain self-possession in pure, unmanifest spirituality. What spirituality conjures is granted to it ambiguously and entangled with mere existence; this throws the critique of Kierkegaard's idea of truth back onto the structure of his concept of existence as the origin of ambiguity.—To understand this concept, it will help to bring Kant's synthesis to mind, which prepared the way for Fichte's and Hegel's systems as much as for Kierkegaard's doctrine of existence. The critique of pure reason was a critique of rational ontology, specifically of Wolff's ontology. This ontology was subjected to its most severe test: that of the contingency of the categorically undeducible material of intuition. If ontology is not to be rescued as the content of experience, it may be conceived only as the form of experience. It shrinks to a synthetic *a priori* judgment to the extent that it is not relegated to the secure and powerless transcendence of the postulates. The gap between the inner and the contingent outer is still mastered in the system of principles: subjectively produced by means of the synthetic unity of apperception, they belong to the immanence of consciousness; as constitutive conditions of all objective knowledge, they are themselves objective. Ontology is preserved in their double meaning: it is protected from contingency through the systematic strength of the spontaneous center and protected from the deceptions of speculative thought through experiential validity. The cost of this security is abstractness: the principles are "necessary" only insofar as they are "universal." The idealist systems undertook once again to recover the lost content of ontology through the elimination of the contingency of the "material," which is itself derived from the synthetic unity of apperception, developed as "content" out of the subjective forms from which "ontology" can be deduced and through "development" posited as identical with subjectivity. This is the model of Kierkegaard's philosophico-historical effort. For Kierkegaard, just as for Hegel, Kant's subjective ontology is rendered powerless by its abstractness. At the same time, however, Kierkegaard recognizes the fraud of the material ontology of the late expositional sections of the Hegelian system—the Hegelian construction of the status quo as meaningful: the identity of the real and the reasonable volatilizes ontology by spreading it out over the whole of existence and thus forgoes any binding measure of exalted existence as of "meaning," a meaning whose ubiquity threatens to reverse into being nowhere at all. Kierkegaard's project is the precise antithesis of the Kantian thesis and the Hegelian synthesis. Against Kant, he pursues the plan of concrete ontology; against Hegel, he pursues the plan of an ontology that does not succumb to the existent by absorbing it into itself. He therefore revises the process of post-Kantian idealism: he surrenders the claim of identity. What remains is, however, not the Kantian landscape of a transcendental subject whose forms of intuition and concepts of order objectify the manifold of perceptual data as experience. Along with Hegelian identity, he sacrifices the Kantian transcendental objectivity. Whereas in Kant, "consciousness in general" persists—this side of the gap—as the guarantor of ontology, Kierkegaard renounces the scientific validity of "results" and contrasts the particular consciousness of the individual person, as concrete, with the contingency of external experience. The individual becomes, for Kierkegaard, the bearer of a material meaning that the philosophy of identity was unable to realize in contingent sensuous material, whereas the abstract Kantian "I think" did not suffice to confirm the existence it had mastered as meaningful. Hegel is turned inside out: world history is for Hegel what the individual is for Kierkegaard. Yet Kierkegaard is not exempted from the obligation of paying the Kantian tribute to contingency. For the person's existence and quiddity, which cannot be understood on the basis of any "meaning," is as contingent as any perceptual data. To prevent the individual's contingency from losing its "meaning," the concrete individual is subjected to a procedure that indeed ensures him of concrete meaning— just as the Kantian "idea" ensures the coherence of the intellect (*Verstand*)—yet renders the individual abstract: the ontological determinations that are sought in him are hollowed out, be it that they—like the terms "meaning," "freedom," and "idea"—are in no way less abstract than the Kantian categories; be it that insofar as they remain concrete, they are overtaken—as determinations of mere facticity—by the same contingency from which the restriction to inwardness was supposed to give protection. This is made perfectly evident by the ambiguity of ontological meaning in Kierkegaard. The origin of this ambiguity is the abstract self. Its abstractness is the counterpole to the abstractness of the universal. It is the abstractness of the particular. This abstractness stands in contrast to the transparentness that is Kierkegaard's aim. True, this transparentness is imageless, yet what lies closest to it remains as impenetrable as are only those images that are seen at the most extreme distance. Kierkegaard gives evidence of this in a passage from *The Concept of Anxiety*; while the passage is concerned with an "egoist," no criterion distinguishes it from his positive presentation of existence: "For selfishness is precisely the particular, and what this signifies only the single individual can know as the single individual, because when it is viewed under universal categories it may signify everything in such a way that it signifies nothing at all. . . . 'Self,' however, signifies precisely the contradiction of positing the universal as the particular. Only when the concept of the particular is given can there be any talk of selfishness; however, although there have lived countless millions of such 'selves,' no science can say what the self is without again stating it quite generally."[20] The self, the hoard of all concretion, contracts in its singularity in such a fashion that nothing more can be predicated of it: it reverses into the most extreme abstractness; the claim that only the individual knows what the individual is amounts to no more than a circumlocution for its final unknowability. Thus the most determinate self remains the most indeterminate. Modern logic did not fail to perceive the indeterminateness of the pure substratum of any form of categorial determination. In Husserl's analysis of noematic "meaning" in the *Ideas*, there is a description that precisely sums up the situation of the Kierkegaardian "self": "There detaches itself as the central noematic phrase: the 'object,' the 'objective unity,' the 'self-same,' the 'determinable subject of its possible predicates'—the pure x in abstraction from all predicates."[21] Just as in Husserl's many synonymous expressions, the logical center of the Kierkegaardian self, the object of all possible predication, the inherently "concrete," becomes an indeterminate, indeterminable, abstraction. Its abstractness is the reflection of the abstractness of the highest universalities to which it is subordinated: the idea, decisiveness, and spirit. That, however, this abstractness characterizes not only the egoistic, "selfish" self, but the "existential" self as well, can be interpretively inferred from an excursus from the *Concluding Unscientific*

Postscript: "What does it mean in general to explain anything? Does it consist in showing that the obscure something in question is not this but something else? This would be a strange sort of an explanation; I thought it was the function of an explanation to render it evident that the something in question was this definite thing, so that the explanation took the obscurity away but not the object. Otherwise the explanation would not be an explanation, but something quite different, namely, a correction."[22] The sort of "explanation" that Kierkegaard demands would be possible only in image and name, and precisely these are excluded by the demand for "transparentness." It is, in addition, generally blocked by Kierkegaard's subjectivistic-nominalistic theory of language, which grounds his doctrine of "communication." Transparentness, however, which helplessly perseveres in the face of its blind, unilluminable, and closed object, completely renounces knowledge in a different manner. The object resists all transparentness. This is evident in the relationship of the category of transparentness to the category of the paradox: "The explanation of the paradox makes it clear what the paradox is, removing any remaining obscurity."[23] If here transparentness, as the name for ontology, is the subordinating concept of the paradoxical, whose obscurity is to be "removed"—how should transparentness accomplish this, if the paradoxical itself remains obscure, indeterminate, and abstract? For indeed all illumination has its boundaries defined by the condition of determinate existence. True illumination will never gnostically volatilize existence into a system of "significations." Nor can illumination ever mean the mere constatation of obscurity; knowledge may be unable to solve its material, yet it may indeed construct its material in figures of the existing in which the material—however obscure and however impoverished of meaning it is for itself—all the same functionally contributes to illumination. The empty and blind "x" is set up as truth only by a pseudo-dialectic in which illumination is identical with categorization under universal concepts and which celebrates its triumphs there where such categorization is no longer possible because it takes the negation, the transcendence, and the explosion of the concept to be its material's highest accomplishment. All that this pseudo-dialectic really demonstrates is the inappropriateness of its categories to its philosophical-historical objects. Kierkegaard was able to deceive himself about this by the force of his opposition to Kant. He thought he had warded off its abstractness along with the transcendental subject, without, however, noticing that the abstractness returns in the narrowing of concretion to the pure this-there. Where he recognized the danger, he defended himself by tearing concretion away from knowledge: "Certitude and inwardness are indeed subjectivity, but not in an entirely abstract sense. It really is the misfortune of the most recent knowledge that everything has become so terribly magnificent. Abstract subjectivity is just as uncertain and lacks inwardness to the same degree as abstract objectivity."[24] If concrete subjectivity were exclusively reserved for praxis, praxis itself would be without orientation and knowledge would have abdicated. For this reason Kierkegaard must unceasingly concern himself with the theoretical interpretation of concrete subjectivity, with the person as the bearer of "meaning." But this theoretical effort necessarily entangles itself in tautology: "The most concrete content that consciousness can have is consciousness of itself, of the individual himself—not the pure self-consciousness, but the self-consciousness that is so concrete that no author, not even the one with the greatest power of description, has even been able to describe a single such self-consciousness, although every single human being is such a one. This self-consciousness is not contemplation, for he who believes this has not understood himself, because he has not seen that he himself is in the process of becoming and consequently cannot be something completed for contemplation. This self-consciousness, therefore, is action."[25] Only the Fichtean turn toward "action," as the unity of theory and praxis, leads out of the tautology. Yet had Kierkegaard insisted on such unity, he would have been consigned to the philosophy of identity. Thus the doctrine of existence at every turn comes up against aporia. Sometimes its center, the "self," is abstract and only tautologically definable; sometimes the self falls to a praxis that would first have to receive its rule from the self; sometimes the conception of the self leads to nebulous positings of identification. In spite of the various constructions, the self becomes obviously fully abstract there where its content was to have been interpreted, in the "psychology": "I may lose my wealth, my honor in the eyes of others, my intellectual powers, and suffer no damage to my soul. I could gain it all and yet suffer damage. What then is my soul? What is this inmost being of mine which can remain unaffected by this loss and suffer damage by this gain? To the despairing man this apparently insubstantial abstraction proves to be 'something.' "[26] The discussion here is of an insubstantial abstraction; the "something," however, its corrective, remains equally abstract. If one wanted, by a questionable method, to search out the grounding nexus of Kierkegaard's concept of existence in praxis, i.e., in its moral theses, it would not gain adequate concreteness. For Kierkegaard, the instrument of moral "action" is the "earnestness" of decisiveness. Through earnestness the anthropological schemata of the self and of existence are to gain their content. But since earnestness may not draw its determinations from the objective world, it is defined by the same "inwardness" to which it is supposed to grant "meaning"; and hence, once again, the thought is tautological: "But this same thing to which earnestness is to return with the same earnestness can only be earnestness itself."[27] Just as earnestness remains tautological, the subject remains its own object: "The phrase 'What has made him earnest in life' must of course be understood, in a pregnant sense, as that from which the individuality in the deepest sense dates his earnestness. Having become truly earnest about that which is the object of earnestness, a person may very well, if he so wishes, treat various things 'earnestly,' but the question is whether he first became earnest about the object of earnestness. This object every human being has, because it is himself.''[28] Ultimately the self, which as existence is the theoretical-anthropological category, and earnestness, the practical category, are directly identified: "Inwardness, i.e. certitude, is earnestness.''[29] This prompts the contrary insight: "This seems a little paltry.''[30] But this insight is immediately turned into self-righteous irony that intends to finish off transcendental idealism: "If at least I had said that it [earnestness] is subjectivity, the pure subjectivity, the encompassing subjectivity, I would have said something, something that no doubt would have made many earnest. However, I can also express earnestness in another way. Whenever inwardness is lacking, the spirit is finitized. Inwardness is therefore eternity or the constituent of the eternal in man.''[31] Thus, when the "impoverishment" becomes evident, the abstractness of the past, of the general categories of eternity, spirit, and infinity, is substituted for the abstractness of the most minute, the abstractness of the self. This becomes drastically evident in the central definition of the self in the *Unscientific Postscript*: "The negativity that pervades existence, or rather, the negativity of the existing subject, which should be essentially reflected in his thinking in an adequate form, has its ground in the subject's synthesis: that he is an existing infinite spirit. The infinite and eternal is the only certainty, but as being in the subject it is in existence; and the first expression for this, is its elusiveness, and this tremendous contradiction, that the eternal becomes, that it comes into being.''[32] Such concepts spin a web around the ethical substratum without opening it up. As a self, it remains indeterminate; as the intersection of conceptual projections, it is not grasped as *this* specific self. "This is the single fashion in which the ethical can manifest itself; in itself, in its positive meaning, it is concealed in the deepest layer of the soul,''[33] that is, it remains totally opaque.

Existence Mythical

Spirit, separated from nature, disdains imagery. This enmity manifests itself as abstractness in the concept of the self, and it is the origin of both the powerlessness of conjuration and the ambiguity of what is conjured. But this enmity is at the same time expression. Abstractness, as opaqueness, bears witness to mere nature, into which Kierkegaard's spiritualism invariably reverses. Like the universal concepts, so the pure this-there remains abstract in Kierkegaard's doctrine of existence. In it the content of the concept of existence expresses itself. It may be said that abstractness is the seal of mythical thought. The ambiguity of the guilty natural context, in which everything undifferentiatedly communicates with everything else, knows no true concretion. Here the names of created things are confounded and blind material or the empty sign remains in its place. The commonplace attribution of the highest concreteness to mythical, archaic thought by virtue of the conceptually unmediated intuition of the this-there is misleading.

Primitive speechless intuition is unable to give its objects lasting boundaries; although it bestows everything individual with its own word, the word rigidifies under its gaze as a fetish that locks itself even deeper in its own existence. The universal concepts, however, distilled from the intuited objects as abbreviations of their common characteristics, are, like these characteristics, dependent upon speechless intuition for their fulfillment. The concrete, already lost in the case of the universal concept and still obscure to pure intuition, is not the secure middle between the two. It is the spark that—in the name—shoots across from the most universal concept to the material of the this-there and ignites.—Material statements about existence that contain more than the proclamation of the factual there-ness of the self or the attempt at its localization through the combination of universal concepts, occur in Kierkegaard only rarely and with the greatest abridgement. Kierkegaard—as Johannes de Silentio and Frater Taciturnus—may have been able to justify his silence with the "concealedness" of the existential substrate, with the insufficiency of the *ratio*, to develop a "system of existence." The concept of existence is presented in positive form, without any supporting apparatus, only on the first several pages of *The Sickness unto Death*; and it receives a (qualifying) commentary exclusively in two passages in the *Training in Christianity*, which—without referring to *The Sickness unto Death*—unmistakably pursue the terminology of the earlier work. It is from these fragments that concrete criticism must start if it wants to do more than to understand existential thought banally in terms of its antithesis to systematic thought, as thought directed toward being, without troubling over the specific idea of being at which, beyond all mere relativity of existence, Kierkegaard's concept of existence aims.—*The Sickness unto Death* begins with the thesis of spiritualism, with the determination of existence as spirit. Guardini has trenchantly noted the danger in this: "Kierkegaard . . . pushes his thesis one-sidedly to an extreme; for this thesis should be weighty, weighty in such a fashion that it becomes catastrophic in that it becomes a functionally, meaningful impossibility. Thus he says: 'Spirit' is identical with the 'self'—a thesis whose destructive consequences cannot be presented here."[34] Creation is reduced to spirit in the self in order to rescue the self from its fallenness to guilt-laden nature. Since, however, man as creation— as "existing," which is precisely how Kierkegaard conceives him in opposition to speculative idealism—is not identical with spirit, nature overcomes him there where he thinks he has secured the supranatural for himself, i.e., in the self, precisely as in something absolutely spiritual. "Man is spirit. But what is spirit? Spirit is the self."[35] This is Kierkegaard's axiom. But is the self spirit? And does not spirit, identified with created being, become a mythical quality? Kierkegaard attempts to escape this implication through his ruling idea of the dialectic as one between "nature and spirit, mythical content and consciousness as qualitatively different, strictly contrary powers."[36] In *The Sickness unto Death* this idea is reduced to its basic formula and joined with the definition of the self as spirit:

"But what is the self? The self is a relation which relates itself to its own self."[37] In that Kierkegaard interprets the self not as existing statically but, functionally, as spirit, it is to transcend the natural world to which its substratum necessarily belongs in its "opaqueness." The commentary in the *Training* makes the functional character of the doctrine of "relationship" evident: "What is it, then, to be a self? It is a duplication. Hence in the relation established here the phrase, 'truly draw to oneself,' has a double meaning. The magnet draws iron to itself, but iron is not a self: hence, in the relation established here, 'draw to itself' indicates a single and simple act. But a self is a duplication, it is freedom: hence in this case 'drawing truly to oneself' means to present a choice. In the case of iron which is drawn, there is not and cannot be any question of a choice. But a self can be truly drawn to another only through a choice, so that 'truly drawing to oneself' is a composite act."[38] This conception of the self as a "relation" reveals its mythical character. The "relation which relates itself to its own self" has no precise meaning if exactly that "x" is not accepted as the substratum of the relation. The definitions of *Sickness unto Death* want, however, in contradistinction to those of the *Unscientific Postscript*, to exclude precisely the "opaque" substratum through the introduction of pure functions. The concept of relation, however, says nothing else than that its elements relate to one another; not that their relation relates to the "whole." The "relation which relates itself to its own self" can therefore, in the first place, not be reflectively comprehended without a "substratum." If, however, the relation which relates itself to its own self is neither the reference to a substratum nor the reflection of the relationship to itself, which would indeed already amount to objectivation, then nothing else could be meant by Kierkegaard's reflective diction than a structure of the relation itself that could then be reflected upon. It must be asked: what distinguishes a "relation" from a "relation which relates itself to its own self"? Only one answer is possible: the latter relation produces, as a unity, the self-relating elements out of itself, just as "life" for the young Hegel is a unity that is self dividing; whereas the former, the mere "relation," posits divergent elements in regard to one another. The relation which relates itself to its own self is a metaphorical designation for the original, productive unity that at once "posits" and unifies the contradictions. Thus not only the Kantian transcendental synthesis but even the macrocosm of the Hegelian, infinitely productive "totality" is hidden in the microcosm of the Kierkegaardian self. Kierkegaard's self is the system, dimensionlessly concentrated in the "point." That in fact a "totality" sustains the plan of the self is betrayed by a passage from *The Concept of Anxiety*. Kierkegaard there demands of the "psychological observer" that "hence he ought also to have a poetic originality in his soul so as to be able at once to create both the totality and the invariable from what the individual always presents in fragmented and erratic form."[39] The transcendental synthesis in the configuration of totality and primordiality is easily sensed. This self, in its primordiality at once totally posited and positing, bears an unmistakable resemblance—as "un-fragmented"—to the organic, the simply natural self. For in that the creature, split between nature and the supranatural, as self, as "a relation which relates to its own self," as a primordial and productive unity spontaneously produces the duality of nature and the supranatural, it has raised itself unnoticed to the status of creator. Accordingly, however, the "spirit," to which the creature has laid claim, is pulled down to the level of the creature and is transformed back into nature. The creature remains mythically self-positing in the undifferentiated nexus of the natural and measures the highest concept of itself on that of organic life. It could only become transparent through transcendence. On its own, it remains self-opaque.—The absurdity of Kierkegaard's doctrine of the "self relating relationship" has its origin here. It attempts to rescue the dark, spontaneous, and self-positing "I" of transparentness by a postulate: "By relating itself to its own self and by willing to be itself the self is grounded transparently in the power which posited it."[40] As a "relation which relates to its own self," it is itself the "power which posited it," and hence its transparentness is a reflection, just as in the images of the *intérieur*, and as such it is indeed semblance. Kierkegaard's "self" remains mythically-ambiguously between autonomy as the immanent production of meaning and a reflection that perceives itself in the semblance of ontology. The reflective element is accentuated in the definition of despair: "Despair is the disrelation in the relation of a synthesis which relates itself to itself. But the synthesis is not the disrelation, it is merely the possibility, or, in other words, the possibility of the disrelation is latent in the synthesis. If the synthesis were the disrelation, there would be no such thing as despair, for despair would then be something inherent in human nature as such, that is, it would not be despair."[41] The disrelation with regard to the synthetic relation can occur as despair only in reflection; without reflection, there can be no "disrelation" in a relation, for a disrelation may only be measured by some further reflected relation. This corresponds to Kierkegaard's resistance to making despair a category of nature in the immediateness of the "relation." But Kierkegaard's portrayal of despair, if despair were identical with "synthesis" as mere immediacy, is to be literally applied to the definition of the self relating relation itself. It becomes "duplication" simply because, in contrast to reflective semblance, the contradiction between ontological transparentness and mythical self-positing could not be mollified. The unity that produces the relation pulls Kierkegaard's self back into the same nature that transparentness vis-à-vis the positing power was to have purged from it. The dialectic of nature and the supranatural proceeds from natural spirit as from their unity; the dialectic does not attain transparentness, and it must constantly begin anew. Therefore the domineering role of "duplication" and "repetition" not only provides the title of a work, but essentially constitutes the image of the *intérieur*. Caught in the circle of natural life, repetition remains mythic and invocational even when Kierkegaard lays claim to it as an "existential" form of correct life. Repetition turns in circles in the mythical center of his philosophy, in the "relation to relation," which is how he defines the self. If Kierkegaard communicates with Nietzsche anywhere more deeply than is vaguely supposed, it is here: the "image of eternity modeled on endless repetition,"[42] which Bloch has shown Nietzsche's eternal return to be, is also the image of what is eternal in the person around which the concepts of Kierkegaard's doctrine of existence collect themselves in vain.

Objective Despair

The mythical essence of existence breaks loose in Kierkegaard's doctrine of despair. The doctrine anticipates the criticism of the concept of existence: "In order to will in despair to be oneself there must be consciousness of the infinite self. This infinite self, however, is really only the abstractest form, the abstractest possibility of the self, and it is this self the individual despairingly wills to be by detaching the self from every relation to the power which posited it, or detaching it from the conception that there is such a power in existence. By the aid of this infinite form the self despairingly wills to preside freely over itself or to create itself."[43] For Kierkegaard, the central insight transforms itself into a delusion where it should become fruitful for the interpretation of the self; if the self sacrifices its claim to autonomy, in return it succumbs to blind devotion to its fateful essence that it itself earlier produced in blind defiance; in Kierkegaard only the despairing undertakes "to refashion the whole thing, in order to get out of it in this way a self such as he wants to have, produced by the aid of the infinite form of the negative self—and it is thus he wills to be himself."[44] Every escape from the entanglement of the encircling concepts is blocked to "existence." All Kierkegaardian existence is in truth despair, and this is the single source of the power of the tenets of *The Sickness unto Death*. Hope has no place in "existence," and the Christian paradox is not bestowed as a miracle of faith on a universal, existential "religiosity A," but despairingly demanded of it. No theology has ever conceived the idea of hope for a "relation," or for the indeterminate substratum of the relation, but solely as hope for the mortal creature. Kierkegaard's explication of existence, however, fractures the creature by deceptively exalting it into transcendence as "spirit." Kierkegaard makes the apersonality of "existence" evident in despair. Indeed, despair is to serve as the counterconcept to existence. But the origin of the distinction is not for him the apersonality of despair but the refusal of the "relation" to be itself. Its apersonality is averted only by the indeterminate substratum of the self. If "reflection"—which as "transparentness" was to open the existential relation to "meaning"—was semblance, this semblance disappears in the doctrine of despair and nothing is able to prevent the fall from existence. For despair is objective for Kierkegaard and independent of all self-knowledge. Kierkegaard accepts as certain "that one form of despair is precisely this of not being in despair, that is, not being aware of it."[45] The self is thereby surrendered to nature; every illumination has lost its power over it; and nothing remains but an apersonal "relation" from which the comfort of the mirror—the "self which relates to itself"—has been withdrawn. The last word of the existential dialectic is death; and Heidegger had good reason to interpret Kierkegaardian existence as "being toward death," however Kierkegaard may have rejected such being as despair. "If in the strictest sense we are to speak of a sickness unto death, it must be one in which the last thing is death, and death the last thing. And this precisely is despair."[46] But it is also "existence." If death is the last word of imageless conjuration, it is also its exemplary image. In despair the primeval figures of existential repetition flash up demonically: Sisyphus and Tantalus as the bearers of the myths of repetition. In death a realm of imagery silently reveals itself: the image of timeless hopelessness in abject, endless, fallen nature. It is the inability to die as negative eternity: "On the contrary, the torment of despair is precisely this, not to be able to die. So it has much in common with the situation of the moribund when he lies and struggles with death, and cannot die. So to be sick unto death is, not to be able to die—yet not as though there were hope of life; no, the hopelessness in this case is that even the last hope, death, is not available. When death is the greatest danger, one hopes for life; but when one has become acquainted with an even more dreadful danger, one hopes for death."[47] In the most extreme depths of the existential dialectic, in the impersonality of despair in which the mere spirit of the existing individual finally sinks through the vortex of an ever-circling repetition, Kierkegaard's subjectivism hits bottom. Certainly, it lands where he least expected: not in ontological meaning, but in eternal meaninglessness. Under a thin, deceptive covering Kierkegaard's doctrine of existence conceals the ontology of hell: "It is in this last sense that despair is the sickness unto death, this agonizing contradiction, this sickness in the self, everlastingly to die, to die and yet not to die, to die the death. For dying means that it is all over, but dying the death means to live to experience death; and if for a single instant this experience is possible, it is tantamount to experiencing it forever. If one might die of despair as one dies of a sickness, then the eternal in him, the self, must be capable of dying in the same sense that the body dies of sickness. But his is an impossibility; the dying of despair transforms itself constantly into a living. The despairing man cannot die; no more than 'the dagger can slay thoughts' can despair consume the eternal thing, the self, which is the ground of despair, whose worm dieth not, and whose fire is not quenched."[48] Thus the explicit description of the punishment of hell, of whose eternity he approvingly speaks,[49] is developed not from Christian dogmatics but directly from the philosophy of existence and its idealistic core. Only the image of hell, however, pulls the person out of the enchantment of his hopeless immanence; and it does so by shattering him.

Reversal of the Existential Dialectic

"But to reach truth one must pierce through every negativity. For there applies what the fairy-tale recounts about a certain enchantment: the piece of music must be played through backwards; otherwise the enchantment is not broken."[50] If the self, the productive unity of the "relation which relates itself to its own self," blocks transparentness in illusory reflection and circling repetition, its power dwindles in the face of the manifest images of the demonic. The demonic cancels the autonomy of the self along with its dynamic configuration. This is ultimately revealed as more than mere mythical obdurateness toward being transparent; it turns out to be the desperate resistance of nature to its dissolution and dismemberment. As "relation," the self is to be secure from the insanity that unrelentingly threatens its disparate elements. Thus the dialectical double meaning of the abstract choice of self: it demands that the immanently imprisoned individual not fall altogether to the mercy of mythical dissociation from which the autonomous act ultimately protects it: "Can you imagine a more horrible end than your nature actually being dissolved? that the potentialities in you with which you now toy might one day toy with you? that you . . . would become a play-ground for a legion of demons? and be deprived of the inmost and holiest thing of all in a man, the unifying power of personality."[51] This is how hell appears to the subject that has been pulled down into its depths; the subject may climb out of it to the extent that the semblance of its self-posited essence is volatized before the actuality of that being that has its source in the collapse of the subject's false, immanent unity. The self that approaches such regions is still mythical. Its faith remains profoundly bound to the "will," as to the mythical figure of idealism. In Kierkegaard's characterization of the "Christian" and "Socratic," sinfulness and willfulness are bound together: "But where does the difficulty lie? It is to be ascribed to a fact of which the Socratic view itself was aware (though only to a certain degree) and sought to remedy, that it lacks a dialectical determinant for the transition from having understood something to the doing of it. In this transition Christianity makes its start; by proceeding along this path it proves that sin lies in the will thus attaining the concept of defiance; and then, in order to make the end thoroughly fast, it adjoins to this the dogma of original sin."[52] If, however, it is the will that incurred sin, it is not able to wipe it out: just as in the fairy tale, so in the transformation of myths; wishes do not permit themselves to be arbitrarily revoked. Sins originating in the autonomous will may not—according to Kierkegaard—be wished away by that same will: "To wish to have it that sin might never have come into the world"—and according to *The Sickness unto Death* sin is precisely despair—"reduces mankind to a more imperfect stage. Sin has entered in, but when the individuals have humbled themselves under it they stand higher than they stood before."[53] Whereas the self thus entrenches itself in its immanence through the freedom to sin in order to escape mythical collapse, it is driven precisely toward this: toward the state of despair, toward total sinfulness. Despair dissociates the self, and the ruins of the shattered self are the marks of hope. In Kierkegaard's work, this remains the innermost (and hence from Kierkegaard hidden) dialectical truth, which could only be disclosed in the posthumous history of his work. It justifies the puzzling phrase—nowhere explicated in his writings—found in the preface to *The Sickness unto Death*, that "in this whole book, as the title indeed says, despair is conceived as the sickness, not as the cure. So dialectical is despair,"[54] reversing into a remedy for the spiritual body as soon as it breaks through the "continuity of sin,"[55] the continuity of the autonomous will. In objective despair, in the ontology of hell, Kierkegaard's philosophy renders the true image of man: shattered, separated, and condemned; no longer in the twilight of freedom and nature but explicitly in the name of judgment and grace. In the idea of judgment, not in that of the autonomy of human spirit, Kierkegaard's concept of the individual is rescued, who—unjudged—would fall to mythology: "What, a judgment! Why, we men have learned, indeed experience teaches, that when there is a mutiny aboard ship or in an army, the guilty are so numerous that the punishment cannot be applied; and when it is a question of the public, 'the highly respected cultured public,' the people, then not only is there no crime, but, according to the newspapers, upon which one can rely as upon the Gospel or divine revelation, this is the will of God. Why is this? The reason for it is that the concept of judgment corresponds to the individual, one does not pronounce a judgment *en masse*; one can put the people to death *en masse*, play the hose on them *en masse*, flatter them *en masse*, in brief can treat the people in many ways like beasts, but to hold judgment over the people as beasts one cannot do, for one cannot hold judgment over beasts; even though ever so many are judged, if there is to be any seriousness and truth in the judgment, it is each individual who is judged. Lo, for this reason God is 'the Judge' because before him there is no crowd but only individuals. . . . Yes, doubtless they are secured if it was only in eternity they became individuals. But they were and are before God constantly individuals."[56] Kierkegaard's "transparentness" would have its time and place in the light of the final judgment. Nature, which as existing, despairing nature perishes, would here, after damnation and reconciliation, become pellucid. In the world of experience, however, that is concrete onto which a trace of this light once falls. To describe the course of concretion through Kierkegaard's mythical-abstract realm amounts to the surveyal of the extensive organization of a system that is intertwined in itself intensively as existence.

Chapter 5
On the Logic of the Spheres

Existence and System

Kierkegaard's doctrine of existence could be called realism without reality. It contests the identity of thought and being, but without searching for being in any other realm than that of thought. Precisely here, however, being evades him: the being of the self is determined functionally, as a "relation," whose movements are to conjure an ontological "meaning," but not in such a fashion that existence itself would become comprehensible. Accordingly, along with ontological meaning and the substratum of the self, that which has been predicated by the self—the structure of the qualities of inwardness, i.e., their "reality"—becomes crucially antinomical. Kierkegaard's philosophy of existence is nothing other than the attempt to master or to justify—in thought—the antinomic of existence as truth content. And, indeed, it means to accomplish this systematically. True, Kierkegaard invariably presents Hegel's "system of existence" as detestable. But in that, for Kierkegaard, existence is drawn together in consciousness; in that the spontaneous act of freedom becomes the most inward determination of subjectivity; in that the image of the individual, as a "total" image, is subordinated to pure determinations of thought; he succumbs to the idealist compulsion for systematics. At the same time, however, he must attempt to express whatever in his plan opposes the system in the form of the system: being, in which thought is borne; ontological meaning that is not identical with thought; discontinuities that cannot be derived from a deductive context—all this, however, is embedded in precisely that spirituality that functions as a system-positing force. Kierkegaard elaborated the paradoxical system of existence in the theory of its "spheres." However carefully he avoided calling this theory a system, he himself disclosed its systematic character by the word "schema"; it is not accidental that the term is reminiscent of Kant: "According to this schema, one is able to orient oneself, and without getting upset if in an aesthetic lecture Christ's name and a whole Christian terminology is used; one needs only to refer to the categories."[1] This schema is laid out twice, the more completely in the *Stages on Life's Way*: "There are three spheres of existence: the aesthetic, the ethical, the religious. The metaphysical is abstraction: there is no man who lives metaphysically. The metaphysical, the ontological, *is* but nowhere in particular; for when it has a location it is in the aesthetic, in the ethical, in the religious, and when it *is* it is the abstraction of or the *prius* for the aesthetic, the ethical, the religious. The ethical sphere is only a transitional sphere, and hence its highest expression is a negative action, repentance. The aesthetic sphere is that of immediacy, the ethical is that of obligation (and this obligation is so infinite that it always outstrips the means of the individual), the religious sphere is that of fulfillment."[2] This is concisely recapitulated and supplemented in the second volume of *Concluding Unscientific Postscript*: "There are thus three spheres of existence: the aesthetic, the ethical, the religious. Two boundary zones correspond to these three: irony, constituting the boundary between the aesthetic and the ethical; humor, as the boundary that separates the ethical from the religious."[3] This schema of the spheres is not deduced; like Platonic ideas, they are axiomatically posited next to one another. The cognitive operation that defines them is that of distinction, the counterconcept to all dialectical "mediation," and is polemically formulated by Kierkegaard: "In our own age everything is mixed up together: the aesthetic is treated ethically, faith is dealt with intellectually, and so forth. Philosophy has answered every question; but no adequate consideration has been given the question concerning what sphere it is within which each question finds its answer. This creates a greater confusion in the world of the spirit than when in the civic life an ecclesiastical question, let us say, is handled by the bridge commission."[4] If the method therefore prohibits communication through "mediation," even the content of the spheres—subjectivity—is withdrawn precisely from that dialectic which, according to the doctrine of existence, specifically constitutes subjectivity as a self-relating relation: "If the individual is in himself undialectical and has his dialectic outside himself, then we have the aesthetic interpretation. If the individual is dialectical in himself inwardly in self-assertion, hence in such a way that the ultimate basis is not dialectic in itself, inasmuch as the self which is at the basis is used to overcome and assert itself, then we have the ethical interpretation."[5] Hence the self, so completely subjected to dialectic in the definitions of *The Sickness unto Death* that it finally succumbs to dissociation in the category of despair, is bluntly assigned an ontic substratum, an "ultimate basis that is not dialectical in itself." Even if the concept of existence was not yet so developed in the *Postscript* as it was later in *The Sickness unto Death*, the contradiction between the hierarchy of spheres and the doctrine of existence is not without objective significance. If in the existential point being and becoming flow undifferentiatedly into each other, still they must part in actual life. Therefore the spheres build a "system" from whose hypostatizations the pure actuality of the "relation" may strive to distance itself; but thus at the same time the spheres, of ontological status, set themselves in opposition to one another; spheres which the existential vortex has destroyed. Thus the doctrine of the spheres is both less and more than a material realization of the "project" of existence. It is less: because the doctrine does not maintain itself in pure actuality, but bears witness to the compulsion toward hypostatization precisely there where Kierkegaard supposes it has been excluded. It is more: because subjectivity, forced for once to interpret itself materially and not simply to sink into itself as into the productive unity, ends up making statements about the existent such as are never achieved by Kierkegaard's doctrine of existence even in the moments of its greatest concentration.

Origin of the Spheres

The systematic character of the hierarchy of the spheres is confirmed by its historical origin. As categories of individual existence, the concepts of the aesthetic, ethical, and religious articulate their development in time. Therefore they are sometimes called spheres, sometimes stages. The stages, dialectical levels of the process of existence, are, however, produced in the closest intimacy with Hegelian systematics. This is evident in the formulation of the concept of the stages in the first volume of *Either/Or* where the structure of the "immediate stages of the erotic" is Hegelian even in its language: "The contradiction in the first stage lay in the fact that desire could acquire no object, but that it, nevertheless, was in possession of its object without having desired it, and therefore could not reach the point of desiring. In the second stage, the object appears in its multifariousness; but in that desire seeks its object in this multifariousness, it still has, in a deeper sense, no object, it is not yet posited as desire. In Don Juan, in contrast [in the third stage] desire is absolutely determined as desire; it is, in an intensive and extensive sense, the immediate synthesis of the two preceding stages. The first stage desired the one ideally, the second stage desired the particular under the qualification of the multifarious; the third stage is a synthesis of these two."[6] The Hegelian rhythm requires that the next step be the transformation of quantity into quality: it is the step from the determinations of immediacy to those of reflection. The architectonic parallel is in fact followed out: the naive quality of erotic "reflection" is represented by the "Diary of the Seducer." If ethical "freedom," by way of reflection, finally confronts aesthetic "immediacy" as a new level of spirit, the presentation of this new level is reminiscent of Hegel to the point of literal reference; Hegelian "speculation" is to have been overcome through "decisiveness": "Marriage is freedom and necessity, but it is also more, for 'freedom' of first love is no more than the emotional freedom: the individual has not been pulled loose from the dregs of natural necessity to consciousness."[7] — The later Kierkegaard seems to have excluded such rudiments of Hegelian systematics through the abrupt reaction against the philosophy of identity. But along with the dialectical structure, Hegelian rhythmics are also maintained. The objections to Hegel do not concern the dynamic being of the "idea," but only its arena in mere existence, where for Kierkegaard the idea is transformed into semblance while transfigured existence solidifies into a thing. The motive of the distinction, which he contrasts to Hegel, does not impugn the Hegelian "idea"; it intends to save the idea itself from Hegel. And it means to do so with Hegel's own instruments. All of Kierkegaard's antisystematic "psychological" investigations, whose goal is the distinguishing of the spheres, operate according to the same form of contradiction that in Hegel brings the particular elements into relation with one another. Even where the ideas have been pulled free from the "process" and, arranged alongside one another, occupy the philosophical landscape, their apparent juxtaposition remains one of mutual contradiction. This is markedly so in *The Concept of Anxiety*: "*Unbelief-Superstition*: These correspond completely to each other: both lack inwardness, but unbelief is passive through an activity, and superstition is active through a passivity. . . . *Hypocrisy-Offense*: These correspond to each other. Hypocrisy begins through an activity, offense through a passivity. . . . *Pride-Cowardice*: Pride begins through an activity, cowardice through a passivity; in all other respects they are identical."[8] Just as these concepts constitute partial contradictions, the "spheres" define the range of intra-human activity through total contradiction. Differing from Hegel, however, contradiction is not sublated by the concept; rather, it remains as a sign of the brittleness of an existence from which ontological meaning is hidden. Total contradiction is called the "leap": "It is therefore a superstition when it is maintained in logic that through a continued quantification a new quality is brought forth. It is an unforgivable reticence when one makes no secret of the fact that things indeed do not happen quite that way in the world and yet conceals the consequence of this for the whole of logical immanence by permitting it to drift into logical movement as does Hegel. The new quality appears with the first, with the leap, with the suddenness of the enigmatic."[9] To the same degree as this is conceived polemically against Hegel and the "system," it remains dependent upon him. Kierkegaard did not exactly hide the origin of the terminology so much as obscure it through its aggressive employment. The terminology can be found explicitly in the *Phenomenology of the Spirit*: "But just as the first breath drawn by a child after its long, quiet nourishment breaks the gradualness of merely quantitative growth — there is a qualitative leap, and the child is born—so likewise the spirit in its formation matures slowly and quietly into its new shape, dissolving bit by bit the structure of its previous world, whose tottering state is only hinted at by isolated symptoms. The frivolity and boredom which unsettle the established order, the vague foreboding of something unknown, these are the heralds of approaching change. The gradual crumbling that left unaltered the face of the whole is cut short by a sunburst which, in one flash, illuminates the features of the new world."[10] Kierkegaard indeed admits: "Hegel made use of the leap, but in logic,"[11] yet he continues: "Hegel's misfortune is exactly that he wants to maintain the new quality and yet does not want to do it, since he wants to do it in logic, which, as soon as this is recognized, must acquire a different consciousness of itself and of its significance."[12] This insubstantial argument bears witness against itself. It gives no criterion for distinguishing the "leap" from the reversal of quantity into quality other than the difference of the (for Kierkegaard) speculative-contemplative "logical" sphere and that of the "ethical" sphere, which is precisely grounded in the act of the leap. The argument is therefore circular. But even as simple explication, this argument is not to be maintained. Whereas Kierkegaard earlier accused Hegel of maintaining that "in logic . . . through a continued quantification a new quality is brought forth," he now criticizes the introduction of a "leap" in a logic where he himself had required it as a corrective. His proposition that a "new quality appears with the first, with the leap," and his "secret of the first" are themselves logical determinations in the Hegelian sense. The real difference from Hegel is not so much the "leap" but that the "spheres" do not undergo synthesis. It remains to be decided whether Hegel's schema of logic, philosophy of nature, and philosophy of the spirit did not supply even here the model for Kierkegaard, since the "leap" in the introduction of the philosophy of nature did not go unnoticed in the Hegel scholarship of Kierkegaard's time. The idealist origin of the "spheres" is therefore beyond question. They are the antithetical elements of the dialectical process that the "self" inaugurates in the effort to autonomously reconstruct ontological meaning. As such elements, the spheres constitute "stages on life's way," reversing into one another. Since, however, "meaning" is not bestowed on the continuity of the process; since the self persists in circular repetition, opaque in the face of blocked truth and incapable of producing it out of itself; the totality of the spheres—even if systematically produced out of the unity of the self—does not consolidate itself into an integral, fully rounded system. It is rather a totality of ruins, and in the depth of the chasms between them a dialectic surges that does not flow uninterruptedly from one to the other. Torn apart by Kierkegaard's dialectic, as though by a natural force, the spheres that it had earlier created as stages become autonomous "ideas" and rule over the existence from which they originated as articulating elements of its unity.

"Constellation"

This rule is, however, mythical. In the distinguishing of the spheres, subjectivity exalts itself as its own judge; and the judgment of its finitude is as illusory as the infinite process is hopeless with which subjectivity qua "existence" undertook the appropriation of grace. If subjectivity has withdrawn into the bottomless and nameless darkness of its total immanence, so the fixed stars—a frozen and distant eternity that arises out of this abyss—glimmer ambiguously to it. The images of these stars are the spheres. Their nomenclature is astral. And just as the most concealed experiences of philosophy are continuously sedimented in its terminological figures, it is not by accident that the term "sphere" calls up the memory of mythical, Pythagorean harmony. The Kantian formula of the starry heaven above and the moral law within appears in Kierkegaard's "spheres" in Baroque abbreviation: the starry heavens have collapsed into the blind self, and the law of its freedom has been transformed into natural necessity. Moral life itself is organized according to natural categories, though not causal but astrological categories. They return incessantly. It is not simply that Kierkegaard is fond of "conjoining" concepts, rather than—like the idealists—deducing them from one another: "All deeper apprehension of existence consists in conjoining."[13] *The Sickness unto Death* is openly astrological: "Such an existence, as is to be seen from the conjunction and position of the categories, will be the most eminent poet-existence."[14] So too is the *Postscript*: "If ever the position of the stars in the firmament has signified something fearful, then the position of the categories in this situation signifies something other than laughter and jesting."[15] Every one of Kierkegaard's "spheres," however, expresses fright. It clings to the magnitude of its universal-conceptual scope. In its emptiness as in the minutest detail, in the blind this-there of existence, the essence of the mythical shows through. The constellations of the spheres are in every case conjuring signs, collectively allegorical. Hence the constant invocation "of" the aesthetic, ethical, and religious, whose objectified character never really corresponds to the demand of the "subjective thinker"; hence such absurd phraseology as: "To stick to my subject, the religious."[16] And hence, again, Kierkegaard's scurrilous methodological deliberations, as in the initial problem set out by *The Concept of Anxiety* (fully misunderstood by Schrempf[17]) of determining "the sense in which the object of the study is a task of psychological interest and the sense in which, after having been the task and interest of psychology, it points directly to dogmatics."[18] The most universal concepts, posited by consciousness to order its multifarious contents, appear to consciousness as alien, meaning conferring powers that define their own course. They direct the individual's fate the more completely the stranger they become to him; the more hidden their human origin; the more, that is, that abstraction progresses in them. Their disparate contours and stark boundaries—drawn by Kierkegaard's rational deductive method in opposition to its own claim—are transformed by the strength of their abstractness directly into distantly threatening mythological constellations. The fruit of his idealistic deductions is an archaic conceptual realism. Certainly this is not the only result. Even though the spheres may rule like demonic abstractions, the astrology that "conjoins them" bears witness to how far the "meaning" of the concrete lies from the merely universal concept to whose scope the object in question belongs. For this reason, astrology attempts to gain control of its object in another fashion. Individual existence is interpreted according to constellations in order to avoid definitions. What remains opaque to mere contemplation; what escapes from the transparent categorial form as content—this is what thought wants to read out of the figures inscribed in the object, in the context of related concepts. As their focal point, the object indeed dictates the law of the figure, but without ever coming to rest on any one of the curves. In contrast to mathematics, dialectics is unable to summarily formulate the laws of figure and focal point. Constellations and figures are its ciphers and its "meaning," immersed in history, and not arbitrarily calculable. As a doctrine of ciphers, Kierkegaard's method of constellation refers back to the manner in which ontology appears in his thought. The spheres, originating idealistically, mythical powers of fate, will not dispense with ontological importance.

Overlapping of Idealist and Ontological Elements

It was precisely insight into the inaccessibility of ontology that obliged Kierkegaard to differentiate the spheres. Since truth is blocked, the continuity of uninterrupted, unintermittent deductions from the "idea" becomes a fiction that shatters in the rifts between the spheres. The totality of the infinite is closed to contingent human consciousness; in the finite, however, distinctions must be made. This is the point of Kierkegaard's criticism of the Hegelian doctrine of positive infinity: "Positive people, or (to indicate by the definite article more definitely what I mean) the Positives, like the positive have a "positive" infinity. This is as it should be: a positive is finished, and when we hear that, we also are soon finished with it. Here we have result in superabundance, which is how it is with both the positive and the Positives. If one would seek enlightenment from Hegel the Master about what is to be understood by a positive infinity, one has a great deal to read, and a great effort to make; but one finally succeeds in understanding him. The one thing a laggard like myself perhaps does not understand is how a live man or a man in a living body becomes such a being that he can come to terms with this 'positive' infinity, which ordinarily is reserved for the Deity and eternity and the deceased. Consequently there is no other way I can understand the thing but by supposing that a result is missing which we, the negative ones who are not finished, might *en passant* look forward to eagerly, wondering if long after the System has been finished astronomy might discover on those distant stars higher beings who could make use of it. It must be left to the higher beings what they will make out of it, but for men it would be the part of prudence not to be too positive, for this really means to be made a jest of by existence. Existence is cunning and possesses many means of enchantment to catch rash adventurers, and he who is caught, yea, he who is caught, out of him is not made exactly what could be called a higher being."[19] Kierkegaard did not recognize how closely his doctrine of spheres borders on an "astrology" the expressions of which it employs; even the conception of a "cunning existence," which he opposes to Hegel, carries traces of mythical deception. Yet the boundaries of the spheres are more than merely the outlines of magical, hypostasized universal concepts. They mark out the distance of the creature from ontology. This is the true intention of Kierkegaard's polemic against Hegelian "mediation." The polemic is fruitless as an attempt to situate ontology beyond the subjective dynamic in the realm of ideas that rule existence as abstractions—whether indifferently or threateningly. The polemic, however, legitimately challenges subjectivity's claim to posit ontology out of itself by the strength of the principle of identity. For this reason, the debate between Hegel and Kierkegkaard cannot be concluded on idealistic terrain. Kierkegaard, in contrast to Hegel, failed to achieve historical concretion—the only authentic concretion; he absorbed it into the blind self, volatilized it in the empty spheres: he thereby surrendered philosophy's central claim to truth—the interpretation of reality—while calling on a theology from which his own philosophy extracted the pith. More emphatically than all previous philosophers, Hegel posited the question of concretion, but succumbed helplessly to it by believing that he had produced it; succumbed to a reality that is not rational vis-à-vis a "meaning" that escaped from it. Both philosophers remain idealists: Hegel by the conceptual definition of life as meaningful, "rational"; Kierkegaard by negating Hegel's claim and tearing "meaning" away from existence with the same insistence that Hegel forces them together. Ontological and idealist elements overlap in Kierkegaard, and it is their interwovenness that makes his philosophy so impenetrable.

Humor, Accident, and "Motivation"

The claim of "absolute" spirit presides both over the surrender of the world as perfectly meaningless and over its glorification by the system of reason. Whether subjectivity allots or denies "meaning" to reality, in both cases it appears as the court charged with making this determination because it is in subjectivity itself that "meaning" inheres. The conceptual realism of the spheres therefore no more reaches the reality of things than does existential withdrawnness. This can be demonstrated unequivocally in Kierkegaard's analysis of humor. For his analysis is founded on the assertion of the radical contingency of the external world, and humor is precisely not adequately defined on this basis: "When a humorist says, for example: 'If only I might live to see the day when my landlord installs a new bell-pull in the house where I live, so that it might be quickly and definitely decided for whom the bell is rung in the evening, then I would count myself the happiest of men.' Everyone who understands repartee understands at once when he hears such a speech, that the speaker has annulled the distinction between fortune and misfortune in a higher madness — because all are sufferers. The humorist comprehends the profundity of the situation, but at the same moment it occurs to him that it is doubtless not worthwhile to attempt an explanation."[20] As plausible as Kierkegaard's explanation of the phenomena seems to be, just so little does his commentary reach the source of light to which the phenomena owes its dull yet inextinguishable glimmer of humor. The simple negation: "in a higher madness," as the contingency of external existence, is not this source of light; neither is the transcendence of the concrete distinction between happiness and unhappiness by a more abstract, universal suffering under a contingent reality. Rather, suffering presents itself on such contingent occasions with the absurd promise of happiness. If a new doorbell is indeed all that is needed, but is never installed, this and not the murky indifference of something "external" is the humor of the passage; it is hope in nonsense, just as in the Oriental fairy tale Nas'r-ed-din lied to the townspeople that a monstrous whale had swum up on the shore; and after they had all hurried there and were already angrily on their way home, he came running to meet them to see if a whale really was not there. What escapes Kierkegaard in the reply of the "humorist" at least touches his aesthetic definition of the "occasion" as the single point of communication between objectless inwardness and the contingent world of things: "The occasion is at one and the same time the most significant and the most insignificant, the most exalted and the most humble, the most important and the most unimportant. Without the occasion, precisely nothing at all happens, and yet the occasion has no part at all in what does happen. The occasion is the last category, the essential transitional category between the sphere of the idea and actuality. Logic should consider this. It can be absorbed as much as it wishes in immanent thinking, it can rush down from nothing into the most concrete form; the occasion it never reaches, and, therefore, never reality. The whole of reality can be ready in the idea, but without the occasion, it never becomes real. The occasion is a category of the finite, and it is impossible for immanent thinking to lay hold of it; for that it is too paradoxical."[21] The irony of the passage, which was perhaps planned by Kierkegaard as a poor aesthetic distortion of the theological paradox, cannot be ignored. It contains not only his fundamental objection to Hegel, but equally a correction of his own doctrine. Even if he took the occasion as the source of the mere subject alien contingency of complete nonsense, still the supposedly immanent ontological "meaning" of the dialectic becomes dependent on the occasion in that an occasion is required to release the dialectic of inwardness, and meaning is therefore lodged beyond subjectivity in the nonsense of the occasion. "You transform something accidental into the absolute, and, as such, into the object of your admiration. This has an excellent effect, especially on excitable souls":[22] the sentence from "The Rotation Method" remains ironic as long as the severed external world remains dark and deprived of any truth. But the flash of light that is reflected back on the world, as soon as the dialectic is referred to truth by way of the "occasion," suffices to reestablish to a certain degree the legitimacy of the collapsed external world. Thus the abstract distinctions between the spheres are ambivalent: they are at the same time determinations of that realism from which Kierkegaard cannot withhold all content by means of mere inwardness. For the "occasion" itself is a category of the logic of the spheres; it is the boundary of the structure of the spheres with the external world.

Confinien and "Leap"

Such boundary demarcations, and their ambivalent function, are also aspects of the internal structure of the spheres. They are explicitly touched upon in the doctrine of the *confinien* (boundaries). This doctrine is developed as a system of allegorical metaphors. The system of the spheres is marked off in opposition to an unreachable objectivity: horizontally it is limited by the contingent world of things, vertically by the opposites of eternity and damnation. Layered between them is subjective life. Its slowest sphere, the "aesthetic," reverses from definitive despair into the condition of objective damnation; its highest *confinium* is "irony." The middle region, the "ethical," is delimited by "humor" from the higher "religious" sphere. The religious sphere itself would be defined by the idea of the holy, apostolic life, which Kierkegaard attempted to sketch, polemically in the "Two Minor Ethico-Religious Treatises," his book against Adler.— Kierkegaard's model of the spheres, however, is in no way limited to a bare, static-undialectical diagram. Occasionally, in the midst of literary criticism, there is discussion of a *confinium* between the aesthetic and the religious. In *The Point of View*, Kierkegaard claims this *confinium* as his own even if it is not inscribed in the topography of the spheres. The ethical itself sometimes appears as a "transitional stage" under the category of the *confinium*. Moreover, the content of the *confinien* varies. Not only irony, but even the "interesting," is defined as a *confinium* between the aesthetic and the ethical spheres, without their relation to irony ever being explicated: "The interesting is a *confinium* between aesthetics and ethics. Accordingly, this examination must constantly wander into the territory of ethics, while in order to be of consequence it must seize the problem with aesthetic fervor and concupiscence."[23] Such variations make it probable that the *confinien* are not so much established on the basis of the interpretation of the phenomena in question as they are derived from the schema of the spheres itself without any regard for their respective contents. This is confirmed by the definitions of the particular *confinien*. Irony and humor are indeed difficult to distinguish: "Irony is a synthesis of ethical passion—which infinitely accentuates inwardly the person of the individual in relation to the ethical requirement—and of culture, which infinitely abstracts externally from the personal ego, as one finitude among all the other finitudes and particularities. . . . Irony is a specific culture of the spirit, and therefore follows next after immediacy; then comes the moralist, then the humorist, and finally the religious individual."[24] The corresponding definition of humor, however, reads: "So again in the case of the humorist and the religious individual, since . . . the dialectic of the religious sphere itself forbids the direct expression, forbids the outward difference. . . . The humorist constantly . . . sets the God-idea into conjunction with other things and evokes the contradiction—but he does not maintain a relationship to God in terms of religious passion *stricte sic dictus*. . . . Religiosity with humor as its incognito is . . . a synthesis of absolute religious passion (the inwardness being dialectically produced) with a maturity of spirit, which withdraws the religiosity away from all externality back into inwardness, where again it is absolute religious passion."[25] Irony and humor are defined as *confinien* by nothing else than the spheres whose *confinien* they are to constitute and by the form of contradiction according to which they respectively unify in themselves the determinations of two spheres. These determinations are explicitly taken up in the definition of humor: "Contrast produces a comic effect by means of the contradiction, whether the relation is that the in and for itself not-ridiculous is used to make ridiculous the riduculous or the ridiculous makes that ridiculous which is in itself not-ridiculous, or the ridiculous and the ridiculous make each other mutually ridiculous, or the in and for itself not-ridiculous and the in and for itself not-ridiculous become ridiculous through the relationship."[26] This contrast, however, pertains as much to humor as to irony in that it distinguishes the affirmation in the form of the communication from its negation through the content of the communication. Thus the *confinien* remain—in spite of their incommensurability with one another—purely deduced forms of mediations, whose task can be fulfilled through interchangeable phenomena. This task is the distinguishing of the spheres. They collide with one another in the contradiction of the *confinien*; the abyss between them, however, and the movement over it is the "qualitative leap." The equivocation—"leap"—is not a mere figure of speech. It is founded objectively in the ambiguity of the plan of the logic of the spheres and of a philosophy whose totality is equally posited and fragmented by total contradiction. This fragmentation is the result of distinction: Kierkegaard abstracts the "spheres" from the phenomena and from one another in order to hypostatize them as ideas. The "leap" yawns between them as an "abyss of meaning" no less than between the "I" and the contingent external world. According to the topological diagram of the spheres, the leaps are the voids which no "mediation" can patch. Yet this topology is not the last word: the plan of the spheres is dynamic. As far as its dynamics are concerned, however, the "leap" is the highest measure of dialectical movement. If Kierkegaard seeks ontology exclusively in the dialectic of subjectivity, this ontology cannot be completely portrayed in the friable stasis of the hierarchy of spheres. Its fissures, then, are only the residual marks of a movement that the hierarchy itself completes. The self-motivated totality of the spheres changes one sphere into another. It is not the subject and its concrete particular life that mediate between them; the subject is, rather, the stage on which spheres disappear and others are revealed. Thus in its origin, as in its fully developed form, Kierkegaard's dialectic transcends the person for whom it was planned, while in the objectivity of the mythical, ambiguous spheres, the autonomous self's claim to dominion disavows itself. Insofar as in the "leap" the spheres can be thought of as dynamic, this is not a movement of phenomena immanent to the spheres that, as "irony," or "humor," transform their concrete figure. Rather, the sphere is transformed altogether: the leap means the reversal of the aesthetic into the ethical, and of the ethical into the religious. It does not, however, mean a translation of the individual content of the spheres, i.e., of the character. This is most evident in a work that is apparently as little concerned with totality and systematic construction as *Fear and Trembling*. Abraham, as the subject of a "dialectical lyric," is an allegorical name for the objective (one could almost say physical) dynamic of the spheres. Formulaically defined, the spheres oppose, attract, and repel one another: on one hand, the sphere of the "universal," of human life and ethics; on the other, the sphere of the "exception," of the transcendent commandment and faith. They do indeed come into contact through the "leap." Yet the one takes the place of the other regardless of the specific content of the individual's experience of faith in which the mythical sacrifice and its reconciling redemption are intertwined. It goes no farther than the name, the "teleological suspension of the ethical," which is illustrated by Abraham rather than becoming evident through its real completion, and the spheres collide without revealing the Word to man, whom the spheres have chosen as their arena. This is in accord with Kierkegaard's postulate: "Only passion against passion provides a poetic collision, not this hurly-burly of minutiae within the same passion."[27]

Dialectic of the Spheres

The nexus of the "collisions" of the spheres as a group constitutes the schema of the dialectic of the spheres. This dialectic rules the hierarchical organization of the spheres altogether, and its model is the doctrine of "aesthetic seriousness" as that of a dialectical cure: "Even aesthetic seriousness, like seriousness of every sort, is profitable to a man, but it can never save him completely. To a certain extent this is true in your case, I believe. Your aesthetic idealism has undoubtedly done you harm, but it has also been profitable for you: you have stared yourself blind gazing at the ideal of the good, so that you must also develop an ideal of the bad; this has protected you from the merely common. Of course your aesthetic seriousness cannot cure you, for you never get further than letting the bad alone for the reason that it cannot be ideally carried out."[28] "Aesthetic seriousness" is dialectical in itself in that it both "harms . . . [and is] . . . profitable"; by the strength of the "ideal,"it is unified as a totality, and in the "leap" of resolution this totality inaugurates a new sphere. This clearly implies a dual model of the dialectic: for Kierkegaard, there is a dialectic immanent to the spheres and one between the spheres. Thus Kierkegaard is not only distinguished in a formal fashion from Hegel, to whose schema the "immanent" dialectic of the spheres would correspond, whereas the dialectic of the "leap" between the spheres would contradict it. This dual model expresses the very aporia of the dialectic of the spheres. This aporia can be grasped in the doctrine of the wonder—the "miracle"—which Kierekgaard presented in the *Training*.[29] According to the concepts of the logic of the spheres, which are not expressly developed here, the miracle would be the *confinien* of Socratic, negative "religiosity A" and of paradoxical "religiosity B"; yet as *confinien*, they would still be situated in the area of "religiosity A." For miracles are not for him "proof" of faith, which according to his thesis is precisely unprovable and only attainable through the "leap." Rather, miracles serve the leap: "A miracle can make one attentive."[30] To this extent the miracles are located externally to faith and are subject to the criticism of the *ratio*. As an article of faith, miracles are for Kierkegaard the absolutization of historical facts, which according to the *Philosophical Fragments* would not be admissible; time itself appears in Kierkegaard's paradox as merely abstract.[31] Hence faith and miracle may be related in two possible ways. (1) The miracle wants to make the nonbelieving "disciple" "attentive." Then he has the right to inquire. If he, for example, compares the Christian miracle stories with their equivalent in other faiths and concludes from the comparison the uncertainty, which now properly makes him "attentive," then he may legitimately reject the faith toward which the miracle should have directed him. (2) The miracle is only for the faithful. Then Christianity quits the "point," the faith in the paradox as well as the subjective dialectic: it is hypostatized. At the same time, the simple question intrudes: how should "nonbelievers"—whom the miracle should make "attentive"—become believers if the miracle is only intended for the "believers"? The dialectical question of "mediation" (*Vermittlung*), specifically that of religiosity A and B, stands behind the theological subtleties. Kierkegaard defamed Hegelian mediation as mere "interposition" (*Mediation*) and wanted to exclude it from the spheres in favor of a "qualitative dialectic": "It is necessary always to hold the different spheres apart by the use of the qualitative dialectic, sharply distinguishing them lest everything come to be all of a piece, the poet becoming a bungler when he wants to take a little of the religious with him, and the religious speaker becoming a deceiver who delays and obstructs his listener by wishing to dabble a little in the aesthetic."[32] It is evident, however, that if "mediation" is excluded from Kierkegaard's dialectic presuppositions and requirements remain at a variance, either the paradox—as a result of the exclusion of every "reference"—becomes in fact something "absolutely different"; that is, it is set up as the pure negation of the totality of the spheres, which the dialectical movement completes while its content in no way becomes graspable by the "faithful." In this case the paradox is a simple limiting condition, and the possibility of positive religion, which Kierkegaard indeed wanted to rescue precisely in the radical distinguishing of the spheres, is lost; the entire "holy history," whose concept he as a Christian maintained, remains a mere "reference" to the paradox, subsidiary to an argument from which Kierkegaard wanted to defend it—as inspired—in the first part of the *Unscientific Postscript.*"[33] The possibility of positive religion withers away; all that is left is the idea of a nameless paradoxy: "So let us call this unknown something: *the God.* It is nothing more than a name we assign to it";[34] even the name of Christ must founder in an earnestly "dialectical" theology. —Or: the paradox is nevertheless "mediated" (*mediert*). Then miracles are mediations and as such ambivalent: for the believer, they illuminate the landscape of faith; for the nonbeliever, they illuminate the way to this landscape. In this ambivalence, however, they are symbols of the "metaphysic" disdained by Kierkegaard, and he finds himself in the place of those he mocks: "standing in front of a Christmas tree."[35] The dialectic of the spheres can be judged accordingly. Where the conception of this dialectic is defined by the categories of the leap, the absolutely different and the paradox, there can be no room for the authentic dialectic. As a movement, the "leap" is not commensurable with any dialectical movement immanent to the sphere; it is not demonstrable in any act of consciousness. Paradoxical in itself and otherworldly, the leap reveals itself to be an act of election: the consummation of an irrational doctrine of predestination that is perhaps the foundation of Kierkegaard's "Baroque." In the face of such severity, the image of a "free," dialectically self-determining subjectivity—a subjectivity which, as the bearer of Kierkegaard's idealism, first makes possible the constitution and counterplay of the spheres—must perish. Inconsistency is therefore inscribed in his dialectic of spheres by the law of its own origin. "Qualitative dialectic"—this is not simply a dialectic between spheres that transform themselves, reversing into one another. It is also a dialectic in which the quality of the self-reversing phenomenon is itself effective and is rescued from the abyss of theological irrationality. Thus it is precisely Hegelian interposition (*Mediation*) that comes to the aid of Kierkegaard's concern for the concrete. This form of the dialectic is not adequately defined by the logical form of contradiction, by logical reversal. It does not merely involve parts of descriptions of melancholy, passion, repentance, and finally despair. It is postulated generally: "It is, by the way, certainly very much to be desired that a sober thinker would for once explain how far this purely logical process, which recalls the grammatical rule that two negatives make an affirmative, and the mathematical rule that two minuses are a plus—how far, I say, this logical process is valid in the world of reality, in the world of qualities; whether after all the qualities are not subject to a different dialectic; whether in this case 'transition' does not play a different role."[36]

Intermittence

Nothing distinguishes this dialectic better from the total dialectic between the spheres than the statement that it is a movement in place. The entire "passion narrative" is its allegory. Precisely here the dialectic is anecdotally elucidated: "In old times the army employed a very cruel punishment, that of riding a wooden horse. The unfortunate man was held down by weights on a wooden horse whose back was razor sharp. One time when this punishment was put in execution and the culprit was groaning in pain, up came a peasant who walked on the rampart and stooped to look at the drill ground where the culprit was undergoing his punishment. Desperate with pain and now further irritated by the sight of this idle gaper, the unfortunate man shouted at him: 'What are you staring at?' But the peasant replied, 'If you can't bear to have anybody look at you, then you can ride around by another street'."[37] This becomes, in theoretical form, the thesis of *The Sickness unto Death*: "To become is a movement from the spot, but to become oneself is a movement in place."[38] This at first seems to indicate the condition of objective inwardness, the atemporal, dimensionless figure of Kierkegaard's philosophy. At the same time this movement in place refers to a remaining within the sphere of dialectically motivated thought, which progresses only by the movement of the total sphere altogether, that is, by the "leap." But this is not all there is to it. The dialectic begins anew in each sphere; its continuity is fractured. The discontinuity of the large movement is confirmed by the movement in place of the psychological and individual movement, and by the model of an "intermittent" dialectic. The latter's true instant is not a going farther but a hesitation, not a process but a caesura; and it is posited at the center of Kierkegaard's existential philosophy as the protest of transsubjective truth against the mythical universal domination of the spontaneous subject. The antinomy between the "differentiation" of ideas and the "process" of subjectivity seeks its most characteristic expression in a dialectical vacuum in which what becomes presents itself eternally and eternity presents itself in motion. Thus the model of the dialectic of a movement in place corresponds precisely to the image of the *intérieur* in which dialectic itself hesitates. This dialectic is expressly formulated as a critique of idealistic continuity: "When it is impossible to think existence and the existing individual nevertheless thinks, what does this signify? It signifies that he thinks intermittently, that he thinks before and after. His thought cannot attain to absolute continuity. It is only in a fantastic sense that an existing individual can be constantly *sub specie aeterni.*"[39] The positive content of the intermittent dialectic is the goal of an organic and often repeated metaphor, that of respiration. "Personality is a synthesis of possibility and necessity. The condition of its survival is therefore analogous to respiration, which is an in- and an a-spiration. The self of the determinist cannot breathe, for it is impossible to breathe necessity alone, which taken pure and simple suffocates the human self. . . . So to pray is to breathe, and possibility is for the self what oxygen is for breathing."[40] The metaphor appears in theological form in the discourse "Christ Is the Way" from *Self-Examination*: " 'O faithless and perverse generation! how long shall I be with you? how long shall I suffer you?' This is a sigh. It is as when a sick man—not on a sick-bed, but on a death-bed, for this is no light sickness, his life is despaired of—raises his head from the pillow and says, 'What time is it?' . . . Only quickly! Even the most frightful thing is less frightful than this— only quickly! A sigh which draws breath deeply and slowly."[41] What is said here of Christ's suffering refers by way of the "follower" equally to the individual and thereby to the intrahuman dialectic. In the place of Hegelian "mediation" between freedom and necessity, intermittence enters as a breath that pauses, concentrates, and begins anew; it is a movement in place, not one of progress and continuity. The metaphor of respiration is to be taken literally: it is the reestablishment of the body in the rhythm of absolute spirituality. The reversal of spiritualism into an organology has found its place here in the schema of the dialectical movement itself. For the instant of the pause, where dialectic comes to a stop, is the same instant when nature, its mythical basis, reverberates in the depth of the sounding of the hour. Humanity is assured of its transience by this instant, just as are the deathly ill by the caesuras marked on the hour. Yet its empty figure, the rhythm of mere time, without any other expression than that of itself, is the voiceless intervention of reconciliation. The endlessly repeated soundings of the hour paradoxically contain the uncertain certainty of the end. Nature, temporal nature dialectically self-contained, is not lost: "Here it is evident that I do not"—in contrast to *The Sickness unto Death*—"assume a radical evil, since I posit the validity of repentance. Repentance, it is true, is an expression for reconciliation, but it is also an absolutely irreconcilable expression."[42] This demonstrates the profound double sense of Kierkegaard's doctrine of emotion. Subjectivity moves dialectically in its affects; in them, however, blocked truth, itself enciphered, also makes itself known. Clearly, this does not occur in the progress of the dialectic, but where the dialectic stops. Subjectivity disappears, admitting transience as its essence. Therefore repentance is more than a merely preparatory dialectical category leading to the "leap"; and it is with good reason that Kierkegaard's opposition to the Fichtean system begins precisely with repentance, which appears as discontinuity. The intervention of divine power in the immanent movement is characterized in Kierkegaard's philosophy by intermittence; only by penetrating the illusion of isolated inwardness is consciousness able "to draw a breath."

Projection

Intermittence inserts lacunas in the continuity of the dialectic of the spheres. Although it is constituted systematically, this dialectic does not form a unity. It does not unequivocally determine the position of the phenomena subsumed by it, which are, on the one hand, torn apart in the "leap" and, on the other, susceptible of repetition. Kierkegaard tried to justify this in his plan of the logic of the spheres by developing a technique that bound the repetition of the refractory phenomena with the schema of the spheres. The spheres, as a system, as to depict— through "projection"—what, as reality, escapes the coercion of the system. Phenomena, with positions in a sphere defined by the system, are perspectively presented in another sphere. In the "aesthetic" sphere, for example, all dialectics, including the "religious," appears as spuriously infinite; the "end" of dialectics in the aesthetic sphere through "decisiveness" becomes comical: "When she [Marie Beaumarchais] tries at times to tear herself free, it comes to nothing, so this is again only a mood, a momentary passion, and reflection constantly remains victorious. 'Interposition' (*Mediation*) is impossible. If she tries to make a new beginning, but so that this beginning is in one way or another the result of her previous reflection, she is at once carried away. The will must be wholly indifferent; it must begin in the strength of its own willing before there can be any talk of a beginning. If this happens, she may indeed find a beginning, but she removes herself from the field of our interest, since we turn her over willingly to the moralists, or whoever cares to attend her. We wish her a respectable marriage, and pledge ourselves to dance on her wedding-day, when fortunately the altered name will help us forget that it was the Marie Beaumarchais of whom we have spoken."[43] Or, similarly, the "universality" of the "ethical" sphere is no more than parodied by the aesthetic sphere; seen from the perspective of immediacy, universality appears as the destruction of individual life, as the transcendence of immediacy: "Death is the common lot of all men, and in so far as the unhappiest man is not yet found, he will have to be sought amongst the mortal."[44] While this is deduced directly from the schema, the projections of the theological theses into the aesthetic sphere are more than mere means for the presentation of the plan of the logic of the spheres. Here the contents express themselves in their historically secularized configuration. The erotic image of the instant is astonishing: "The instant is everything, and in the instant, woman is everything; the consequences I do not understand. Among these consequences is the begetting of children. Now I fancy that I am a fairly consistent thinker, but if I were to think until I became crazy, I am not a man who could think this consequence; I simply do not understand it. Only a husband could make sense of it.''[45] The "instant" appears "aesthetically" as strictly timeless and hence lacks the character of becoming, the "consequence." Hence the paradoxical instant is distorted, reduced to an empirical-univocal determination, whereas in Kierkegaard's theology it forces together becoming and incommensurable being as the point where time and eternity touch. Here it is precisely the "consequence"— for Kierkegaard: the disciple of Christ in the passion—that is to determine the authenticity of the "instant." Even the famous passage on the unintelligibility of religious writings for heretics is not sufficiently comprehensible on the basis of the need for disguise, but only as part of the projective depiction of the spheres, which converges with the former: "Of course, this deplorable state has its effect on an author who, in my opinion, very properly joins Clement of Alexandria in writing in such a way that the heretics are unable to understand it.''[46] Intrigue is the projective depiction of a dialectical movement between the spheres within one particular sphere. Clearly a more determinate content is implicit in the thesis of "unintelligibility." In Kierkegaard "higher" spheres may not be arbitrarily depicted in "lower" spheres; the "leap" precludes adequate projection, and in the necessity of dissimulations the system of the spheres shows itself as a totality in fragments. The projection of the phenomena of a higher sphere onto a lower means falsification and, therefore, every statement of the "religious" sphere remains incomprehensible for the aesthetic sphere because it is already falsified by mere depiction.

Transcendences

Thus the phenomena are no longer directly deducible from the formal unity of the system. Rather they are subordinate to its highest material "meaning," the theological truth contents that Kierkegaard collects in the "religious" sphere. The relations between the spheres cannot be calculated as images derived from their predetermined definitions; rather, they can be realized only as "transcendences" in which the truth contents are revealed. This means, however, that the phenomena neither mediate as *confinien*, nor provide distorted images of phenomena from other "spheres"; rather, without any mediation, the same phenomenon belongs to disparate spheres, specifically to those of the "exception": the "religious" and the "aesthetic." Corresponding to this is the material plan of these spheres. Both spheres are set apart from intrahuman autonomy: the "aesthetic" sphere is situated prior to "decisiveness"; the "religious" sphere is set apart because its autonomy is wiped out by the "leap" into absolute difference.

Through the transcendence of both extremes, the ontological question is posed in the hierarchy of the spheres—a question only apparently answered by the "distinctions" of the spheres and cut off by the system. That definition is ontological that grants authenticity only to the aesthetic and religious spheres; while making the ethical sphere a "transitional stage" and relativizing it as the sphere of intrahuman autonomy. Theological truth crashes down to human level as aesthetic truth and reveals itself to man as a sign of hope. For this reason the aesthetic figure of the "poet" is a *"terminus a quo* for Christian religious existence":[47] "So if a religious author wishes to deal with this mirage"—"that religion and Christianity are something one first has recourse to when one grows older"[48]— "he must be at the same time an aesthetic and a religious author. But one thing above all he must not forget, the intention of the whole undertaking, that what must come decisively to the fore is the religious. The aesthetic works thus become a means of communication"[49]—through transcendence. He in whom such communication is consummated is the "exception." In the "exception," the "aesthetic" transcends to the "religious." The "exception," however, is nothing else but the incarnation of objectless inwardness itself; and it is of key importance not only in psychological terms, but for the logic of the system itself. Kierkegaard's historical model, the bearer of ontological fulfillment, is the "exception" that devalues the ethical in the hierarchy of the spheres. Guardini has correctly recognized that the "attempt to grasp marriage as a moral totality in which the individual evolves" fails because "the consequence is asserted":[50] the consequence of a state of consciousness for which the objectless individual and the enciphered "meaning" are bound for better or for worse. It could almost be said that in Kierkegaard the image of man is identical with that of the "exception"; for Kierkegaard, man exists humanly only by becoming an exception—insofar as he emancipates himself from contingency, anonymity, and reified universality. Both the "genial" aesthetic and the "religious" existence are for him "exceptions." He ultimately included the ethical universality of marriage in reification, expounded Christianity as strictly opposed to marriage, and fiercely ridiculed the style of life praised by William in one of the novellas of *The Instant*. Most commentators have explained this as part of Kierkegaard's personal fate. This takes the sting out of his polemic: its disdain for stable, middle-class life. It is, rather, to be asked if—in the name of a misanthropic transcendence of the extreme spheres—the ethical altogether, and even the bourgeois private sphere represented by his "ethical" writings, do not stand under the verdict and irony of the "exception." The doctrine of the late writings that the "meaning" of existence is suffering and that only in the negativity of suffering can positive meaning be represented is the theological designation of a category psychologically termed "exception." If suffering is the sign of subjugation to nature, natural life transcends itself in profoundest contradiction to the stated intention of Kierkegaard's spiritualism. At one point Kierkegaard admits this possibility: "Woman because of her immediacy is essentially aesthetic, but just because she is essentially this, the transition to the religious is also direct. Feminine romanticism is in the very next instant the religious."[51] Only by transcending are the phenomena pulled free from the significations that the logic of the spheres, as a schema of autonomous movement, bestowed upon them; they become incommensurable and concrete. To block these phenomena from such concretion is, however, the greatest concern of the "ethic" of the universal as of the logic of system of the spheres: "I sit and clip myself, take away everything that is incommensurable in order to become commensurable."[52] Thus the system of the spheres finally collapses over the question of concretion, which originally distinguished it from Hegelian systematic universality. Labyrinthically intertwined, the dialectic of the spheres permits space for the entrance of the concrete in its intermittent caesuras, in the light shafts of concrete illumination. The figure, however, that this dialectic finally constitutes is a cipher of the ultimate contradiction: its own demise. For Kierkegaard, autonomous spirit, infinitely dynamic and trapped in itself, may only be truly rescued in death. If, in contradistinction to the system, the relations between its spheres are paradoxical, the totality of the system is entirely paradoxical: it is directed toward the transcendence of the system. Therefore the traditional, theological interpretation of Kierkegaard is more correct than the psychologically informed interpretation when it poses paradoxy as the highest theme and not the immanence of a "spiritual life" whose systematic unity omits — along with the ultimate paradoxy — the cells of concretion. Yet the theological interpretation remains obediently dependent on Kierkegaard to the extent that it unquestioningly concedes paradoxy as the theological answer. The task is rather: to reveal the structure of the paradoxy itself as dialectical and systematic and at the same time to construct its proper content. This content becomes evident not so much in the theological concept of the symbol as in mythical sacrifice as it is represented in the reversal and ruin of Kierkegaard's idealism.

Chapter 6
Reason and Sacrifice

Self-Destruction of Idealism

Of those modern philosophies in which the self-imprisoned consciousness of idealism is aware of its own imprisonment and attempts to escape from its immanence, each develops an exclusive category, an undeviating intention, a distinguishing trait that, under the rule of the idea of totality acknowledged by all these philosophies, is intended to mollify the rigidity of this imprisonment. Ultimately, however, this category dissolves the idealist construction itself, which then disintegrates into its antinomies. Thus Hegel, the most extreme exponent of the idea of totality and to all appearances anything but a critic of idealism, developed a dialectical process that employed the claim to totality so dynamically that particular phenomena never result from the systematic subordinating concept; instead the system—from which reality truly results—is to be synonymous with the quintessence of fulfilled actuality. Kierkegaard tirelessly ridiculed Hegel for deferring every statement that would be binding for real existence until some imaginary completion of the system. But precisely in this regard Kierkegaard is more similar to Hegel than he would have cared to recognize. For through such deferment of the whole, the particular present—and even more the past—gains a concrete fullness that Kierkegaard's repetitions seek in vain to procure.—Similarly, Feuerbach moved his enlightenment concept of humanity, as a corrective, to the center of his philosophy; a concept that can no longer be contained by autonomous spirit. Similarly, again, Marx ultimately subordinated all his thought to the category of exchange-value, of the commodity. Indeed even this category, as the quintessence of the phenomena of capitalist society, maintains allegiance to the concept of totality. However, it shifts the emphasis of explanation from the side of consciousness to that of the "material" in such a fashion that the unity of the "idea" of capitalist society is destroyed by contents that do not arise continuously from any idea because they place the reality of the idea itself in question. Although all these categories originate in the self-enclosing infinity of the system, they draw the systematic structures into themselves like whirlpools in which they disappear. Kierkegaard's case is no different. He becomes a critic of the system because consciousness, as consciousness of an existence that is not deducible from itself, establishes itself as the ultimate contradiction of his idealism. From the totality of consciousness, which is extensive yet produced in a single point, his thought returns to this one point in order to gain the single category that will break the power of the system and restore ontology. The point that he seizes, his own fulcrum, is the archimedean point of systematic idealism itself: the prerogative of thought, as its own law, to found reality. The category that dialectically unfolds here, however, is that of paradoxical sacrifice. Nowhere is the prerogative of consciousness pushed further, nowhere more completely denied, than in the sacrifice of consciousness as in the fulfillment of ontological reconciliation. With a truly Pascalian expanse, Kierkegaard's dialectic swings between the negation of consciousness and its unchallenged authority. His spiritualism, the historical figure of objectless inwardness, is to be understood according to the immanent logic of the crisis of idealism. For Kierkegaard, consciousness must have pulled itself free from all external being by a movement of "infinite resignation"; through choice and decisiveness, it must have freely posited every content in order finally, in the face of the semblance of its own omnipotence, to surrender its omnipotence and, foundering, to purify itself of the guilt it acquired in having supposed itself autonomous. The sacrifice of consciousness, however, is the innermost model of every sacrifice that occurs in his philosophy. It constitutes the nexus of the mythical and the intrahistorical in his categorical structure. For sacrifice indeed wants to absolve nature, and nature has its determining power at Kierkegaard's historical moment and even for his knowledge in the spirit of the isolated individual. Just as, for Kierkegaard, the spirit of the individual stands as the archetype not only of all spirit, but of nature itself, which does not appear except as "spirit," so sacrifice, the final category of nature to which he raises himself and at the same time the final category of the destruction of the natural, is in his terms a sacrifice of spirit. With the greatest tension of which system-building idealism was still capable, he carried out this sacrifice both for the system as a whole and in all phenomena that fall within the system. The category of sacrifice, by means of which the system transcends itself, at the same time and fully contrary to expectation, holds Kierkegaard's philosophy systematically together as its encompassing unity through the sacrificial abstraction of all encountered phenomena. In intellectual sacrifice the mythical origin of sacrifice appears most unalloyed; its historical function appears most spontaneously. The two meet on the stage of spirit and carry out the dialogue of idealism as mythical thought's own play of lamentation. Idealism, however, is ultimately revealed as mythical in that although it indeed transcends itself, it is unable to immanently fulfill the claim to reconciliation that it announces. Nature, withdrawn into human spirit, hardens itself in idealism and usurps the power of creation. While the ruin that idealism brings upon itself is therefore able to free it from the semblance of autonomy, reconciliation as catharsis cannot be vouchsafed for a fully collapsing idealism.

Mythical Sacrifice

Of the many commentators, only Monrad gives any insight into the relation between Kierkegaard's sacrifice and the mythical. As part of a sketch of Kierkegaard's character, he quotes a passage from the *Havamal* of nordic mythology: "Odin speaks: I know that I hung from a wind-blown tree nine nights long, wounded by a spear, consecrated to Odin: I myself, consecrated to myself."[1] Monrad emphasizes the phrase "consecrated to Odin: I myself, consecrated to myself"; it could in fact serve as the motto of a theology of sacrifice in which the individual must "perish" to become "himself." Nothing is added here by the observation of more recent Danish authors of Kierkegaard's "genuinely nordic character."[2] The relation is evident in the material. The god sacrifices himself, that is, autonomously; for himself, that is, remaining in the natural domain of his own domination. Ultimately the sacrifice transpires, as the continuation of Monrad's passage makes evident, because the god wanted "to procure a higher knowledge through the transcendence of runes";[3] even Kierkegaard's philosophical intention of "transparentness," including the model of the cipher, is contained in the passage from the *Edda*. Kierkegaard himself compares the concept of philosophy with mythology: "No philosophy . . . no mythology . . . has ever had this idea."[4] The idea, however, that should overcome philosophy and the context of mere nature is that of the paradox. — Kierkegaard himself perceived in the aesthetic sphere that sacrifice is mythical. He wrote of Euripides' "Iphigenia in Aulis": "Agamemnon is about to sacrifice Iphigenia. Aesthetics demands silence of Agamemnon, inasmuch as it would be unworthy of the hero to seek comfort from any other person, just as out of solicitude for the women he ought to hide it from them as long as possible. On the other hand, in order to be a hero, the hero also has to be tried in the dreadful spiritual trial that the tears of Clytemnestra and Iphigenia will cause. What does aesthetics do? It has a way out; it has the old servant in readiness to disclose everything to Clytemnestra. Now everything is in order."[5] What is specified here as the aesthetic character of sacrifice is in truth mythical: it is the silence of speechless submission to fate; the mute struggle

that the hero puts up against fate as he submits and by submitting inserts a caesura in the fateful circle. The servant's speech, however, is no aesthetic "way
out"; rather, his disembodied voice is the echo of fate itself that announces its
consummation to the taciturn hero. The paradox also offers up a sacrifice, one
comparable to the silent hero, and therefore falls prey to that mythology that Kierkegaard imagines never to have "had this idea." For just as the hero, deprived of
all hope, is handed over as absolution to blind natural forces, paradoxy sacrifices
hope, the favorite child of spirit, to spirit itself as expiation. In this fashion Kierkegaard himself "aesthetically" bans the paradoxical, to which he "religiously"
succumbs specifically in the mythical figure of memory. As mere imageless
spirit, memory destroys the pictorial configuration of hope: "I can describe hope
so vividly that every hoping individual will acknowledge my description; and yet
it is a deception, for while I picture hope, I think of memory."[6] This already
points the way, by means of a "transcendence of spheres," to Kierkegaard's
Christology: while hope here falls to the mercy of memory that is as mythical as
the recollection of what has always been, in the Christology all worldly existence
is ultimately consecrated to the simply different that cancels the "deception" of
existence but without reconciling it. The mythical figure of pure spirit ascends
out of the hell of memory: "No power in the play, no power on earth, has been
able to coerce Don Juan, only a spirit, an apparition from another world, can do
that. If this be understood correctly, then this will again throw light upon the
interpretation of Don Juan. A spirit, a ghost, is a replication; this is the mystery
which lies in its apparition; Don Juan can do everything, can withstand everything, except the replication of life, precisely because he is immediate sensuous
life, whose negation the spirit is."[7] Thus power over natural life remains dedicated to its annihilation in spirit rather than to reconciliation. The annihilation of
natural life, originating in the statue of the commander, is correctly understood as
ghostly. For here it is not merely natural life that is destroyed by spirit; spirit itself
is annihilated natural life and bound to mythology. For this reason, spirit is without hope, and, even in Kierkegaard's doctrine of faith, paradoxy distorts hope as
the simple annihilation of nature by spirit: "And next the spirit brings hope, hope
in the strictest Christian sense, this hope which is hope against hope. For in every
man there is a spontaneous hope, in one man it may be more vitally strong than
in another, but in death (i.e. when thou dost die from) every such hope dies and
transforms itself into hopelessness. Into this night of hopelessness (it is in fact
death we are describing) comes then the life-giving spirit and brings hope, the
hope of eternity. It is against hope, for according to that merely natural hope
there was no hope left, and so this is hope against hope."[8] In spite of its force-
fulness, this image of hope is false. Hope does not unfold in this image in the
absurdity of a life that is natural, fallen to nature, and yet at the same time created. Rather the absurdity turns against hope itself. By annihilating nature, hope
enters the vicious circle of nature; originating in nature itself, hope is only able to

truly overcome it by maintaining the trace of nature. The twilight of Kierkegaardian hope is the sallow light of the twilight of the gods that proclaims the
vain end of an age or the aimless beginning of a new one, but not salvation.
Thus, in the dialectic of hope, Kierkegaard's paradoxy proves to be caught up in
nature by virtue of its antinatural spiritualism. His polemic against mythical hope
becomes mythical hopelessness just as the movement of "existence" changes
into the despair that initiated its flight into the labyrinth. According to its stated
intention, his interpretation of Christianity is directly opposed to any mythological interpretation. He would like to exclude every mythical content that propa-
gates itself in images; with the greatest severity, he criticizes "childish
religiosity"[9] for its "immediacy"; and he equally repudiates infant baptism and
anabaptism as "external" because of their theological symbolic form, which he
attributes to myth. Blinded, however, it escapes him that the image of sacrifice is
itself mythical and occupies the innermost cell of his thought, accessible equally
by way of his philosophy as by his theology. The sacrifice of Christ and the "disciple" of reason cannot be finally distinguished. The claim "that Christ came
into the world to suffer,"[10] paradoxical and yet all too laconic, transforms the
Christian doctrine of reconciliation itself into the mythical. However unrelentingly he undertook to extirpate the mythical origin of sacrifice through dialectics
and however effectively the ambiguity of this mythical origin supported him in
this, he nevertheless unintentionally betrays the mythical essence of his theology
in otherwise unimposing sentences: "If Christianity once changed the face of the
world by overcoming the crude passions of immediacy and ennobling the state, it
will find in culture a resistance just as great."[11] Thus the dialectical refraction of
subordination to nature, of the "crude passions of immediacy," is to become a
danger for Christianity itself, is to break Christianity — with the result that Christianity reverts to subordination to nature. The fact that Kierkegaard, to mollify
nature, polemically substituted the reified and questionable concept of culture for
a reconciling dialectic that issues from nature changes nothing in this situation.

"Gnosis"

There is thus a mythologization of Christianity in the last instance, although in all
preceding instances, nature had been driven out of Christianity. Christ's death
itself is for Kierkegaard not so much an act of reconciliation as a propitiating
sacrifice. However the *Training in Christianity* may employ the phrase "reconciling death,"[12] the "doctrine of reconciliation" is still explicitly defined as
atonement: "It is taught that Christ has made satisfaction for hereditary sin."[13]
In vain, Kierkegaard denies that which to him marks Christ and likewise man as
an "exception": "It was not in order to appease the angry gods that Abraham
transgressed the universal"[14] — but why else? For all authentic existence is atone-

ment for Kierkegaard: in *The Instant* he demands that Christians "live as sacrificed men in this world of falsehood and evil."[15] All thereby violate "the universal." Moral requirements are properly promulgated only in a life for which
reconciliation is a continuous possibility; if life is sacrificed, ethos disappears
with it in the abyss of the natural. The distinction of good and evil no longer
holds under the domination of death. For this reason, ethics constitutes for Kierkegaard a "transitional stage"; since no life is begrudged it, it cannot prove itself.
Sacrifice is that point in the system where the tangent of an abstract and unreachable "meaning" touches the closed circle of life, and his doctrine insists on this
"point" without progressing along the circumference; if, according to the paradox, it is only here that he can participate in "meaning," he must pay for it
according to a graceless mythical calculus with the loss of the living person. In
his ethics human life sets itself, powerlessly, against sacrificial annihilation. —
Through sacrifice, the difference between Christ and man is abolished. If Christ,
as sacrifice, falls to the mercy of the natural, in sacrifice the individual raises
himself up, sacrificially, as a follower. Of Christ, it is said: "This story, the story
of constant maltreatment which finally ended in death, or shall I say the story of
this suffering, is the story of his whole life. It can be told in several ways. It can
be told briefly in two words, nay even in one: it was the story of the passion."[16]
Thus the story is mythically reduced to a sacrifice, systematically reduced to a
single point, as in the morose thesis that "indeed every day of His life was a day
of burial for Him who was appointed to be a sacrifice."[17] The life of the individual is "relegated" — through sacrifice — to nothing else: "Now if for any individual an eternal happiness is his highest good, this will mean that all finite sat-
isfactions are volitionally relegated to the status of what must be renounced in
favor of an eternal happiness."[18] Renounced by the strength of the "follower":
the Christian is to "make 'the pattern' so vividly present that" he experiences
"such suffering as if in contemporaneousness you had recognized Him for what
he is. All ado made afterwards, all ado about building his tomb etc., etc., etc.,
etc., etc., is, according to the judgment of Jesus Christ, hypocrisy and the
same blood-guilt as that of those who put him to death. This is the Christian
requirement. The mildest, mildest form for it after all is surely that which I have
used in *Training in Christianity*: that you must admit that this is the requirement,
and then have recourse to grace"[19] — a grace for which Kierkegaard knows no
other criterion than suffering. The mythical content of suffering is hardly mastered by Christology and by being a follower; occasionally this mythical content
breaks through, autonomously, and sacrifice is presented in its true natural form:
as expiation, performed for the sinful corps of the present "generation." "The
thought goes very far back in my recollection that in every generation there are
two or three who are sacrificed for the others, are led by frightful sufferings to
discover what redounds to the good of others. So it was that in my melancholy I
understood myself as singled out for such a fate."[20] The emancipation from the

Christian prototype, the separation of the sacrifice from the name and fulfillment of Christ, the fetishistic autonomization of the sacrifice are—in this passage—no accident of expression. In fact his philosophy develops the cult of sacrifice with such tenacity that it finally becomes a gnosis, which Kierkegaard as a Protestant would have otherwise passionately opposed. Gnosis erupts in late idealism when—through spiritualism—mythical thought gains power over Christian thought and, in spite of all talk of grace, draws Christianity into the graceless immanence of the course of nature. Kierkegaard's gnostic doctrines are presented as "literary works" and fantasies. This is perhaps not simply on formal grounds the result of the requirements of the material, as set out in the *Concluding Unscientific Postscript*, but also in order to mask the heterodox character of these doctrines—a requirement that Kierkegaard must have been aware of. Yet these gnostic doctrines return so relentlessly; they present such a tight nexus of motives; they pursue so strictly the course of transcendence defined by the system of spheres; that the critic of the mythical content of Kierkegaard's philosophy finds its real basis in them. The mythical character of sacrifice becomes evident in the fateful necessity of the "offense," over which God is supposed to have no control: "This precisely is the sorrow in Christ: 'He can do no other,' He can humble himself, take the form of a servant, suffer and die for man, invite all to come unto him, sacrifice every day of his life and every hour of the day, and sacrifice his life—but the possibility of the offense he cannot take away. Oh, unique work of love! Oh, unfathomable sorrow of love! that God himself cannot, as in another sense he does not will, cannot will it, but, even if he would, he could not make it impossible that this work of love might not turn out to be for a person exactly the opposite, to be the extremest misery! For the greatest possible human misery, greater even than sin, is to be offended in Christ and remain offended. And Christ cannot, 'love' cannot render this impossible. Lo, for this reason He says, 'Blessed is he who shall not be offended in me.' More he cannot do."[21] Indeed, it is not the sacrifice itself, but its acceptance by the creature that is withdrawn from the control of the deity; just as in the astrology of the spheres, so in the demonic "offense," necessity rules. God's sadness over the unreachable, the "lost" person, responds gnostically to this necessity as the final word of Kierkegaard's theology. In ambiguous reconciliation divine love itself laments: "Behold, he therefore brought to completion this work of love, he offered the sacrifice (in which for his part he exulted), but not without tears. Over this— what shall I call it?—historical painting of inwardness there hovered that dark possibility. And yet, if this had not hovered over it, his work would not have been that of true love."[22] Thus the "historical painting of inwardness" as the theological prototype of all melancholy: God's mournfulness over humanity is itself mythical. In the image of this mournfulness, the creator founders and falls helpless; in sacrifice he is devoured by nature. This is the self-evident and gnostic heresy posited by Kierkegaard's doctrine of the imprisonment of God in his own "incognito," just as this imprisonment follows rationally for Kierkegaard from the paradox of the immediate unity of divine and human nature: "And now in the case of the God-Man! He is God, but chooses to become the individual man. This, as we have seen, is the profoundest incognito, or the most impenetrable unrecognizableness that is possible; for the contradiction between being God and being an individual man is the greatest possible, the infinitely qualitative contradiction. But this is His will, His free determination, therefore an almightily maintained incognito. Indeed, he has in a certain sense, by suffering himself to be born, bound himself once and for all; his incognito is so almightily maintained that in a way he is subjected to it, and the reality of his suffering consists in the fact that it is not merely apparent, but that in a sense the assumed incognito has power over him."[23] If a theology of the "strictly different" were prohibited from any pronouncement over "God's mournfulness," it must be fully confounded since it denies God's freedom and subsumes the incarnate God to a necessity that he cannot "revoke." Kierkegaard's theology cannot escape this entanglement because the conception of the paradoxy and absolute difference of God is itself bound to the autonomous spirit as God's systematic negation, an autonomous spirit that ultimately cancels divine transcendence by construing God dialectically out of itself and its own necessity. Just as in the depths of perdition the dialectic of pure spirit turns toward deliverance, it plummets from the heights of sacrifice into mythology, which subjects its god to abstract fate: "But the unrecognizableness of the God-Man is an incognito almightily maintained, and the divine seriousness consists precisely in the fact that it is so almightily maintained that He Himself suffers under His unrecognizableness in a purely human way."[24] Haecker criticizes Kierkegaard's spiritualism: "The Individual is to become spirit, as he is intended to be, pure spirit if possible; this is an almost gnostic error on Kierkegaard's part";[25] and this gnosis proceeds from the definition of man as purely spiritual to a theology that classifies god in the categories of pure spirit, as which man appears to god. The result is that god disappears into that nature that is in truth precisely man's spirituality. Mythical dialectic consumes Kierkegaard's god, as did Kronos his children.

Paradox Sacrifice of Mere Spirit

The mythical sacrifice itself is carried out in Kierkegaard by spiritualism, the historical figure that nature takes on in his thought. It is the sacrifice of mere spirit into which all reality has been transformed. The model of this sacrifice is paradoxy: a movement of thought, completed in pure thought, and negated as totality in this movement of thought, in order, sacrificed, to draw toward itself the "strictly different," its absolute contrary. What, according to Kierkegaard, characterizes demonic nature and despair in *The Sickness unto Death*, namely the impulse toward self-destruction and annihilation, returns in "consciousness at its apex" — in absolute spirituality. "However, one should not think slightingly of the paradoxical; for the paradox is the source of the thinker's passion, and the thinker without a paradox is like a lover without feeling: a paltry mediocrity. But the highest pitch of every passion is always to will its own downfall; and so it is also the supreme passion of reason to seek a collision, though this collision must in one way or another prove its undoing. The supreme paradox of all thought is the attempt to discover something that thought cannot think."[26] The paradoxical character of sacrifice is already marked by the determinant of hereditary sin, which, itself exclusively spiritual, is to be absolved through sacrifice: "Sin is: before God in despair not to will to be oneself, or before God in despair to will to be oneself. But is not this definition, even though in other aspects it may be conceded to have advantages (and among them this which is the weightiest of all, that it is the only scriptural definition, for the scripture always defines sin as disobedience), is it not after all too spiritual? To this one must first of all make answer that a definition of sin can never be too spiritual (unless it becomes so spiritual that it does away with sin); for sin is precisely a determinant of spirit."[27] If, however, the creature's sin is defined by spirit, its atonement appears just as much posited by spirit as it is contrary to spirit and therefore paradoxically: "But the religious consists precisely in being religiously concerned about oneself infinitely, and not about visions; in being concerned about oneself infinitely, and not about a positive aim, which is negative and finite, because the infinitely negative is the only adequate form for the infinite."[28] The sacrifice of consciousness is carried out according to its own categories, rationally. It is no accident that Kierkegaard is fond of using mathematical metaphors in his doctrine of the Christian paradox: "Like the straight line that is tangent to the circle at only one point — so was He, in the world and yet outside the world, only serving one master."[29] Thus Kierkegaard's paradoxy is here compared to the mathematical-rational paradox of a point that "has no extension," just as, in fact, the point serves as the model of every Kierkegaardian paradox from the *Journal of a Seducer* on. The idea of the point, however, which cannot be purely represented visually, refers to the autonomous *ratio* as its origin. The "spontaneous center" of idealism, the abstract transcendental unity of apperception, the Kantian "principle," is itself a point. That Kierkegaard's paradox is to be understood as precisely this point of spontaneous production may be extracted literally from the *Philosophical Fragments*: "The conclusion of belief is not so much a conclusion as a resolution, and it is for this reason that belief excludes doubt."[30] The category of "resolution," which Kierkegaard expressly terms "ethical," subsuming it thereby to "freedom" and autonomy, is to be, paradoxically, the "religious starting point": "The resolution is not man's strength, it is not man's courage, it is not man's talent (these are only immediate analogies which do not furnish an objective measure for the immediacy of love, since they belong to the same sphere and are not a new immediacy), but it is a religious starting-point."[31] Thus Kierkegaard legitimates "religious" paradoxy by a spontaneous act of consciousness. This has the consequence that all sacrifice in the domain of consciousness assumes the form of the paradoxical. It is not the symbolic, objective completion of sacrifice that is decisive for Kierkegaard, but rather, that with each sacrifice the autonomy of thought be destroyed by determinations of thought. Opposed to this analysis is the common objection to any "intellectualization" of Kierkegaard, who — it is said — had whatever fundamental religious experiences that he represented in the form of rational paradoxes as the tribute of his thought to "his age." This objection arbitrarily tears apart time and thought, which are interwoven in him in such a fashion that the modern is the site of the archaic, while the archaic becomes incorporeal vapor as soon as any inquiry into it is made. Kierkegaard did not present fundamental religious experiences as rational paradoxes; the locus of mythical sacrifice in his work is the historical figure of consciousness: objectless inwardness. This objectless interiority did not carry on a timeless discussion with God; by breaking free from the outer world through the strength of its historical position and inserting itself into an indissoluble dialectic as the quintessence of creation and equally as the guarantor of the meaningfulness of this dialectic, the alleged dialogue in fear and trembling can be nothing other than the deceptive echo that answers back out of nothingness to a self-confined spirituality. Rational sacrifice is not the mere copy of an ontic sacrifice; absolute spirit is incapable of any other sacrifice than itself. Kierkegaard's "profundity" — if one insists on the misused concept — is by no means located in his recreation of an absolute, fundamental religious meaning in the guise of idealism. He presented mythical content as concomitantly historical, as the "fundamental meaning" of idealism, in the moment of its historical collapse. — The primacy of rational paradoxy in Kierkegaard's sacrificial realm can be verified immanently by the fact that paradoxy is not limited to the spiritual Christology; it does not converge with the traditional paradoxy of theological symbols. If sacrifice is the dialectical structure of his oeuvre, and if the leap and negation in every case complete the surrender of the "sphere" from which they derive, every sacrifice is alloted paradoxy as the sign of its systematic seal of authenticity. The astonishing catalog of paradoxes listed in one passage of the *Concluding Unscientific Postscript* can be explained in no other way: "The reader will remember: A revelation is signalized by mystery, happiness by suffering, the certainty of faith by uncertainty, the ease of the paradoxical-religious life by its difficulty, the truth by absurdity."[32] What would be blasphemous in the face of the once inspiring symbol fits passively into the form of a universally rational legality according to its "applications," as if this legality were one that stamped the "cases" as content of whatever paradoxy and turned it materially against the *ratio*. The paradox is Kierkegaard's fundamental, categorial form; he undertakes the synthesis of multiplicity paradoxically, and in the categorial unity and totality the rational origin persists that the determinate paradoxies respectively disavow. Such paradoxies therefore occur in every "sphere." The oneness of time and eternity is already conceived "aesthetically"; this is evident not only in the parody of seduction but in a positive form in the doctrine of art: "Through Don Juan [Mozart] is introduced into that eternity that does not lie outside of time but in the midst of it, which is not veiled from the eyes of men, where the immortals are introduced, not once for all, but constantly, again and again, as the generations pass and turn their gaze upon them, find happiness in beholding them, and go to the grave, and the following generation passes them again in review, and is transfigured in beholding them."[33] The "ethical" stage is constituted by paradoxy in precisely the same way: "The highest expression of immediate love is that the lover feels himself as nothing in the presence of the beloved, and this feeling is mutual, for to feel oneself as something conflicts with love."[34] Love is defined, therefore, by the simple negation of that self to which, according to Kierkegaard's doctrine, the full content of the doctrine depends. Corresponding to the paradoxy of emotion is that of the moral commandment itself: "This shows that the individual is at once the universal and the particular. Duty is the universal which is required of me; so if I am not the universal, I am unable to perform duty. On the other hand, my duty is the particular, something for me alone, and yet it is duty and hence the universal."[35] Even the non-Christian "religiosity 'A' " is ultimately paradoxical, and in such a precise sense that its delimitation from the Christian becomes impossible. Paradoxy therefore furnishes the unifying subordinating concept of Kierkegaard's positive theology: "Was Job proved to be in the wrong? Yes, eternally, for there is no higher court than the one that judged him. Was Job proved to be in the right? Yes, eternally, by being proved to be in the wrong before God."[36] The all-inclusive function of paradoxy is made possible by its abstractness, by the inclusion of all specific contents in it as their categorial form. This abstractness, however, is again grounded in sacrifice, the essence of paradoxy, and is therefore not to be fulfilled or corrected through the multiplicitousness of the contents. The coherence of the living person, according to Kierkegaard the "reality" of the self, is sacrificed in the paradox: "The religiousness which is fetched directly from reality is a dubious religiousness; it may be that aesthetic categories are employed and worldly wisdom acquired; but when reality has not been able to crush an individual and he falls by himself, the religious factor is clearer."[37] The collapse of the individual is, however, concretely the annihilation of time and therefore the surrender of the immanent coherence of life itself. For Kierkegaard, time distinguishes the realm of human existence from the realm of merely fallen nature: "But the historical is the past (for the present pressing upon the confines of the future has not yet become historical). How then can it be said that nature, though immediately present, is historical, except in the sense of the said ingenious speculation? The difficulty comes from the fact that nature is too abstract to have a dialectic with respect to time in the stricter sense. This is nature's imperfection, that it has no history in any other sense.''[38] But for Kierkegaard the historicity of Christ in the paradox remains precisely as abstract as he perceives the paradox to be in the processes of mere nature because the Kierkegaardian sacrifice is nothing other than that of mere nature: ''If the contemporary generation had left nothing behind them but these words: 'We have believed that in such and such a year the God appeared among us in the humble figure of a servant, that he lived and taught in our community, and finally died,' it would be more than enough. The contemporary generation would have done all that was necessary; for this little advertisement, this *nota bene* on a page of universal history, would be sufficient to afford an occasion for a successor, and the most voluminous account can in all eternity do nothing more.''[39] In such a construction of the paradoxy, the appearance of Jesus in time becomes arbitrarily interchangeable because, indeed, time occurs in the paradox exclusively as an abstract, contentless *nota bene*. This suffices to show how fundamentally Kierkegaard's doctrine of the paradox, as a unity of time and eternity, turns against its own fundamental thesis, according to which ''the historical fact that the God has been in human form is the essence of the matter.''[40] In fact Kierkegaard's paradox omits that concrete moment of time that it precisely should have maintained and that instead appears as simple temptation: ''There is in the immediate contemporaneity,'' as in the experience of the temporally concrete life of Christ, ''an unrest, which does not cease until the word goes forth that it is finished. But the succeeding tranquillity must not be such as to do away with the historical, for then everything will be Socratic'';[41] or the ''contemporaneity'' is called ''an intermediate situation, having its significance indeed, and not eliminable without, as you would say, turning back to the Socratic order of things, but nevertheless without absolute significance for the contemporary.''[42] Just as in the ''point'' concrete time is wiped out by sacrificial paradox, so the image of eternity also fades into the most extreme abstractness; natural life is sacrificed, and the sacrifice that occurs remains bound to natural (be it even spiritual) life, unable to posit determinate transcendence: ''Nor is it true that the absolute telos becomes concrete in the relative ends, for the absolute distinction that was fixed between them in the moment of resignation will secure the absolute *telos* against fraternization at every moment.''[43] In that the telos becomes incomparable, it also becomes indeterminate; in that it demolishes all pictorial mythology, it sinks into the imageless mythology of pure negation. What Kierkegaard was reluctant to state as Christ is expressed by Job in the doctrine of the paradox in ''religiosity A'': ''It is a weak point in the structure of the Book of Job that God appears in the clouds and also appears as the most accomplished dialectician; for what makes God the terrible dialectician he is, is precisely the fact that one has him at very much closer quarters, and therewith the softest whisper is more blissful, and the softest whisper is more terrible, than seeing him enthroned upon the clouds and hearing him in the thunder. Hence one cannot argue dialectically with him, for God brings to bear all the dialectical power in the soul of the man concerned against this man.''[44] If in such sentences Kierkegaard's dialectic meant to raise itself above mythology, it here falls entirely to its mercy. For although the mythical images of transcendence are destroyed in the instant of "faith,"in the same instant human consciousness itself usurps the power of the absolute through the paradoxy that it posits. "Subjectivity is truth": the paradox reveals the horrible lineaments of the sacrificial mask. In the demonic sacrifice of consciousness, man is still the ruler of a sinful creation; through sacrifice he asserts his rule, and the name of the divinity succumbs to his demonic nature. Here the philosophical criticism of Kierkegaard converges with the psychological question that current research prefers to pose and that can indeed be answered rigorously only on the basis of knowledge of the philosophical content itself: was Kierkegaard a true believer? To ask this of the person is neither legitimate nor possible; the text of the last conversations with Boesen alone prevents its affirmation. Philosophically, in the face of the mythical essence of Kierkegaard's paradoxy, the question can be decided negatively, and indeed according to the evidence furnished by the concept of the "follower." This concept ultimately becomes the guarantor of theological substance itself, but in such a fashion that this substance is secularized in the paradox: "Just as the ascension shatters or defies natural law (such in fact is the objection doubt raises), so the pressing need of the follower shatters the purely human sources of comfort (how could these give comfort to men who must suffer because they have done well?), and presses for another sort of comfort, pressingly needs the ascension of their lord and master, and believingly presses through to the ascension. So it always is with human need, 'from the eater cometh forth meat': where the need is, it produces as it were that which it needs. And the followers verily had need of his ascension in order to hold out in such a life as they led—so therefore it was a certainty to them.''[45] However carefully, perhaps even ambiguously, this is formulated, in that the sacrifice of the follower in the "uncertainty" of faith constitutes the single criterion of truth, this truth is turned over to a pragmatism that, although it is still concealed in the point, could have been grasped by its consequences if Kierkegaard had ever relinquished the "point." Kierkegaard's theology would have disintegrated had it ever established itself as such. In sacrifice immanence reaches out beyond itself only to plunge into the blind relentless context of nature in which the immanent follower is to procure assurance of the transcendent ascension, rather than the reverse. The theology quoted by the sacrifice is subordinate to intraworldly categories to the extent that the sacrifice again intervenes, occasionally if not continuously, as *deus ex machina*, and subjective immanence submerges in the void of abstract negation. Lukács's thesis that Kierkegaard's "leap" was simply a helpless flight from meaninglessness is justified by the same interpretation that makes Kierkegaard a "nihilist"; and although the methodology of Ludwig Marcuse's cultural-philosophical cogitations is questionable, his results are critically unchallengeable where he classifies Kierkegaard as a "romantic" and comes to the conclusion that "the ideal of faith, which he sketches, is indeed ultimately romantic fantasy, not an image of existence"[46] and where he says of the paradox that "this romantic credo *quia absurdum* is not inner certainty in the face of all sorts of cognitive aporia; the cognitive aporia themselves are to render certainty"[47]—in the mythical sacrifice of reason. Reason, which in Hegel as infinite reason produces actuality out of itself, is in Kierkegaard, again as infinite reason, the negation of all finite knowledge: if the former is mythical by its claim to universal sovereignty, the latter becomes mythical through universal annihilation. Kierkegaard's continuously repeated assurances that he was not one of the faithful are therefore not to be taken as an expression of Christian modesty but as the truth of the matter. Precisely the assurances—conjuring formulas like the words "scripture" and "paradox"—are too stereotypically repeated to ever confirm the revived sentiment of modesty; they do not sternly ward off imposture from religion, but rather the reconciling word from the mythical circle that it would burst. In the ideal of speaking "without authority," the profound knowledge of the heterodoxy of paradoxy—which Kierkegaard sets up as the standard of Christianity—becomes obdurately impenitent. This explains Kierkegaard's zealous concern for the "boundary," which fills his book against Adler: in priestly fashion, it would rather secure the ritual tradition of the cult of sacrifice than a Christianity that, if it were truly held, would know itself secure as revealed truth even in depravation and misrepresentation; it is instead threatened by demons because it is itself demonic. This is what gives the mythical tone to a passage in *For Self-Examination*: "In the case now anyone among us dares to step out ethically in the role here indicated, appealing moreover as an individual to a direct relationship with God [as does Adler] then I shall instantly (so it is I understand myself at this instant, but I cannot even know whether the next instant I may not be deprived even of the conditions for being able to do it, the next instant, perhaps while I am getting this published), I shall instantly be at his service, by undertaking what before God I shall understand as my task. This task of mine will be to follow him, the Reformer, step by step, never budging from his side, to see if step by step he is in the true character of his role, is actually the Extraordinary."[48] A border-guard mentality, unchallengeable discipline, the power of fascination—these the deluded Kierkegaard owes not, as he claims, to the purity of his Christian doctrine, but to its mythical reinterpretation in the paradox. Here the excessiveness of the created is revenged mercilessly on the manufactured system. As booty for the sacrifice of reason, reason receives whatever falls within its region. Sacrificed reason governs as a demigod.

Passio

The governance of sacrificed reason—in Kierkegaard's philosophy—traces the outlines of passion.[49] Along with melancholy, anxiety, and despair, *passio* is counted by him among the affects that, as ciphers, take the place of a blocked truth, yet at the same time give witness to the merely agitated subjectivity. *Passio* aims at the sacrifice of the self, whose passion is that of self-destruction: "If the individual is inwardly defined by self-annihilation before God, then we have *religiousness A.*"[50] And *passio* is a subjective category: the natural urge of spirit, continually reconceived by Kierkegaard on the model of erotic inclination. Kierkegaard even intended to assure himself of the transcendental content of faith by the psychological content of passion. "But the highest passion in a person is faith";[51] thus the double sense of his concept of *passio* encourages misinterpretations, which are condensed, most drastically, in the title of Vetter's book, *Piety as Passion*. This double sense is, however, dialectical. It is the old double sense of *passio* which, according to Benjamin's formulation, constitutes the "high pass of mythology": passion and sacrificial suffering. It is not accidental that Kierkegaard's "ethical" passion—from which he indeed thought he had "excised everything incommensurable," had banished nature—requires such an opaque and equivocal determination as that of sympathy: "sympathy is an essential quality of man, and every resolution in which sympathy is not given its due, in which it fails to gain adequate expression, is not in the largest sense an idealizing resolution."[52] The ambiguousness of sympathy is mythical. It is expressed, in Kierkegaard's "ethical sphere," through *passio*, which as the passion of the intellect preserves its natural instinctual character. This instinct is able to articulate itself vividly. Its dialectic appears bound to the totality of "existence," which the dialectic expiates altogether through annihilation. Its claim to totality, however, is bound to absolute spirit's claim to domination. If this claim disappears, passion receives another dialectical form than that of atonement and complete annihilation. Passion may then fulfill itself in its impulses according to the rhythm with which it encounters them individually, without submitting to the rigid subordinating concept; the steps of fulfillment are transformed by it into those of reconciliation. It is Kierkegaard's second plan of the dialectic, the dialectic of the mythical itself, which reawakens in the depth of his philosophy and turns against a sacrificial mythology that could have "isolated" the plan but indeed not subsumed it in its paradoxies. If passion, as an all-powerful, infinite, insatiable natural power knows only its own destruction wherever it finds any satisfaction in the finite, then despair, previously passion's demonic totality, loses its power over passion and the dialectical sickness unto death is transposed into the force of reconciled-historical life. It is not, as Kierkegaard's doctrine of total sin and total expiational sacrifice supposes, a "superficial understanding" that permits the assumption that "the doctrine of reconciliation is the qualitative difference between paganism and Christianity."[53] Reconciliation is the imperceptible gesture in which guilty nature renews itself historically as created nature; unreconciled, it remains obsessed with its greatest gesture, that of sacrifice.

Christianity distinguishes itself from mere natural religion in the name of reconciliation and not in the nameless execution of the paradox. What Kierkegaard mythically neglects in Christianity, he recognizes, in truth with greater Christianity, in myth itself; in the nordic "Saga of Agnes and the Merman," which he recounts, transforms, and comments upon in *Fear and Trembling*. For here the dialectical transition from passion to reconciliation is understood, if not as already fulfilled, then indeed as without sacrifice: "The merman is a seducer who rises up from his hidden chasm and in wild lust seizes and breaks the innocent flower standing on the seashore in all her loveliness and with her head thoughtfully inclined to the soughing of the sea. This has been the poets' interpretation until now. Let us make a change. The merman was a seducer. He has called to Agnes and by his wheedling words has elicited what was hidden in her. In the merman she found what she was seeking, what she was searching for as she stared down to the bottom of the sea. Agnes is willing to go with him. The merman takes her in his arms. Agnes throws her arms around his neck; trusting with all her soul, she gives herself to the stronger one. He is already standing on the beach, crouching to dive out into the sea and plunge down with his booty/ then Agnes looks at him once more, not fearfully, not despairingly, not proud of her good luck, not intoxicated with desire, but in absolute faith and in absolute humility, like the lowly flower she thought herself to be, and with this look she entrusts her whole destiny to him in absolute confidence./ And look! The sea no longer roars, its wild voice is stilled; nature's passion, which is the merman's strength, forsakes him, and there is a deadly calm / and Agnes is still looking at him this way."[54] The "change" that Kierkegaard has undertaken is so small and perfect that it can be compared only with what the sagas once underwent at the hands of the attic tragedians: the enigmatic step that leads out of mere nature by remaining within it; the reconciling redemption of sacrifice. Sacrifice disappears, and in its place dialectic holds its breath for an instant; a caesura appears in its progress, as is represented, graphically, by the solidus before "And look!" Certainly, to the eyes of Kierkegaard the existentialist, reconciliation passes by overhead like a radiant meteor that never reaches the earth. Sacrifice, as renunciation, once more breaks into the fleetingly reconciled landscape: "Then the merman breaks down. He cannot withstand the power of innocence, his natural element is disloyal to him, and he cannot seduce Agnes. He takes her home again/ he explains that he only wanted to show her how beautiful the sea is when it is calm, and Agnes believes him./ Then he returns alone, and the sea is wild, but not as wild as the merman's despair. He can seduce Agnes, he can seduce a hundred Agneses, he can make any girl infatuated / but Agnes has won, and the merman has lost her. Only as booty can she be his; he cannot give himself faithfully to any girl, because he is indeed only a merman."[55] This he remains through renunciation: sacrifice throws him back again into the mythical element, into the "passion of nature," which "forsakes him" in the instant of reconciliation, dissolved by the fulfilling gesture of the girl who holds true to nature till the end. In sacrificial renunciation, however, the merman becomes "demonic": he falls silent. His silence binds him to mere nature. Thus Kierkegaard himself understood it: "We shall now give the merman a human consciousness and let his being a merman signify a human preexistence, in consequence of which his life was entrapped. There is nothing to hinder his becoming a hero, for the step he now takes is reconciling. He is saved by Agnes; the seducer is crushed, he has submitted to the power of innocence, he can never seduce again. But immediately, two forces struggle over him: repentance, Agnes and repentance. If repentance alone gets him, then he is hidden; if Agnes and repentance get him, then he is disclosed."[56] In scarcely another passage is Kierkegaard's idealism of objectless inwardness more self-evidently mythical than here where he holds up to himself the image of reconciliation. Objectless inwardness must silently endure, like the refractory natural demon. The sole organ of reconciliation, however, is the word. "Meanwhile, there is no doubt that the merman can speak";[57] this speech, as "the disclosed," would draw him out of mythology, to which he is banned by his silence — the archaic silence of his unmediated natural existence as well as the dialectical silence of "repentance" shut within itself and sacrificially annihilating itself without ever finding the reconciling word. The "merman" is truly the "preexistence" of Kierkegaardian inwardness: in silence its dialectical sacrifice reveals itself as archaic. This confirms his idealism as the historical figure of the mythical. Where, however, nature — free of resignation — perseveres as desirous instinct and eloquent consciousness, it is able to survive, whereas in sacrifice nature succumbs to itself; nature, which truly cannot be driven out with a pitchfork and returns until genius is reconciled with it.

Chapter 7
Construction of the Aesthetic

Crisis of Melancholy

"Just as man—by nature—desires what is able to sustain and revive the lust of life, so does he who is to live for the eternal need constantly a dose of pessimism, so that he should not dote upon this wretched world, but rather learn loathing and weariness of and disgust at its foolishness and lies."[1] What is stylized so puritanically in *The Instant* that it seems to be an old-fashioned quotation from a sermon of repentance nevertheless contains the richest dialectic in the form of a summary thesis, and betrays it dialectically. In Kierkegaard's philosophy passion and sacrifice originate in melancholy as their natural source in order to extinguish nature itself in melancholy as in the spiritual body. Yet nature is not dissolved in the passion of its annihilation; melancholy accompanies Kierkegaard as a "mediating" element through all stages, before sacrificing itself in the point. For this reason melancholy is still to be found in his later writings, where one would think it would be overcome by a polemical-paradoxical Christianity. Melancholy, fractured, has nonetheless survived the ruin that, as a whole, it earlier visited upon its own totality. What remains, however, is divided like the despair that with the sudden shock of the sickness unto death breaks through the foundation of subjectivity, polarizing itself objectively into judgment and grace. Mythical self-assertion through melancholy is anathematized: "Aye, let the storm break forth in still greater violence, making an end of life, and of the world, and of this brief speech, which has at least the advantage over all things else, that it is soon ended? Let that wild vortex, which is the inmost principle of the world, although this escapes the attention of men, who eat and drink and marry and increase in heedless preoccupation—let it break forth, I say, and in pent-up resentment sweep away the mountains and the nations and the achievements of culture and the cunning inventions of mankind, let it break forth with the last terrible shriek which more surely than the trump of doom proclaims the destruction of everything; let it move, and moving whirl along this naked cliff on which we stand, as lightly as thistledown before the breath of our nostrils!''[2] Thus melancholy is concentrated in the image of catastrophe as the extreme limit of its potential. ''Herein consists also the significance of his melancholy. Its nature is the concentration of possibility,''[3] and ''the most perfect mockery of the world would have to become earnestness''[4] in the presence of this image. Sacrifice is powerless in this situation; rather, melancholy breaks down before the reality of judgment: ''It appears to me that there is something infinitely disconsolate in such an isolation, and I cannot help thinking how dreadful it is when a man awakes to another life on the Day of Judgment and again stands there quite alone.''[5] The demonic possibility, however, is that of total, defiant self-assertion. Shattered melancholy means something quite different. Its ruins are the ciphers on which Kierkegaard reflects, and hope is integral to the absurdity of its desire. The order of the spheres is inverted. There where Kierkegaard supposes only the discontinuity and contingency of total melancholy, the natural impulse, even if denied fulfillment, clings to the names of its objects; in his philosophy hope nowhere insists more stubbornly than in the aesthetic ''Diapsalmata,'' whose fragmentariness, according to Kierkegaard's hierarchy of spheres, results from the incapacity of the aesthetic to achieve continuity. Thus in a melancholy reminiscence on a child named Louis: ''How true human nature is to itself. With what native genius does not a little child often show us a living image of the adult world. Today I really enjoyed watching little Louis. He sat in his little chair; he looked about him with obvious pleasure. The nurse Mary went through the room. 'Mary,' he cried. 'yes, little Louis,' she answered with her usual friendliness, and came to him. He tipped his head a little to one side, fastened his immense eyes upon her with a certain gleam of mischief in them, and thereupon said quite phlegmatically, 'Not this Mary, another Mary.' What do we older folks do? We cry out to the whole world, and when it comes smiling to meet us, then we say: 'Not this Mary.' ''[6] Kierkegaard's commentary helplessly misses the point of his own narrative. It is not hopelessness in the autonomous, infinite wish, but hope in the finite that is described; a hope that is frustrated in the factual world, in the 'milieu,' by this girl and no other but which still, utopianly and concretely, grasps in the name what is denied to it by the world of alienated objects. For this reason, the child does not appear as a banally ironic image of ''the adult world'' in the vain reduction of a melancholy retrospective. Rather, the impulse of his impatience is mournful; an impulse that, to be fulfilled, should not be sacrificed to reality through ''decisiveness,'' but nourished dialectically. The motives of the

"Diapsalmata" may, in terms of literary history, have their origins in romanticism. Yet they are distinguished from the romantic just as much as by the distinctness of their definition as by the strict impossibility of their fulfillment, an impossibility whose figure defines the form of hope in Kierkegaard's work. Thus, in the name, even an observation that starts off fully romantic becomes true to the finite, but displaced wish: "The tremendous poetic vigor of folk literature expresses itself, among other ways, in the strength to desire. The desires of our age are in comparison with these both sinful and dull, since we desire what belongs to our neighbor. The characters in folk literature are very well aware that the neighbor as little possesses what they are seeking as they themselves do. And when they do indulge in sinful desire, it is so terrible as to cause men to tremble. This desire does not allow itself to be cheapened by the cool calculation of probabilities of sober reason. Don Juan still struts across the stage with his 1,003 mistresses. No one dares to smile, out of respect for the venerable tradition. If a poet were to venture the like in our age, he would be hooted off the stage."[7] Kierkegaard has found the formula for what here exceeds the impulse to restore lost immediacy and fullness of life: "My soul has lost its potentiality. If I were to wish for anything, I should not wish for wealth and power, but for the passionate sense of the potential, for the eye which, ever young and ardent, ever sees the possible."[8] Such "potentiality" is not so much a mirage of what has been lost as an unfulfilled, thin, prophetic, but nevertheless exact schema of what is to be. It is, however, the schema of that truth to which Kierkegaard's question of origin is directed; that enciphered and distorted truth that, while autonomous subjectivity cannot create it, melancholic subjectivity is indeed able to read it. In this figure melancholy brings home what existence destroyed. In contradiction to the superficial intention of systematic completeness, the "Diapsalmata" work toward the "original script of human existence." Nowhere are their metaphors more powerful than here: "I am as shrunken as a Hebrew *shewa*, weak and silent as a *daghesh lene*; I feel like a letter printed backward in the line, and yet as ungovernable as a three-tailed Passha, as jealous for myself and my thoughts as a bank for its notes, and as generally introverted as any *pronomen reflexivum*. If only it were true of misfortunes and sorrows as it is of conscious good works that they who do them have their reward taken away — if this held true of sorrow, then were I the happiest of men: for I take all my troubles in advance, and yet they all remain behind."[9] It is perhaps not by accident that the metaphor chooses Hebrew letters, the signs of a language that theologically makes the claim to being the true language. Theological truth, however — and here, beyond the paradoxical sacrifice, Kierkegaard's own ontological position presumably lies — is guaranteed precisely by its encipherment and distortedness; the "collapse" of fundamental human relations reveals itself as the history of truth itself. This is shown, totally against Kierkegaard's own intention and therefore all the more convincingly, in a passage of an essay on Marie Beaumarchais; script appears as a model of despair, only to transform itself, gently, into a model of hope: "And thus she will pass her time until at last she has consumed the object of her grief which was not the cause of her grief, but the occasion through which she always sought an object for her grief. If a man possessed a letter which he knew, or believed, contained information bearing upon what he must regard as his life's happiness, but the writing was pale and fine, almost illegible—then would he read it with restless anxiety and with all possible passion, in one moment getting one meaning, in the next another, depending on his belief that, having made out one word with certainty, he could interpret the rest thereby; but he would never arrive at anything except the same uncertainty with which he began. He would stare more and more anxiously, but the more he stared, the less he would see. His eyes would sometimes fill with tears; but the oftener this happened the less he would see. In the course of time, the writing would become fainter and more illegible, until at last the paper itself would crumble away, and nothing would be left to him except the tears in his eyes."[10] Endless, useless reading should represent the empty infinity of the reflection of the "aesthetic" (in this case the immediately loving) individual; reflection that, according to the doctrine of the system of spheres, can be broken only by "decisiveness." Yet no truer image of hope can be imagined than that of ciphers, readable as traces, dissolving in history, disappearing in front of overflowing eyes, indeed confirmed in lamentation. In these tears of despair the ciphers appear as incandescent figures, dialectically, as compassion, comfort, and hope. Dialectical melancholy does not mourn vanished happiness. It knows that it is unreachable. But it knows also of the promise that conjoins the unreachable, precisely in its origin, with the wish: "Never have I been happy; and yet it has always seemed as if happiness were in my train, as if glad genii danced about me, invisible to others but not to me, whose eyes gleamed with joy."[11] Such hope rejects all mythical deception, all claim to having once existed, by this *never*: it is promised as unattainable; whereas, if it were directly asserted as reality, it would regress to the mythological and phantasmagorical, surrendering itself to the lost and past. For the true desire of melancholy is nourished on the idea of an eternal happiness without sacrifice, which it still could never adequately indicate as its object. Although the wish that follows this aim is unfulfillable and yet full of hope, it originates in its aim, and just as it circles around happiness, the wish circles, fulfilled, in happiness itself. Accordingly, in Kierkegaard homesickness for happiness answers the disguised utopian wish as the eschatological rescue of his gnosis: "The trick would be to feel homesick notwithstanding one is at home. Expertness in the use of illusion is requisite for this."[12] Here illusion is located in the unreachable figure of hope as in homesickness at home. As the desire for happiness, however, illusion has its content not in the infinite, but in a finiteness that, as a dividing wall, saves body and name better than the open horizon of thought in which they drift away. Thus in the diapsalm concerning the roast, pragmatism goes farther than Kierkegaard's romantic irony gives it credit for: "One must be very naive to believe that it will do any good to cry out and shout in the world, as if that would change one's fate. Better take things as they come, and make no fuss. When I was young and went into a restaurant, I would say to the waiter, 'A good cut, a very good cut, from the loin, and not too fat.' Perhaps the waiter did not even hear me, to say nothing of paying any attention to my request, and still less was it likely that my voice should reach the kitchen and influence the cook, and even if it did, there was perhaps not a good cut on the entire roast. Now I never shout any more."[13] Happiness would taste like this precisely described piece of meat; the former is as unreachable in the hierarchy of significations as is the latter in a shabby restaurant. Reification is as inimical to happiness as the bad organization of the inn is to the roast, and it is promised just as certainly as the roast in its smell.

Passing Away of Existence

Nature and reconciliation communicate in melancholy; from it the "wish" arises dialectically, and its illusion is the reflection of hope. It is illusion because not happiness itself but only its images are given to the wish and in them the wish, which is nourished by them, is at the same time filled with longing because, according to Kierkegaard, the eye, the organ of the wish, "Is most difficult to satisfy."[14] This insatiability is aesthetic. What crumbles into disparate, incommensurable definitions of the aesthetic in the face of the claim to power of his systematic idealism, what is irreducible to the spontaneous core of subjectivity, crystalizes however irregularly, yet coherently, under the gaze of melancholy. The sphere of the aesthetic, which Kierkegaard, employing the categories of his paradoxical system of existence, divides up into a traditional doctrine of art, the sensual immediacy of existence, the speculative deception of objective metaphysics, and the subjective *how* of communication—just to be able to discard it as discontinuous; this sphere, painfully furrowed by a subjectivity that leaves its traces behind in it without ever mastering it, receives its structure from images that are present for the wish, without having been produced by it, for the wish itself originates in them. This realm of images constitutes the absolute opposite of the traditional Platonic realm. It is not eternal, but historical-dialectical; it does not lie in perfect transcendence beyond nature, but dissolves darkly into nature; it is not imageless truth, but promises paradoxically unreachable truth in opposition to its semblance; it does not open itself to Eros, but shines forth in the moment of collapse—in the historical collapse of the mythical unity of unmediated existence; in the mythical dissociation of the historically existing individual. The figures that assemble themselves at this point carry marks of a suffocating objectless inwardness. Kierkegaard leaves no doubt that the origin of their luminosity is putrefaction; they often remain behind as monuments of a withered and alienated nature. But no matter how far behind, they are ahead of the living. Kierkegaard understood this better as a "psychologist" than as a systematizer of existence: "In every man there is a talent, understanding. And every man, the most knowing and the most limited, is in his knowing far ahead of what he is in his life, of what his life expresses."[15] By this lead of knowledge over existence, the knowing subject participates in truth through semblance, a participation which imageless existence, in its empty depth, never achieves. For the trace of truth becomes accessible to the wish that perseveres in the face of the merely existent; if the existent were cast off as contingent, the existence of inwardness would not offer truth, for inwardness knows no truth beyond its own life. Before the trace of truth, however, mere existence passes away. What Kierkegaard says polemically of speculative reason, which usurps the *intellectus archetypus*, characterizes positively that "aesthetic" deportment that asserts itself in spite of his doctrine of existence: "But for the speculating philosopher the question of his personal eternal happiness cannot arise precisely because his task consists in getting more and more away from himself so as to become objective, thus vanishing from himself and becoming what might be called the contemplative energy of philosophy itself."[16] Thus the autonomous self would have to "vanish" into truth, whose trace reaches the self by aesthetic semblance in the ephemeral images of which the self's mighty spontaneity is powerless. If the expansive self in its full dimension is lost in sacrifice, it survives in its transience by making itself small. It is possible that knowledge inheres in Kierkegaard's ethical abstraction, in the "exclusion of the incommensurable" that transcends mere sacrifice; that is, as knowledge of inconspicuousness as is maintained by the longing of the romantics for the "philistine": "They who carry the treasure of faith are likely to disappoint, for externally they have a striking resemblance to bourgeois philistinism, which infinite resignation, like faith, deeply disdains."[17] Kierkegaard describes the believer, who resembles the philistine, not as one who lives the good life, immediately in his humble station, but as a fleeting, unimposing figure: "The instant I first lay eyes on him, I set him apart at once; I jump back, clap my hands, and say half aloud, 'Good Lord, is this the man, is this really the one—he looks just like a tax collector!' But this is indeed the one. I move a little closer to him, watch his slightest movement to see if it reveals a bit of heterogeneous optical telegraphy from the infinite, a glance, a facial expression, a gesture, a dashness, a smile that would betray the infinite in its heterogeneity with the finite. No! I examine his figure from top to toe to see if there may not be a crack through which the infinite would peek. No! He is solid all the way through."[18] This is not a sacrificial figure, nor a bourgeois "moralist" of the everyday realm of obligation, marriage, and well-ordered activity. His origin is to be found rather in traditions: those of the wise man who is unrecognized and hidden from himself; in the saint whose mortal being disappears imperceptibly. The "telegraphy from the finite," a missive of judgment in *The Sickness unto Death*, is for him the secret communication of grace. It is his ability "to express the sublime absolutely in the pedestrian . . . the one and only marvel,"[19] and he performs it. The subjective astrology of the spheres is powerless; neither the freely choosing self nor its sacrifice in the paradox has any power over it. Settled in the discarded precipitate of the aesthetic—insignificant, cast off, but enduring—is that which the pathos of total subjectivity conjured in vain. "Then I lay at your side and vanished from myself in the immensity of the sky above and forgot myself in your soothing murmur! You, my happier self, you fleeting life that lives in the brook running past my father's farm, where I lie stretched out as if my body were an abandoned hiking stick, but I am rescued and released in the plaintive purling!—Thus did I lie in my theater box."[20] This speculative image of passing away and salvation is concealed, almost irresponsibly, behind the theory of farce found in *Repetition*, which it follows; a theory in which not only Kierkegaard's doctrine of art, but his entire systematics of the concept of existence disintegrates: "Every general aesthetic category runs aground on farce; nor does farce succeed in producing a uniformity of mood in the more cultured audience. Because its impact depends largely on self-activity and the viewer's improvisation, the particular individuality comes to assert himself in a very individual way and in his enjoyment is emancipated from all aesthetic obligations to admire, to laugh, to be moved, etc. in the traditional way. For a cultured person, seeing a farce is similar to playing the lottery, except that one does not have the annoyance of winning money. But that kind of uncertainty will not do for the general theater-going public, which therefore ignores farce or snobbishly disdains it, all the worse for itself. A proper theater public generally has a certain restricted eagerness; it wishes to be—or at least fancies that it is—ennobled and educated in the theater. It wishes to have had—or at least fancies that it has had—a rare artistic enjoyment; it wishes, as soon as it has read the poster, to be able to know in advance what is going to happen that evening. Such unanimity cannot be found at a farce, for the same farce can produce very different impressions, and, strangely enough, it may so happen that the one time it made the least impression it was performed best. . . . The otherwise so reassuring mutual respect between theater and audience is suspended. Seeing a farce can produce the most unpredictable mood, and therefore a person can never be sure whether he has conducted himself in the theater as a worthy member of society who has laughed and cried at the appropriate places. One cannot, as a conscientious spectator does, admire the fine character portrayal that a dramatic performance is supposed to have, for in a farce all of the characters are portrayed according to the abstract criterion "in general." Situation, action, the lines—everything is according to this criterion. Therefore one can just as well be made sad as ecstatic from laughter."[21] The spontaneous intervention of the viewer in the work, which supposedly defines farce as a form, only apparently has its origin in the principle of autocratic subjectivism. For this intervention is directed against the unity of the aesthetic object, a unity that itself testifies to the unity of subjective synthesis. It is enacted against the unity of the aesthetic object in momentary impulses that remain as incommensurable one to the other as laughter and sadness vis-à-vis the farce: they are responses to the alternation of images—"situations"—in whose "in general" the existence of the *dramatis personae*, as of the existing person, disappear. What Kierkegaard takes the license to say about the anarchy of farce could itself be dangerous to the hierarchy of spheres and challenges it, if only "aesthetically,"in the critique of the tragic: "Does the light-armed comedy hasten past the ethical to the unconcerned position of metaphysics? Does it want only to arouse laughter by making the contradiction manifest? And does tragedy on the other hand, heavy-armed as it is, remain mired in the ethical difficulty so that though the idea triumphs the hero is destroyed? placing the auditor in a rather discouraging position? For if he would like to be a hero, he must succumb without grace; and if he has no reason to fear for his life, since it is only heroes who must die, this is also bitter enough."[22] The tragic is, however, in every instance the presentation of a sacrifice, and Kierkegaard's critique of the hero's fall did not need to become speechless at the sight of the victim. For this reason, he occasionally defends the "aesthetic" against the "religious" earnestness that indeed alone draws the conclusions from sacrificial paradoxicalness: "In practice there is nothing more ludicrous than to see religious categories employed with profound and stupid earnestness where one ought to employ aesthetic categories with humor and jest."[23] The limitation of existential and religious "earnestness" makes room for those sympathies with materialist authors. This sympathy cannot be adequately explained by enmity toward Hegel or by the general structure of Kierkegaard's "dialectical" thought, for they are opposed to the predominant intention of this dialectic and are only able to intervene in the fissures of existential doctrine: "Writers such as Boerne, Heine, Feuerbach, etc., have great interest for an experimenter. They are for the most part very thoroughly informed about the religious, i.e. they know definitely that they want to have nothing to do with it. This is a great advantage over the 'systematic' writers who, without knowing in what the religious properly consists, undertake to explain it, at one moment deferentially, at another superciliously, but always incompetently. An unhappy, a jealous lover can know about love as well as a happy one, and so too one who is offended at the religious can in his way know about the religious just as well as the believer. Therefore, since our age furnishes few examples of men who in a great sense are believers, one has reason to be glad that there are some right clever men who are scandalized at religion."[24] They are scandalized on account of a wish that does not accommodate itself to sacrifice and rises in the collapse of existence, becoming luminous as it passes away: "If you have nothing else to say but that this is not to be endured, then you will have to look about for a better world."[25] Not the hubris of grandeur with which the 'moralist' so scornfully reproaches the "aesthete," but rather the reverse of the hubris of greatness is his best attribute. It is the cell of a materialism whose vision is focused on "a better world" — not to forget in dreams the present world, but to change it by the strength of an image that indeed may be as a whole "portrayed according to the abstract criterion 'in general' " whose contours are concretely and unequivocally filled in every particular dialectical element.

Images and Spheres

The quintessence of such images is Kierkegaard's "aesthetic sphere." Its unity is based on its contents and not on the manner of its subjective constitution. It is the region of dialectical semblance, in which truth is promised historically through the collapse of existence, whereas the "ethical" and "religious" spheres, on the contrary, remain those of subjective, sacrificial conjuration, forfeiting hope with the abnegation of semblance. At the end of *In vino veritas*, Kierkegaard gives a metaphor of the aesthetic sphere that captures this more precisely than any of William's conceptual efforts because it grasps the realm of images itself in an image. After the banquet, "Constantine took leave of them as host, informing them that there were five carriages at their service, so that each might follow his own inclination, drive whither he would, alone, or, if he would in company, and with whomsoever he would."[26] And the passage continues with the following image: "Thus it is that a rocket by the force of powder rises as a single shot, stands for an instant still, collected as one entity, then disperses to all the winds."[27] This is none other than the idea of the aesthetic sphere. Liberated from the subjective dialectic, eclipsing it entirely, pausing in the eternity of the instant, as an illusory unity, dispersing the light of hope over those things to which it belongs, as does the rocket to the modern antiquity of pyrotechnics. Just how much the form of the aesthetic, as a historical-primordial form, is comparable to the form in which the innermost cell of Kierkegaard's philosophy, the *intérieur*, today presents itself to an observer is irrefutably confirmed by the subsequent course of the earlier narrative: "The figures and the groups they formed made a fantastic impression upon me. For that the morning sun shines upon field and meadow and upon every creature which at night found rest and strength to arise jubilant with the sun — with this we have a sympathetic and wholesome understanding; but a nocturnal party beheld by morning illumination, in the midst of a smiling rustic environment, makes an almost uncanny impression. One begins to think of ghosts that are surprised by the dawn of day, of elves that cannot find the crevice through which they are accustomed to vanish because it is visible only in the dark, of unfortunates for whom the difference between day and night has become obliterated by the monotony of their suffering."[28] Kierkegaard's image is more interesting than when it is seen in terms of the cheap antithesis of original innocence and corruption. Those gentlemen in dress-coats do not profane the pure nature of morning: before its purity they are transformed into natural spirits by means of their costume—the most transient thing about them—whereby eternity itself shines through as the content of transience. The hope that inheres in the aesthetic is that of the transparence of decaying figures. Or, in the theological terms of Kierkegaard's later presentation of 'holy history': "In a certain sense, it is true, glory shines through here as well."[29] For just as Kierkegaard's verdict on the aesthetic sphere hardly matches with its contents, so its images are hardly restricted to the domain that his doctrine of existence has granted it. If the paradoxical remains at the mercy of nature, it does not extend over all mythical images; the final such image in front of which the paradoxical stops—the "N.B." of the "Passion Narrative"—is the first auspicious image of aesthetic semblance. Kierkegaard's distinctly Baroque characteristic is to be recognized in the significance that his philosophy attributes to the phenomenon of the crucifixion of Christ: "Think then of a child, and give this child delight by showing it some of those pictures one buys on the stalls, which are so trivial artistically, but so dear to children. This one here on the snorting steed, with a tossing feather in his hat, with a lordly mien, riding at the head of the thousands upon thousands which you do not see, with hand outstretched to command, 'Forward!' forward over the summits of the mountains which you see in front of you, forward to victory—this is the Emperor, the one and only, Napoleon. And so now you tell the child a little about Napoleon.—This one here is dressed as a huntsman; he stands leaning upon his bow and gazes straight before him with glance so piercing, so self-confident, and yet so anxious. That is William Tell. You now relate to the child something about him, and about that extraordinary glance of his, explaining that with this same glance he has at once an eye for the beloved child, that he may not harm him, and for the apple, that he may not miss it. And thus you show the child many pictures, to the child's unspeakable delight. Then you come to one which intentionally was laid among the others. It represents a man crucified. The child will not at once nor quite directly understand this picture, and will ask what it means, why he hangs like that on a tree. So you explain to the child that this is a cross, and that to hang on it means to be crucified, and that in that land crucifixion was not only the most painful death penalty but was also an ignominious mode of execution employed only for the grossest malefactors."[30] Of all the images, only one—dialectically—endures: "For just as a reproach to the Jews there was written above his cross, 'The King of the Jews,' so this picture, which regularly is published every year as a reproach to the human race, is a remembrance which the race never can and never should be rid of, it never should be represented differently; and it will seem as if it were *this* generation which crucified him, as often as *this* generation for the first time shows this picture to the child of the new generation, explaining for the first time how things go in this world; and the child, the first time it hears this, will become anxious and sorrowful, for his parents, for the world, and for himself; and the other pic-

tures—surely as the ballad relates"—the ballad of Agnes and the merman—
"they must turn their faces away, the pictures being so different."[31] Accordingly,
for Kierkegaard the original experience of Christianity remains bound to the
image; in the image one generation gives the other the idea of Christ; his image—
like his name—endures as an irreducibly mythical residue. But it endures dialectically: it is at the same time the overcoming of the demonic in nature; it is the
ultimate image, as it is the ultimate sacrifice; before the image of Christ all other
images must "avert their eyes." His image goes beyond all art; it is "insignificant from the artistic point of view" and yet itself an image; thus it rescues the
aesthetic even as the aesthetic is lost, and remaining paradoxical, opens the way
to reconciliation. Therefore many of the metaphors of *The Sickness unto Death*,
while never finding a place in the rigorous logic of existence, are akin to the
major themes of the "Diapsalmata" and the "aesthetic sphere": "It is (to
describe it figuratively) as if an author were to make a slip of the pen, and that
this clerical error became conscious of being such—perhaps it was no error but in
a far higher sense was an essential constituent in the whole exposition—it is then
as if this clerical error would revolt against the author, out of hatred for him were
to forbid him to correct it, and were to say, 'No, I will not be erased,I will stand
as a witness against thee, that thou art a very poor writer.' "[32] Just as the isolated
and enciphered letter is not subordinated to the total, "existential" expression of
the author, so in Kierkegaard's theology enciphered images oppose the existential
sacrifice and in the midst of its abstracting annihilation grants the solace of their
concretion. That which sets itself up against subjective idealism in the aesthetic
sphere, the ontological character of a "text," whose truth the individual means
to secure as a mere sign; the depersonalization of the self from which a meaningful letter emancipates itself—this determines Kierkegaard's theological stage
in the doctrine of objective despair. The parenthetical possibility, however, that
ultimately the "typographical error" itself would prove to be meaningful is the
nonsensical caesura that brings hope into existence through its collapse. Existence, despair, and hope—it is with this rhythm, not the monotonous rhythm of
the absolute "I" and total sacrifice, that Kierkegaard's ontology must be measured, and it appears in the disparate images into which the abstract unity of
existence is dialectically divided. In these images the "aesthetic" and the "religious" spheres go over into each other and not simply—as Kierkegaard supposes
on systematic grounds—as an "exception" that has no part in life. It occurs
rather in a depersonalization of the living in which life, while passing away, yet
breathes and rests free of sacrifice. Its metaphor is sleep. Kierkegaard uses the
image to characterize the two extreme spheres. It is found in the "aesthetic"
"Diapsalmata": "I divide my time as follows: half the time I sleep, the other half
I dream. I never dream when I sleep, for that would be a pity, for sleeping is the
highest accomplishment of genius."[33] In the *Training in Christianity*, however, it
is said of the believer: "Blessed is he who is not offended but believes, who (like

a child who is taught to say these words as it falls asleep) says, 'I believe' . . . and then sleeps; yea, blessed is he, he is not dead, he sleepeth.''[34] Such sleep is the dialectical double meaning of *passio*: "I must have my sleep to maintain passion in the long run.''[35] For in sleep *passio* obeys nature and yet receives the promise of blissful awakening.

Subjective "How" and Enmity toward Art

In the sleeper the spontaneity of the "I" comes to rest, without, however, being annihilated. If the aesthetic images that surround him are—as ontological semblance—located beyond subjective autonomy, Kierkegaard's theory of the subjective "how" and its correlate, the verdict on the "aesthetic sphere," lose their ultimate legitimation. For the knowledge of the subjective thinker, and all art, always remains—in Kierkegaard's view—"communication": "Objective thinking is . . . conscious only of itself, and is not in the strict sense of the word a form of communication at all, and certainly no artistic communication, in so far as artistry would always demand reflection on the recipient, and an awareness of the form of the communication in relation to the recipient's possible misunderstanding.''[36] Communication, however, is bound to autonomy: to the autonomy of the person communicating who imposes a form on a certain "content" and to that of the fictional and abstract recipient whose interest in "understanding" determines the form. Communication vitiates the law inherent in the object itself. "The greater the artistry, the greater the inwardness''[37]—this may be the regulating principle of Kierkegaardian "communication," but it is not a law of art. However conciliatory such communication might appear in the service of human understanding, it yet belongs exclusively to the realm of abstract inwardness. Only alienated, mute contents can be adapted, dressed up, and "communicated" as "content" to suit a subjective will; only to the extent that they are not binding are they made so by individual existence. The "how" of communication remains a subjective surrogate for the compelling appearance that threatens to perish of its own abstractness. For this reason, Kierkegaard's doctrine of communication is paradoxically concerned with the idea of a "neighbor," whom his absolute subjectivity has long since lost track of. The doctrine must orient itself by this neighbor, contingent and unknown as he is, because in its complete abstraction it acquires no law of form from the concreteness of its contents. It tries powerlessly to conjure this law of form through the repetitions of "double reflection." Artworks are eloquent by means of their law of form in the uncompromising presentation of truth through their semblance. Kierkegaard's unmanifest "existential" communication remains a monologue precisely with regard to the "neighbor" that does not exist for it. His "subjective how" reflects distortedly the power of truth over the manner of its appearance, a manner that can never be separated arbitrarily from it as if it were a mere sign, for truth itself exists exclusively in the dialectic in which it "appears". The "how"—developed by Kierkegaard in opposition to the shallow dualism of form and content—gains its philosophical justification as the expression of objective laws in the manifestation of truth. Yet his doctrine qualifies this justification by consigning it to subjectivity which superadds truth to the matter at hand as something new; by dividing truth from the material in which it appears; by ascribing truth to existence and contingency to the material. However fruitful the linguistic-critical norms prove to be when applied to the material at hand—norms which Kierkegaard poses with the "subjective how" of a philosophy that threatens to succumb to scientism—the theoretical justification of these norms through pure subjectivity misses the point of philosophy and art. For this reason Kierkegaard anathematizes the "aesthetic sphere" and finally art altogether. This malediction has been less compellingly formulated by the existential philosophers than by the theologian who relies not on the concept of subjective decisiveness but on the obligation to be Christ's follower, harking back to the prohibition on graven images: "Only the 'follower' is the true Christian. The 'admirers' have in fact a pagan relationship to Christianity, and hence admiration gave rise to a new paganism in the midst of Christendom, namely, Christian art. I do not wish in any way to pass judgment upon any one, but I regard it as my duty to pronounce what I feel. Would it be possible for me, that is to say, could I bring myself to the point, or could I be prompted, to dip my brush, to lift my chisel, in order to depict Christ in color or to carve His figure? The fact that I am incapable of doing it, that I am not an artist, is here irrelevant, I merely ask whether it would be possible for me to do it if I had the capacity. And I answer, No, it would be for me an absolute impossibility. Indeed, even with this I do not express what I feel, for in such a degree would it be impossible for me that I cannot conceive how it has been possible to anyone. A person says, 'I cannot conceive of the calmness of the murderer who sits sharpening the knife with which he is about to kill another man.' And to me, too, this is inconceivable. But truly it is also inconceivable to me whence the artist derived his calm, or the calmness is inconceivable to me with which an artist has sat year in and year out industriously laboring to paint a portrait of Christ—without chancing to reflect whether Christ desired perhaps to have a portrait made by his master-brush, however idealized it might be. I cannot conceive how the artist preserved his calm, how it is that he did not notice Christ's displeasure and suddenly cast down brush and colors and all, as Judas did the thirty pieces of silver, casting them far, far away from him, because he suddenly understood that Christ required only "followers', that he who here on earth lived in poverty and wretchedness, not having whereon to lay his head, and who lived thus not accidentally, because of the harshness of fate, desiring for himself different conditions, but of his own free choice, by virtue of an eternal resolve—that such as he hardly desired or desires that after his death a man should throw away his time, perhaps his eternal blessedness, by painting him. I cannot conceive it, the brush would have fallen out of my hand the very second I was about to begin, and perhaps I might not have survived it."[38] As a likeness of the living, art is sacrificed to the followers in death: "How a man is to fare in this world is something which the Gospel (in contrast with novels, romances, lies, and other amusements) does not amuse itself by considering. No, for the Gospel these seventy years are like an instant, and its talk hastens on to the decision of eternity."[39] Yet the later Kierkegaard's antagonism toward art cannot simply be reduced to the category of sacrifice. For at the same time, as the final rejoinder of the dialectic of semblance, his antipathy for art expresses the longing for an imageless presence. Kierkegaard's material aesthetic itself indicates the theological concept of the symbol as the idea of an imageless self-presentation of truth. For this reason he entirely excludes from the verdict on art the children's storybook image of the crucifixion, which is as little subject to aesthetic semblance as to any law of form. Kierkegaard's inconspicuousness does not mean the simple annihilation of semblance in death, but its finite extinguishing in truth, which, were it to be incarnated would cause the images to disappear in which truth has its historical life. This is indicated by a noteworthy passage in the second part of *Either/Or*, which, while expressly defending the "aesthetic legitimacy" of an inconspicuous existence, effectively specifies the limit of the images more precisely than can be achieved by the mythical abstraction of the self: "In this instance duration cannot be concentrated, for the point is time in its extension; and therefore neither poetry nor art can represent the ideal husband. At the end of fifteen years he has apparently got no further than he was at the beginning, yet he has lived in a high degree aesthetically. His possession has not been like dead property, but he has constantly been acquiring his possession. He has not fought with lions and ogres, but with the most dangerous enemy: with time. But for him eternity does not come afterwards as in the case of the knight, but he has had eternity in time, has preserved eternity in time. He alone, therefore, has triumphed over time. For the knight, in contrast, has merely killed time, just as any man kills time when it has not reality for him; this, however, is no final victory. Thus the married man lives truly poetically and solves the great riddle: he lives in eternity and yet hearing the hall clock strike, and hearing it in such a way that the stroke of the hour does not shorten but prolongs his eternity — a wondrous paradox. . . . And now even if this is something which cannot be represented in art, we need not regret it. Let it be your comfort as it is mine that the highest and most beautiful things in life are not to be heard about, nor read about, nor seen, but, may only be lived. Conjugal love is therefore more aesthetic than romantic love precisely because it is so much more difficult to represent."[40] If happiness itself, the focal point of wish and cipher of all images, knows no images, then Kierkegaard's doctrine of a "burden of hope"[41] which imposes the doctrine's images, resplendent and fruitful, upon happiness, can be redeemed. Of course, in Kierkegaard the idea of such truth becomes confused with the simple iconoclasm of subjective abstraction and repudiates aesthetic semblance without pursuing the course of the dialectic to its end, a course which the translucence of semblance makes evident in semblance itself. Kierkegaard undialectically takes the images for finite goods that obstruct the infinite good of happiness. According to the doctrine found in the *Postscript* "eternal happiness, as the absolute good, has the remarkable trait of being definable solely in terms of the mode of acquisition. Other goods, precisely because the mode of acquisition is accidental, or at any rate subject to a relative dialectic, must be defined in terms of the good itself."[42] As little, however, as happiness may be defined by its "mode of acquisition," just so little may the "goods" be defined by "themselves" in their reified finitude, but only from the perspective in which they appear historically-dialectically to the wish as finite yet unattainable. Kierkegaard, however, takes the emptiness of the fully abstracted concept for imageless happiness itself. Therefore the dialectic of images that are at once more finite, unreachable, and transparently promising becomes for Kierkegaard a merely mythical deception; their dialectical structure becomes the ambiguity of the contingent: "What the philosophers say about reality is often as disappointing as a sign you see in a shop window, which reads: 'Pressing Done Here.' If you brought your clothes to be pressed, you would be fooled; for the sign is there only to be sold."[43] This criticism neglects the best dialectical truth in philosophy as much as in art: the truth that presents itself in semblance. In fact, Kierkegaard nowhere better described the reconciling figure in which his own philosophy joins nature and history, than in a passage directed against Hegel that meant to destroy this figure as semblance, while yet its semblance, recognized and maintained, serves truth as its truest counterimage: "Some bend eternity into time for the imagination. Conceived in this way, eternity produces an enchanting effect. One does not know whether it is dream or actuality. As the beams of the moon glimmer in an illuminated forest or a hall, so the eternal peeps wistfully, dreamily, and roguishly into the moment."[44]

Fantasy in the Fragment

Here it is fantasy—repudiated by Kierkegaard—that conceives semblance as the instrument of an unbroken transition from the mythical-historical to reconciliation, whereas his doctrine exclusively recognizes the self and the leap. "In a speculative-fantastic sense we have a positive finality in the system, and in an aesthetic-fantastic sense we have one in the fifth act of the drama. But this sort of finality is valid only for fantastic beings."[45] Yet as an opponent of fantasy Kierkegaard reveals the deepest insight into its essence, just as the organization of the "Diapsalmata" legitimates itself as a work of exact fantasy. "For the imagination is itself more perfect than the sufferings of reality, it is timelessly qualified, soaring above the sufferings of reality, it is capable of presenting perfection admirably, it possesses all the splendid colors for portraying it; but suffering, on the other hand, is something the imagination cannot represent, except in a rendering that represents it as already perfected, that is, softened, toned-down, foreshortened. For the imaginary picture, that is, the picture that the imagination presents and fixes, is after all, in a certain sense, unreality, it lacks the reality of time and duration and of the earthly life with its difficulties and sufferings. . . . An actor clad in rags (even if in defiance of stage convention they were actual rags) is, as the mere deceit of an hour, a totally different thing from being clad in rags in the everyday life of reality. No, however great the effort of imagination to make this imaginary picture of reality, it cannot be accomplished.''[46] If indeed fantasy is unable to grasp concretely the ultimate image of despair—as in Poe's story ''The Pit and the Pendulum'' the most horrifying secret of the pit is not depicted—this incapacity is not a weakness but a strength. The element of reconciliation that makes its transient appearance in fantasy still suffices to dissolve despair, whereas existence irresistibly rushes into that very despair. The inability of fantasy to represent despair is its surety of hope. In fantasy nature surpasses itself: nature, the impulse of fantasy; nature, which—in fantasy—recognizes itself; nature, which through the minutest displacement by fantasy presents itself as rescued. Through displacement: for fantasy is not contemplation that leaves the existing as it is; contemplating, it enters unnoticed into the existing to complete its composition as an image. Kierkegaard recognized the model of its composition, far from any autonomous aesthetic ''form,'' in the activity of a child cutting out pictures: ''At times we see the more mature individuality who satiates himself on the strong food of actuality and is not really influenced by a well-executed painting. But he can be stirred by a Nuernberg print, a picture of the kind found on the market not long ago. There one sees a landscape depicting a perfect rural area in general. This abstraction cannot be artistically executed. Therefore the whole thing is achieved by contrast, namely, by an accidental concretion. And yet I ask everyone if from such a landscape he does not get the impression of a perfect rural area in general, and if this category has not stayed with him from childhood. In the days of childhood, we had such enormous categories that they now almost make us dizzy, we clipped out of a piece of paper a man and a woman who were man and woman in general in a more rigorous sense than Adam and Eve were.''[47] The ''in general'' of the Nuernberg print is similar to that of the farce, but is described by Kierkegaard more exactly, making it more amenable to interpretation than in the theory of the farce. It is not the abstractness and range of the concept, but the minute precision and concreteness of a model— in one variety it is familiar as a ''pattern''—in which individual differences of existence disappear only to be resurrected, saved ontologically, as prototypical features of the completed figure. Like names, the pattern attaches contingency, as "accidental concretion," to the most universal concept; and more, it binds it to the natural-historical prototype, Adam and Eve, whom anamnesis appropriates for the instant and for all time by developing their contours, as their "second nature,"[48] out of the chaos of the sheet of paper. Through fantasy, as recollection, genius continuously restores original creation—not as the creator of its reality but by the reintegration of its given elements in an image. The moments of fantasy are the festivals of history. As such, they belong to the free, liberated time of childhood, and their material is as historical as the storybook. Just as in the child creation reproduces itself in miniature, fantasy imitates creation through miniaturization. "This is the sophistical inclination of imagination, to have the whole world in a nutshell this way, a nutshell larger than the whole world and yet not too large for the individual to fill."[49] It is not, however, its sophistical inclination, but purely and simply the idea by which fantasy proceeds. Fantasy achieves the transition only in the nutshell, in the nutshell that is indeed "larger than the whole world" of what merely is, because it goes beyond it infinitesimally. Therefore it is not the total self and its total structure, but exclusively the fragment of collapsing existence, free of all subjective "meaning," that is a sign of hope; its fault lines are the true ciphers, at once historical and ontological. One of the diapsalmata mournfully compares the idea of a fissured, fragmentary individual to that of an enigmatical disparate text: "My life is absolutely meaningless. When I consider the different periods into which it falls, it seems like the word *Schnur* in the dictionary, which means in the first place a string, in the second, a daughter-in-law. The only thing lacking is that the word *Schnur* should mean in the third place a camel, in the fourth, a dust-brush."[50] The insight of *The Sickness unto Death* gets more to the heart of the matter than the systematizer's lament: "The earthly and temporal as such are precisely what falls apart into the particular. It is impossible actually to lose or be deprived of all that is earthly, for the determinant of totality is a thought-determinant."[51] Through recollection, fantasy transforms the traces of the collapse of a sinful creation into a sign of hope for one that is whole and without sin and whose image it forms out of ruins: "A completely finished work has no relation to the poetic personality; in the case of posthumous papers one constantly feels, because of the incompletion, the desultoriness, a need to romance about the personality. Posthumous papers are like a ruin, and what haunted place could be more natural for the interred? The art, then, is artistically to produce the same effect, the same appearance of carelessness and the accidental, the same anacoluthic flight of thought; the art consists in producing an enjoyment which never actually becomes present, but always has an element of the past in it, so that it is present in the past. This has already been expressed in the word: posthumous."[52] If the history of sinful nature is that of the collapse of its unity, it moves toward reconciliation even while collapsing, and its fragments bear the fissures of collapse as propitious ciphers. In these terms Kierkegaard's thought—that through sin the individual stands higher than before — is authenticated; it is the basis of his doctrine of the ambivalence of anxiety, the sickness unto death, as a means of salvation. Unintentionally, his negative philosophy of history as the expression of mere "existence" reverses itself, and presents itself to the idealist's lamenting gaze as a positive, eschatological philosophy of history.

Transcendence of Longing

The ontological "project" that criticism seeks to crystalize out of Kierkegaard's philosophy — in spite of Kierkegaard's dominant intentions and those of the systematic structure — has nothing in common with the totality of his "religious" sphere, though at the most perhaps something with his "faith," which he rebuts in *Fear and Trembling*: "a faith that faintly seeks its object on the most distant horizon."[53] This "most remote possibility of faith"[54] is the law by which the depth of beauty is measured. This law is implicit in the single metaphor in which Kierkegaard gives concrete witness to the idea of reconciliation: the merman, a reconciled power of nature through his love of Agnes, is called: "beautiful as a guardian angel."[55] Every aesthetic form is directed toward truth and disappears in it. It is not by accident that Kierkegaard compared the course of music to a descent from on high: "If in the overture one comes down from these higher regions, then it may be asked where one lands best in the opera, or how does one get the opera to begin?"[56] He compared, however, the transition of arrival with the "shock of awakening" — drawing on another opera, the "Magic Flute."[57] If, as Kierkegaard writes, "longing alone is not sufficient for salvation,"[58] still the images of beauty devolve upon longing through which the course of deliverance, disappearing, must travel if it is ever to lead to landing and awakening; longing is, accordingly, the dialectical substratum of a "doctrine of reconciliation"[59] that Kierkegaard's theology of sacrifice would like to emancipate from longing. Longing is not extinguished in the images, but survives in them just as it emanates from them. By the strength of the immanence of their content, the transcendence of longing is achieved. Their inconspicuousness is for the sake of the inconspicuous, and it wishes nourishment finally for those who are deprived. This is how the "aesthetic" and the "religious" coincide in poverty, as Kierkegaard teaches: "Do you think that it is almost a kind of childishness in me to persist in seeking this quality among the poor and the suffering? Or maybe you have degraded yourself by adopting the shocking division that assigns the aesthetic to the distinguished, the rich, the mighty, the highly educated, and at the most assigns religion to the poor? Well, it seems to me that the poor do not come out badly in this division. And do you not see that the poor in having the religious have also the aesthetic, and that the rich, in so far as they have not the religious, have not the aesthetic either?"[60] For the "aesthetic" does not exist for the poor in aesthetic objects but in the concrete images of their desire; only in their ful-fillment without sacrifice do these images open themselves up to the poor. For this reason, on one occasion, Kierkegaard makes poverty the guarantor of hap-piness: "What is the happiest existence? It is that of a young girl of sixteen years when she, pure and innocent, possesses nothing, not a chest of drawers or a ped-estal, but has to make use of the lowest drawer of her mother's escritoire to keep all her magnificence: the confirmation dress and a prayer-book."[61] In such sen-tences, whose simplicity is exposed to every ideological hazard, poverty and des-titution call up comfort and reconciliation, as in this draft of Kierkegaard's letter to his fiancee: "In my mournfulness I have had only one wish: to make her happy; right now, I am unable; now I go to her side and like a master of ceremo-nies I lead her triumphantly and say: make room for her, give the best spot for 'our beloved, and dearest little Regina.' "[62] The inconspicuous hope of this image tempers even the violent image of death: "What is death? Only a brief stop along the once traveled road."[63] The banality of reconciliation is sublime: "This is how it is in time. As for eternity, it is my hope that we shall be comprehensible to one another, and that there she will forgive me."[64] For the step from mourning to comfort is not the largest, but the smallest.

Notes

Key to Kierkegaard Citations

Standard English translations have been used wherever possible. They have, however, frequently been adapted or corrected.

   I. *Either/Or*, volume I, translated by David F. Swenson and Lillian Marvin Swenson with revisions and a foreword by Howard A. Johnson (New Jersey: Princeton University Press, 1971).

  II. *Either/Or*, volume 2, translated by Walter Lowrie with revisions and a foreword by Howard A. Johnson (New Jersey: Princeton University Press, 1971).

 III. *Fear and Trembling* and *Repetition*, edited and translated by Howard V. Hong and Edna H. Hong (New Jersey: Princeton University Press, 1983).

  IV. *Stages on Life's Way*, translated by Walter Lowrie (New Jersey: Princeton University Press, 1940).

   V. *The Concept of Anxiety*, edited and translated with introduction and notes by Reidar Thomte in collaboration with Albert B. Anderson (New Jersey: Princeton University Press, 1980).

  VI. *Philosophical Fragments*, originally translated and introduced by David Swenson; new introduction and commentary by Niels Thulstrup; translation revised and commentary translated by Howard V. Hong (New Jersey: Princeton University Press, 1967).

 VII. *Concluding Unscientific Postscript*, translated by David F. Swenson and Walter Lowrie (New Jersey: Princeton University Press, 1968).

VIII. *Fear and Trembling and The Sickness unto Death*, translated with an introduction and notes by Walter Lowrie (New Jersey: Princeton University Press, 1974).

  IX. *Training in Christianity and the Edifying Discourse Which 'Accompanied' It*, translated with an introduction and notes by Walter Lowrie (New Jersey: Princeton University Press, 1972).

   X. *The Point of View, etc., including The Point of View for My Work as an Author*, translated with an introduction and notes by Walter Lowrie (London: Oxford University Press, 1939).

  XI. *For Self-Examination and Judge for Yourselves!*, translated by Walter Lowrie (New Jersey: Princeton University Press).

 XII. *Attack Upon "Christendom,"* translated with an introduction and notes by Walter Lowrie; new introduction by Howard A. Johnson (New Jersey: Princeton University Press, 1972).

XIII. *Christian Discourses; The Lilies of the Field and the Birds of the Air; Three Discourses at the Communion on Fridays*, translated with an introduction by Walter Lowrie (New Jersey: Princeton University Press, 1974).

 XIV. *The Concept of Irony*, translated with an introduction and notes by Lee M. Capel (Bloomington: Indiana University Press, 1965).

Motto. Edgar Allan Poe, "A Descent into the Malestroem", *Best Tales of Edgar Allan Poe* (New York: Modern Library, n.d.), p. 34.

Notes

Unless otherwise indicated, translations of foreign-language quotations are my own—translator.

Foreword: Critique of the Organic

1. T. W. Adorno and Max Horkheimer, *The Dialectic of Englightenment*, translated by John Cumming (NY: Herder and Herder, 1972), 51.

2. Adorno, *Aesthetic Theory*, revised translation by R. Hullot-Kentor (London: Routledge and Kegan Paul, in preparation); *Aesthetische Theorie*, edited by Rolf Tiedemann and Gretl Adorno (Frankfurt: Suhrkamp Verlag, 1971), 84.

3. Adorno, *Kierkegaard: Konstruktion des Aesthetischen* (Frankfurt: Suhrkamp Verlag, 1962), 293.

4. Adorno, this translation, 131.

5. Ibid., 118.

6. Ibid., 110.

7. Ibid., 131.

8. Leo Lowenthal, "Recollections of Adorno," *Telos* 61 (Fall, 1984), 160–61.

9. Adorno, "Kierkegaard's Doctrine of Love," *Zeitschrift fuer Sozialforschung*, 8, 413–29.

10. *Kierkegaard: Konstruktion des Aesthetischen*, 294–95.

11. Walter Benjamin, "Kierkegaard: Das Ende des philosophischen Idealismus," *Gesammelte Schriften*, v. 3, edited by Hella Tiedemann–Bartels (Frankfurt: Suhrkamp Verlag, 1972), 383.

12. F. J. Brecht, *Kant Studien*, v. 40 (1935), 327.

13. Helmut Kuhn, *Zeitschrift fuer Aesthetic und allgemeine Kunstwissenschaft*, v. 28 (1934), p. 104.

14. Anon., *Koelner Vierteljahrschrift fuer Soziologie*, v. 12 (1934), 198.

15. Karl Loewith, *Deutsche Literaturzeitung*, v. 4 (1934), 28.

16. Adorno, "The Essay as Form," translated by R. Hullot-Kentor and Frederic Will, *New German Critique* 32, 141–43.

17. Adorno, *Minima Moralia*, translated by E. F. N. Jepcott (London: NLB, 1978), 71.

18. See R. Hullot-Kentor, "Adorno's Aesthetics: The Translation," *Telos* 65 (Fall, 1985), 143–47.

19. *Minima Moralia*, 71.

20. This translation, 29.

21. Adorno, "Vers une musique informelle," *Gesammelte Schriften*, v. 16, edited by Rolf Tiedemann (Frankfurt: Suhrkamp Verlag, 1978), 500.

22. *Minima Moralia*, 71.

23. Without any German it is hard to imagine what this does to a sentence. But it is something like saying: "He takes seriously himself."

24. "Vers une musique informelle," 528–30.

25. Adorno, "Der wunderliche Realist: Ueber Siegfried Kracauer," *Gesammelte Schriften*, v. 11, edited by Rolf Tiedemann (Frankfurt: Suhrkamp Verlag, 1974), 388.

26. This review got as far as being typeset before it was blocked by the National Socialist censors. It is currently among Kracauer's posthumous papers at the Deutches Literatur Archiv am Neckar, Marbach.

27. This translation, 85.

28. How interpretation is to proceed was the question that ultimately divided Adorno from Benjamin. Benjamin wanted to present montages of images; they would speak out of their dense juxtaposition. In the vast quotations assembled in *Kierkegaard*, this book stands closest of all of Adorno's writings to Benjamin's ideal: many of these passages are expected to speak for themsleves. A good part of the obscurity of the study originates here. Adorno ultimately rejected montage as a form that would only relive the dream, not interpret it, and return the work to the historicism that was to be overcome. In Adorno's later studies quotations become sparser and the weight of interpretation increasingly falls to the work of dialectical concepts.

29. This translation, 11.

30. Ibid.

31. This translation, 41.

32. See Susan Buck-Morss, *The Origins of Negative Dialectics* (NY: Free Press, 1977), and Carlo Pettazzi, "Studien zu Leben und Werk Adornos bis 1938" *Text + Kritik*, Special Adorno Issue, ed. H. L. Arnold, 28–37.

33. See Fred R. Dallmayr, "Adorno and Phenomenology," *Cultural Hermeneutics* 3 (1976), 367–405.

34. Adorno, "Der Begriff des Unbewussten in der transzendentalen Seelenlehre, *Gesammelte Schriften*, v. 1, edited by Rolf Tiedemann (Frankfurt: Suhrkamp Verlag, 1973), 156.

35. Hanns Eisler, *Composing for the Films* (Oxford: Oxford University Press, 1947), 77–78. As Adorno mentions in a note appended to the German edition of this book [Adorno and Eisler, *Komposition fuer den Film*, edited by Rolf Tiedemann (Frankfurt: Suhrkamp Verlag, 1976), 144–46], he was actually the principal author of the English edition as well, but renounced co-authorship to avoid American political entanglements that he feared would result in legal complexities that would interfere with his desire to return to Europe. The book is of great interest for the study of film, though largely unknown because it has been out of print so long.

36. "Vers une musique informelle," 538.

37. Adorno, "Faellige Revision: Zu Schweppenhaeusers Buch ueber Kierkegaard und Hegel," *Gesammelte Schriften*, v. 20.1, edited by Rolf Tiedemann (Frankfurt: Suhrkamp Verlag, 1987), 258.

38. Ibid., 263.

39. Ibid., 256.

40. Ibid., 39.

41. Ibid., 37.

42. Ibid., 48.

43. Ibid., 52.

44. Ibid., 53.

45. Ibid., 52.

46. Ibid.

47. Walter Benjamin, *The Origin of the German Play of Lamentation* [title corrected], translated by John Osbourne (London: NLB, 1977), 180.

48. Marcel Proust, *Swan's Way*, translated by C. K. Monscrieff (NY: Modern Library Editions), 100.

49. Ibid.

50. Ibid., 101.

51. Ibid.

52. Adorno, "The Idea of Natural History," translated by R. Hullot-Kentor, *Telos* 60 (Summer, 1984), 120.

53. Ibid., 117.

54. Adorno, *Philosophische Terminologie*, v. 1, ed. Rudolf zur Lippe (Frankfurt: Suhrkamp, 1974), 82.

55. Ibid., 83.

56. Adorno and Ernst Krenek, *T. W. Adorno und Ernst Krenek: Briefwechsel*, edited by Wolfgang Rogge (Frankfurt: Suhrkamp, 1974), 34–35.

57. The manuscript of Adorno's *Habilitationschrift* is among his papers at the Adorno Archiv in Frankfurt.

58. This translation, 3.

59. Adorno, "Introduction to the Writings of Walter Benjamin," translated by R. Hullot-Kentor, in *Walter Benjamin: Critical Essays and Reflections*, edited by Gary Smith (Cambridge: MIT Press, 1988), 16.

60. This translation, 126.

61. Adorno's effort to document hope perhaps explains the important distortion late in the book where, in a discussion of Kierkegaard's famous revision of the story of the Merman and Agnes, Adorno mistakes the Merman for a "guardian angel," who is in fact Agnes.

62. *Aesthetic Theory*, revised edition.

63. Adorno probably knew no Danish. But in "Kierkegaard's Doctrine of Love" he does throw in a word of Danish, perhaps knowledgably, perhaps for clarification, perhaps to obfuscate a deficiency. A biography of Adorno has still not been written.

64. Peter von Haselberg, "Wiesengrund-Adorno," *Text + Kritik*, Special Adorno issue, 10.

Chapter 1. Exposition of the Aesthexia

1. Georg W. F. Hegel, *Phenomenology of Spirit*, trans. A. V. Miller (Oxford: Oxford University Press, 1977), 3– 4.

2. Ibid., 6–7.

3. Georg Lukács, *History and Class Consciousness*, trans. Rodney Livingstone (Cambridge, Mass.: MIT Press, 1968), xlxi.

4. III, 205 (Nachwort von Hermann Gottsched).

5. Ibid., 206.

6. X, 100.

7. Theodor Haecker, *Søren Kierkegaard und die Philosophie der Innerlichkeit* (Munich, 1913), 8.

8. I, 301–2.

9. III, 90; cf. ibid.

10. Kierkegaard, *Crisis in the Life of an Actress*, trans. Stephen Crites (London: Collins, 1967), 56.

148 □ NOTES

11. Lukács, *The Soul and the Forms*, trans. Anna Bostock (Cambridge, Mass.: MIT Press, 1974), 37.
12. August Vetter, *Froemmigkeit als Leidenschaft. Eine Deutung Kierkegaards* (Leipzig, 1928), 60–61.
13. I, 415.
14. IV, 33.
15. Ibid., 42.
16. Kierkegaard, *Die Tagebuecher*, 2 vols., selected and translated by Theodor Haecker (Innsbruck, 1923), vol. 2, 344.
17. Ibid., 345 ff.
18. Ibid., vol. 1, 21–22.
19. Christopher Schrempf, *Søren Kierkegaard. Eine Biographie*, vol. 1 (Jena, 1927), 40 ff.; cf. ibid., vol. 2 (Jena, 1928), 100 ff.; vol. 2, 155 ff.
20. Cf. Erich Przywara, S.J., *Das Geheimnis Kierkegaards* (Munich and Berlin, 1928), 11 ff.
21. Cf. Kierkegaard, *Tagebuecher*, vol. 1, 46.
22. Cf. Vetter, *Froemmigkeit*, 114 and 322–23.
23. X, 50.
24. Cf, I, 333.
25. II, 317 (Nachwort von Schrempf); cf. Schrempf, *Søren Kierkegaard*, vol. 1, 71.
26. I, 363–64.
27. Iv, 40.
28. I, 330.
29. III, 82–83.
30. X, 87.
31. IX, 198.
32. VIII, 206.
33. Ibid.
34. Cf. I, 48.
35. II, 182.
36. VII, 67–68.
37. Ibid., 68–69.
38. Ibid., 73.
39. Ibid., 72.
40. Przywara, *Das Geheimnis Kierkegaards*, 29.
41. II, 319 (Nachwort von Schrempf).
42. Hegel, *Aesthetics: Lectures on Fine Art*, trans. T. M. Knox (Oxford: Clarendon Press, 1985), 1201.
43. IV, 382.
44. II, 278.
45. VII, 459.
46. I, 48.
47. III, 106.
48. I, 46.
49. VII, 283.
50. IV, 414.
51. Ibid., 422.
52. Ibid., 369.
53. Ibid., 423.
54. I, 51.
55. Ibid.

56. Cf. II, 139.
57. Ibid., 138.
58. Ibid., 139.
59. Ibid., 139.
60. Cf. I, 49–50.
61. IV, 164.
62. Hegel, *The Philosophy of History*, trans. J. Sibree (New York: Dover Publications, 1956), 409.
63. I, 51.
64. Karl Rosenkranz, *Aesthetik des Haesslichen* (Koenigsberg, 1853), 180–81.
65. I, 49.
66. Ibid., 46.
67. Ibid., 52–53.
68. Cf. Ibid., 52.
69. Ibid., 65.
70. Ibid., 66.
71. Ibid., 53.
72. Ibid., 55.
73. Ibid., 55–56.
74. Ibid., 68.
75. VII, 297.

Chapter 2. Constitution of Inwardness

1. VII, 554.
2. Ibid., 552.
3. XII, 111.
4. IX, 152.
5. III, 121.
6. VII, 403.
7. II, 261.
8. Walter Benjamin, *Origin of the German Play of Lamentation* [title corrected], trans. John Osborne (London: NLR Press, 1977), 162–63.
9. Cf. Theodor Haecker, *Soeren Kierkegaard und die Philosophie der Innerlichkeit* (Munich, 1913), 33.
10. V, 15.
11. VIII, 255.
12. IV, 174.
13. Ibid., 238.
14. VII, 318.
15. X, 75.
16. XIV. 289–90.
17. VII, 292; cf. IV, 401–2.
18. XIV, 290.
19. I, 3.
20. VIII, 206.
21. VII, 284; cf. IV, 323.
22. II, 246.
23. Ibid., 247.
24. Ibid., 248.
25. Ibid., 248.

26. Ibid., 249.

27. Ibid., 252.

28. Ibid., 252.

29. Cf. ibid., 253.

30. X, 16.

31. IV, 124.

32. Ibid., 238.

33. Theodor Haecker, "Der Begriff der Wahrheit bei Søren Kierkegaard." Lecturer in *Hochland* 26 (1928/29) (no. 11; August 1929), 477.

34. Ibid.

35. Sven Helander, *Marx und Hegel. Eine kritische Studie ueber sozialdeomkratishce Weltanschauung* (Jena, 1922), 64; cf. Bendetto Croce, *Lebediges und Totes in Hegel's Philosophie* (Heidelberg, 1909), 78.

36. Eduard Geismar, *Søren Kierkegaard. Seine Entwicklung und seine Wirksamkeit als Schriftsteller* (Goettingen, 1929), 319.

37. II, 254–55.

38. V, 28–29.

39. Ibid., 29–30.

40. Ibid., 31.

41. Ibid., 33.

42. Ibid., 30.

43. Ibid., 31.

44. Ibid., 47.

45. IV, 377.

46. V, 52–53.

47. IX, 158.

48. Ibid., 181–82.

49. II, 137.

50. IX, 144.

51. Ibid., 67.

52. I, 137.

53. XII, 194–95.

54. II, 19.

55. VII, 318.

56. II, 31–32.

57. X, 37–38.

58. Ibid., 145.

59. XII, 144–45.

60. Ibid., 98.

61. Ibid., 271.

62. Cf. IV, 418 and VII, 196.

63. IX, 227–28.

64. Ibid., 22.

65. Ibid., 230.

66. XII, 81.

67. III, 27.

68. O. P. Monrad, *Søren Kierkegaard. Sein Leben und seine Werke* (Jena, 1909), 30.

69. Geismar, *Søren Kierkegaard.*

70. I, 349–50.

71. X, 87.

72. IV, 192.
73. I, 384–86.
74. IV, 437.
75. XI, 36.
76. VIII, 237.
77. Ibid., 238.
78. Ibid., 241.
79. Ibid., 255.
80. III, 151–52.
81. XI, 73.
82. Ibid., 47.
83. Cf. ibid., 73–74.

Chapter 3. Explication of Inwardness

1. VII, 59.
2. Ibid., 121.
3. Ibid., 553.
4. Karl Marx and Friedrich Engels, *The Holy Family*, in *Collected Works*, vol. 4 (New York: International Publishers), 36.
5. II, 184.
6. Ibid., 267.
7. IV, 62.
8. Schrempf, *Søren Kierkegaard. Eine Biographie*, vol. 1 (Jena, 1927), 63.
9. III, 121.
10. II, 122.
11. Ibid., 122.
12. Ibid., 125–26.
13. IV, 101.
14. Ibid.
15. X, 118.
16. VI, 23.
17. Ibid., 25.
18. Ibid.
19. X, 110.
20. XIV, 303.
21. I, 28.
22. II, 180.
23. I, 3.
24. VIII, 245.
25. XIV, 128.
26. Ibid., 129.
27. Ibid., 129.
28. Ibid., 131.
29. Ibid., 131.
30. Ibid., 131–32.
31. Ibid., 133–34.
32. Ibid., 135.
33. Walter Benjamin, *Origin of the German Play of Lamentation* [title corrected], trans. John Osborne (London: NLR Press, 1977), 166. (The *facies hippocratica* [Hippocratic face] is described by Francis Adams in his introduction to *The Genuine Works of Hippocrates* [New York: William

Wood, 1886], 195: This countenance, suffering from "the worst," is marked by "a sharp nose, hollow eyes, collapsed temples, the ears cold, contracted, and their lobes turned out: the skin about the forehead being rough, distended and parched; the color of the whole face being green, black, livid, or lead colored"—translator's note.)

34. I, 74.
35. Ibid., 75–76.
36. XIV, 134.
37. Ibid., 135.
38. I, 323.
39. Ibid., 154–55.
40. Ibid., 303.
41. V, 136.
42. Ibid., 123.
43. Ibid., 124.
44. VIII, 175.
45. VI, 24.
46. V, 124.
47. Ibid., 135.
48. Ibid., 119.
49. Lukács, *History and Class Consciousness*, trans. Rodney Livingstone (Cambridge, Mass.: MIT Press, 1968), 146–47.
50. I, 395.
51. III, 69.
52. Ibid.
53. VII, 65.
54. IV, 276.
55. VI, 24.
56. III, 173.
57. XIII, 226.
58. VIII, 180–81.
59. II, 25.
60. IV, 345–46.
61. I, 30.
62. IV, 262.
63. I, 167–68.
64. II, 165.
65. IV, 171.
66. Ibid., 406.
67. Ibid., 134.
68. Ibid., 390.
69. Ibid., 356.
70. X, 62.
71. Benjamin, *Origin of the German Play of Lamentation*, 80.
72. Cf. II, 186–87.
73. Cf. IV, 298–99.
74. Cf. ibid., 330–31.
75. Benjamin, *Origin of the German Play of Lamentation*, 85.
76. X, 76.
77. I, 423.
78. IV, 201.

79. Ibid., 220.
80. I, 82.
81. Ibid., 41.
82. Ibid., 142.
83. II, 278.
84. Ibid., 183.
85. III, 97.
86. XII, 201.
87. II, 229–30.
88. X, 132.
89. I, 30.

Chapter 4. Concept of Existence

1. Martin Heidegger, *Being and Time*, trans. John Macquarrie and Edward Robinson (New York: Harper and Row, 1962), 31. (On the translation of *Dasein* and *Existenz*, see the Foreword.)
2. Ibid., 34.
3. III, 200.
4. Cf., 430–31.
5. Heidegger, *Being and Time*, 32.
6. VII, 176–77.
7. Ibid., 176.
8. Ibid., 173.
9. Ibid., 176.
10. Ibid., 172.
11. Ibid., 181.
12. Ibid., 182.
13. Ibid., 178.
14. Ibid., 177.
15. Romano Guardini, "Der Ausgangspunkt der Denkbewegung Søren Kierkegaards." in *Hochland* 24 (1926/27) (no. 7; April 1927), 17.
16. Ibid.
17. Ibid.
18. V, 127.
19. II, 263.
20. V, 77–78.
21. Edmund Husserl, *Ideas*, trans. W. R. Boyce Gibbons (New York.: Collier, 1931), 337.
22. VII, 196.
23. Ibid.
24. V, 141.
25. Ibid., 143.
26. II, 225.
27. V, 149.
28. Ibid., 150.
29. Ibid., 151.
30. Ibid.
31. Ibid.
32. VII, 75–76.
33. II, 226.
34. Guardini, "Der Ausgangspunkt der Denkbewegung Søren Kierkegaards," 23.
35. VIII, 146.

36. Cf. this volume, p. 58.
37. VIII, 146.
38. IX, 159–60.
39. V, 55.
40. VIII, 147.
41. Ibid., 148.
42. Ernst Bloch, *Durch die Wueste*, Kritische Essays (Berlin, 1923), 110.
43. VIII, 201.
44. Ibid., 202.
45. Ibid., 156.
46. Ibid., 150.
47. Ibid., 150–51.
48. Ibid., 151.
49. Cf. ibid., 211, VI, 80.
50. VIII, 177.
51. II, 164.
52. VIII, 224.
53. II, 94.
54. VIII, 143.
55. Ibid., 236.
56. Ibid., 253–55.

Chapter 5. On the Logic of the Spheres

1. VIII, 507.
2. IV, 430.
3. VII, 448.
4. Ibid., 288.
5. Ibid., 507.
6. I, 83.
7. II, 61–62.
8. V, 144–45.
9. Ibid., 30.
10. Hegel, *Phenomenology of Spirit*, trans. A. V. Miller (Oxford: Oxford University Press, 1977), 6–7.
11. V, 30.
12. Ibid.
13. VII, 472.
14. VIII, 208.
15. VII, 433.
16. X, 158.
17. V, 166 (Nachwort von Schrempf).
18. Ibid., 9.
19. IV, 401–2.
20. VII, 401.
21. I, 236.
22. Ibid., 296.
23. III, 83.
24. VII, 449.
25. Ibid., 451–52.
26. Ibid., 461.

27. III, 92.
28. II, 230.
29. IX, cf. 98–99.
30. IX, 99.
31. Cf. VI, 72.
32. VII, 390–91.
33. Ibid., 28.
34. VI, 49.
35. IX, 33.
36. VIII, 228.
37. IV, 206.
38. VIII, 169.
39. VII, 293.
40. VIII, 173.
41. XI, 83–84.
42. II, 179–80.
43. I, 186–87.
44. Ibid., 219.
45. Ibid., 427–28.
46. III, 225.
47. X, 132.
48. Ibid., 31.
49. Ibid., 32.
50. Romano Guardini, "Der Ausgangspunkt der Denkbewegung Søren Kierkegaards." In *Hochland* 24 (1926/27) (no. 7; April 1927), 29.
51. IV, 163.
52. III, 214.

Chapter 6. Reason and Sacrifice

1. O. P. Monrad, *Søren Kierkegaard. Sein Leben und seine Werke* (Jena, 1909), 3.
2. Eduard Geismar, *Søren Kierkegaard. Seine Entwicklung und seine Wirksamkeit als Schriftsteller* (Goettingen, 1929), 14ff.
3. Monrad, *Søren Kierkegaard*, 4.
4. VI, 137–38.
5. III, 87.
6. I, 35.
7. Ibid., 111–12.
8. XI, 101.
9. Cf. Vii, 523 ff.
10. VII, 529.
11. Ibid., 536.
12. IX, 181.
13. V, 28.
14. III, 58.
15. XII, 205.
16. IX, 168.
17. Ibid., 169.
18. VII, 350.
19. XII, 243.
20. X, 79.

21. VIII, 257.

22. Ibid., 258.

23. IX, 131.

24. Ibid., 131–32.

25. Theodor Haecker, *Søren Kierkegaard und die Philosophie der Innerlichkeit* (Munich, 1913), 33.

26. VI, 46.

27. VIII, 212.

28. IV, 438.

29. XI, 178.

30. VI, 104.

31. IV, 159.

32. VII, 387.

33. I, 49.

34. IV, 119.

35. II, 268.

36. III, 212.

37. IV, 406.

38. VI, 94.

39. Ibid., 130–31.

40. Ibid., 130.

41. Ibid., 133–34.

42. VI, 132.

43. VII, 359.

44. IV, 292.

45. XI, 89.

46. Ludwig Marcuse, *Søren Kierkegaard. Die Ueberwindung des romantischen Menschen*, in *Die Dioskuren*, vol. 2 (Munich, 1923), 226.

47. Ibid., 232.

48. XI, 218.

49. In order to distinguish *Leidenschaft* from *Passion*, both of which are usually translated as "passion," the German has been translated as "passion" and the latter by the Latin *passio*—translator's note.

50. VII, 507.

51. III, 121.

52. IV, 117.

53. VIII, 220.

54. III, 94.

55. Ibid., 94–95.

56. III, 96.

57. III, 97.

Chapter 7. Construction of the Aesthetic

1. XII, 264.

2. I, 166.

3. IV, 385.

4. II, 325.

5. Ibid., 326.

6. I, 34–35.

7. Ibid., 22.

8. Ibid., 40.

9. Ibid., 22.

10. Ibid., 188.

11. Ibid., 39.

12. IV, 30.

13. I, 32.

14. II, 180.

15. XI, 133.

16. VI, 54.

17. III, 38.

18. Ibid., 38–39.

19. Ibid., 41.

20. Ibid., 166.

21. Ibid., 159–60.

22. IV, 396.

23. Ibid., 421.

24. Ibid., 409.

25. II, 130. Adorno correctly cites this other "world" from the German translation; the original, however, and the English translation concern another "auditorium" (translator's note).

26. IV, 89.

27. Ibid., 90.

28. Ibid., 70.

29. XI, 175.

30. IX, 174–75.

31. Ibid., 175.

32. VII, 207.

33. I, 27.

34. IX, 79.

35. IV, 285.

36. VII, 70.

37. VII, 72.

38. IX, 247–48.

39. XI, 127.

40. II, 140–41.

41. VII, 385.

42. VII, 382.

43. I, 29.

44. V, 152.

45. VII, 110.

46. IX, 185–86.

47. III, 158.

48. Georg Lukács, *The Theory of the Novel*, trans. Anna Bostock (Cambridge, Mass.: MIT Press, 1978), 62.

49. III, 157.

50. I, 35.

51. VIII, 194.

52. I, 150.

53. III, 20.

54. Ibid., 20.

55. Ibid., 95. Adorno has misread Kierkegaard. It is Agnes that is being described, not the Merman.

56. I, 129.

57. I, 78.

58. V, 58.

59. V, 58.

60. II, 126.

61. IV, 246–47.

62. H. Lund, *Søren Kierkegaards Verhaeltnis zu seiner Braut. Briefe und Aufzeichnungen aus dem Nachlass*, translated into German by E. Rohr (Leipzig, 1904), 113; cf. Erich Przywara, *Das Geheimnis Kierkegaards* (Munich and Berlin, 1928), 166.

63. IV, 297.

64. Ibid., 350.

Index

Index

Compiled by Hassan Melehy

"First and Last Declaration, A," 24-25, 48
Flaubert, Gustave, 18
For Self-Examination, 38, 44, 119
Form: and content, 16-17, 20; and written
 expression, xiii-xiv
Formalism: and aesthetics, 17-18, 20-23
Freud, Sigmund: Adorno's study of, xi-xii

Geismar, Eduard, 32, 41, 48, 155 n. 2
George, Stefan, 22
Gnosis: and sacrifice, 112-13
God: and ethics, 50-51; and infinity, 28; and
 mysticism, 30-31; and paradox, 116-17;
 and sacrifice, 112-13. *See also* Christianity,
 Religion, Spirit
Goethe, Johann Wolfgang von: Benjamin's
 study of, xv
Gottsched, Herman, 4-5, 11
Gryphius, Andreas, 63
Guardini, Romano, 72, 79, 104
Guilty/Not-Guilty, 6

Haecker, Theodor, 5, 11, 26, 31, 113, 148 n.
 16
Haselberg, Peter von, 147 n. 64
Havamal, 108
Hebbel, Friedrich, 18
Hegel, G. W. F., xiii, xvii, 5, 7, 16, 21, 22,
 27, 28, 32, 56, 58, 70, 73, 94, 98, 106,
 119, 130, 137; aesthetics of, 17, 19, 20;
 and allegory, xix-xx; and infinity, 92-93;
 and mediation, xviii; and ontology, 74; and
 philosophy as science, 3-4; and self, 80;
 and spheres, 88-90; and subjectivity, 70-71
Hegelian language: in Adorno, xxi
Heidegger, Martin, xii, xxiii, 69, 83, 153 n. 1
Heine, Heinrich, 130
Helander, Swen, 150 n. 35
Hirsch, Emanuel, 32
History: and absolute, 36; and Christianity, 36;
 and Christians, 38; and idea, 37; and
 individual, 32-38; and inwardness, 35-36;
 and myth, 53-54; and nature, x-xi; and
 paradox, 116-18; and scripture, 25; and
 situation, 37-38; and truth, xv. See also
 Dialectic, Spirit
*History and Class Consciousness (Geschichte
 und Klassenbewusstsein),* 147 n. 3, 152 n.
 49
Hoffmann, E. T. A., 6

Holy Family, The (Die heilige Familie), 151 n.
 4
Homer, 17
Horkheimer, Max, 145 n. 1
Humor: and religion, 96; and spheres, 93-95
Hunold, Christian Friedrich, 62
Husserl, Edmund, xvi, 75

"I." *See* Self, Subjectivity
Ibsen, Henrik, 18
Idealism: and astrology, 92-93; and
 consciousness, 107; critique of, xiii, xiv,
 xvii-xix; and enlightenment, xviii; and
 existence, xii; and myth, 56-57; and
 subjectivity, 27-30; and totality, 106-7
*Ideas: General Introduction to a Pure
 Phenomenology,* 75
Image: and Christianity, 131-33, 135-36; and
 dialectic, 137; and eternity, 135-37
Immanence: and dialectic, 31-32; and
 psychoanalysis, 13
In Vino Veritas, 6, 7, 10, 131
Individual: and history, 32-38; and subjectivity,
 30
Infinity: idealist conception of, 28-29; and
 spheres, 92-93
Instant, The, 25, 36-37, 39, 66, 104, 111, 123
Intérieur: bourgeois, as center of Kierkegaard's
 philosophy, xvi, xviii; and inwardness, 47;
 and reflection, 41-42; and subjectivity,
 40-46
Interpretation: and truth-content, xv-xvi
Inwardness: and aesthetics, 64-67; and
 dialectic, 30-32; and existence, 72; and
 history, 35-36; and *intérieur,* 47; and
 melancholy, 59-62, 64; sociology of,
 47-51; and spiritualism, 51-53; and
 subjectivity, 29-30
"Iphigenia in Aulis," 108
Irony: and ethics, 96

Jaspers, Karl, xii
Job, Book of, 117
Journaux intimes, 9
Judgment: and melancholy, 123-24; and self,
 85

Kafka, Franz, xxii, 25
Kant, Immanuel, 18, 49, 73, 76, 87, 91;
 Adorno's study of, xi-xii, xiv-xv, xvi-xvii;

Theory and History of Literature

Theory and History of Literature

Theodor W. Adorno (1903-1969), philosopher, sociologist, composer, and musicologist, is one of this century's major figures in cultural criticism. Along with Max Horkheimer, he was a founder of the Institut für Sozialforschung at the Johann Wolfgang Goethe University in Frankfurt. Fleeing the Nazis in 1933, he spent the war years in the United States and returned to Germany in 1949 to teach and re-establish the Institut. Adorno's books include: *The Dialectic of Enlightenment* (1944), *The Philosophy of New Music* (1948), *Negative Dialektik* (1966), and *Aesthetic Theory* (1970).

Robert Hullot-Kentor is a Mellon Faculty Fellow at Harvard University. He earned his doctorate in comparative literature at the University of Massachusetts and has studied at the Université de Paris and Frieburg Universität. Hullot-Kentor has taught at Hobart and William Smith Colleges, Boston University, and the Université de Bordeaux. He has published articles on Adorno in *Telos* and *New German Critique*, and is now writing a study of Adorno's *Aesthetic Theory*.